SPANISH

A ROUGH GUIDE DICTIONARY PHRASEBOOK

D0033497

Compiled by

LEXUS

Credits

Compiled by Lexus with Fernando Léon Solís
Lexus Series Editor: Sally Davies
Rough Guides Phrase Book Editor: Jonathan Buckley
Rough Guides Series Editor: Mark Ellingham

First edition published in 1995 by Rough Guides Ltd,
62–70 Shorts Gardens, London WC2H 9AB.
Reprinted in 1995 and 1996.
Revised in 1999.

Distributed by the Penguin Group.

Penguin Books Ltd, 27 Wrights Lane, London W8 5TZ
Penguin Books USA Inc., 375 Hudson Street, New York 10014, USA
Penguin Books Australia Ltd, 487 Maroondah Highway,
PO Box 257, Ringwood, Victoria 3134, Australia
Penguin Books Canada Ltd, Alcorn Avenue,
Toronto, Ontario, Canada M4V 1E4
Penguin Book (NZ) Ltd, 182–190 Wairau Road,
Auckland 10, New Zealand

Typeset in Bembo and Helvetica to an original design by Henry Iles.
Printed in Spain by Graphy Cems.

British Library Cataloguing in Publication Data
A catalogue for this book is available from the British Library.

ISBN 1-85828-577-1

Help us get it right

Lexus and Rough Guides have made great efforts to be accurate and
informative in this Rough Guide Spanish phrasebook. However, if you
feel we have overlooked a useful word or phrase, or have any other
comments to make about the book, please let us know. All contributors
will be acknowledged and the best letters will be rewarded with a free
Rough Guide phrasebook of your choice. Please write to 'Spanish
Phrasebook Update', at either Shorts Gardens (London) or Hudson Street
(New York) — for full addresses see opposite. Alternatively you can email us
at mail@roughguides.co.uk

Online information about Rough Guides can be found at our Web site
www.roughguides.com

CONTENTS

Introduction

The Rough Guide Spanish dictionary phrasebook is a highly practical introduction to the contemporary language. Laid out in clear A–Z style, it uses key-word referencing to lead you straight to the words and phrases you want – so if you need to book a room, just look up 'room'. The Rough Guide gets straight to the point in every situation, in bars and shops, on trains and buses, and in hotels and banks.

The main part of the Rough Guide is a double dictionary: English-Spanish then Spanish-English. Before that, there's a page explaining the pronunciation system we've used, then a section called **The Basics**, which sets out the fundamental rules of the language, with plenty of practical examples. You'll also find here other essentials like numbers, dates and telling the time.

Forming the heart of the guide, the **English-Spanish** section gives easy-to-use transliterations of the Spanish words wherever pronunciation might be a problem, and to get you involved quickly in two-way communication, the Rough Guide includes dialogues featuring typical responses on key topics – such as renting a car and asking directions. Feature boxes fill you in on cultural pitfalls as well as the simple mechanics of how to make a phone call, what to do in an emergency, where to change money, and more. Throughout this section, cross-references enable you to pinpoint key facts and phrases, while asterisked words indicate where further information can be found in the Basics.

In the **Spanish-English** dictionary, we've given not just the phrases you're likely to hear, but also all the signs, labels, instructions and other basic words you might come across in print or in public places.

Finally the Rough Guide rounds off with an extensive **Menu Reader**, giving a run-down of food and drink terms that you'll find indispensable whether you're eating out, stopping for a quick drink, or browsing through a local food market.

¡buen viaje!
have a good trip!

Basics

Pronunciation

In this phrasebook, the Spanish has been written in a system of imitated pronunciation so that it can be read as though it were English, bearing in mind the notes on pronunciation given below:

air   as in h**air**
ay   as in m**ay**
e   as in g**e**t
g   always hard as in **g**oat
H   a harsh 'ch' as in the Scottish way of pronouncing lo**ch**
ī   as the 'i' sound in m**i**ght
ow   as in n**ow**
y   as in **y**es

Letters given in bold type indicate the part of the word to be stressed.

As **i** and **u** are always pronounced 'ee' and 'oo' in Spanish, pronunciation has not been given for all words containing these letters unless they present other problems for the learner. Thus **María** is pronounced 'mar**ee**-a' and **fútbol** is '**foot**bol'.

Abbreviations

adj	adjective	pl	plural
f	feminine	pol	polite
fam	familiar	sing	singular
m	masculine		

Note

In the Spanish-English section and Menu Reader, the letter **ñ** is treated as a separate letter, as is customary in Spanish. Alphabetically, it comes after **n**.

An asterisk (★) next to a word in the English-Spanish section means that you should refer to the Basics section or conversion tables for further information.

Nouns

All nouns in Spanish have one of two genders: masculine or feminine. Generally speaking, those ending in **-o** are masculine:

el zapato
el thap**a**to
the shoe

Those ending in **-a**, **-d**, **-z** or **-ión** are usually feminine:

la cama
la k**a**ma
the bed

la pensión
la pens-y**o**n
the boarding house

A small number of nouns ending in **-o** and **-a** (usually professions) can be either masculine or feminine:

el/la guía
el/la g**ee**-a
the tourist guide

el/la médico
el/la m**ay**deeko
the doctor

Plural Nouns

If the noun ends in a vowel, the plural is formed by adding **-s**:

el camino
el kam**ee**no
the path

los caminos
loss kam**ee**noss
the paths

la camarera
la kamar**ai**ra
the waitress

las camareras
lass kamar**ai**rass
the waitresses

If the noun ends in a consonant, the plural is formed by adding **-es**:

el conductor	los conductores
el kondooktor	loss kondooktoress
the driver	the drivers

la recepción	las recepciones
la rethepth-yon	lass rethepth-yoness
the reception desk	the reception desks

If the noun ends in a **-z**, change the **-z** to **-ces** to form the plural:

el andaluz	los andaluces
el andalooth	loss andaloothess
the Andalusian	the Andalusians

Articles

There are different words for articles ('the' and 'a') in Spanish depending on the number (singular or plural) and gender of the noun. The definite article 'the' is as follows:

	singular	plural
masculine	**el**	**los**
feminine	**la**	**las**

el cuchillo/los cuchillos	la piscina/las piscinas
el koochee-yo/loss koochee-yoss	la peestheena/lass peestheenass
the knife/the knives	the swimming pool/ the swimming pools

When the article **el** is used in combination with **a** (to) or **de** (of) it changes as follows:

a + el = al
de + el = del

vamos al museo	cerca del hotel
bamoss al moosay-o	thairka del otel
let's go to the museum	near the hotel

Plural Articles

The indefinite article (a, an, some) also changes according to the gender and number of the accompanying noun:

	singular	plural
masculine	**un**	**unos**
	oon	**oo**noss
feminine	**una**	**unas**
	oona	**oo**nass

un sello	**unos sellos**
oon **say**-yo	**oo**noss **say**-yoss
a stamp	some stamps

una chica	**unas chicas**
oona cheeka	**oo**nass cheekass
a girl	some girls

Adjectives and Adverbs

Adjectives must agree in gender and number with the noun they refer to. In the English–Spanish section of this book, all adjectives are given in the masculine singular. Adjectives ending in -o change as follows for the plural:

el precio alto	**los precios altos**
el pr**e**th-yo **a**lto	loss pr**e**th-yoss **a**ltoss
the high price	the high prices

The feminine singular of the adjective is formed by changing the masculine endings as follows:

masculine	feminine
-o	-a
-or	-ora
-és	-esa

un cocinero estupendo	**una cocinera estupenda**
oon kotheenairo estoopendo	oona kotheenaira estoopenda
a wonderful cook	a wonderful cook
un señor encantador	**una señora encantadora**
oon sen-yor enkantador	oona sen-yora enkantadora
a nice man	a nice woman
un chico inglés	**una chica inglesa**
oon cheeko eenglayss	oona cheeka eenglaysa
an English boy	an English girl

For other types of adjective, the feminine forms are the same as the masculine:

un hombre agradable	**una mujer agradable**
oon hombray agradablay	oona mooнair agradablay
a nice man	a nice woman

Unlike English, Spanish adjectives usually follow the noun.

The plurals of adjectives are formed in the same way as the plurals of nouns, by adding an **-s**:

una tumbona roja	**dos tumbonas rojas**
oona toombona roнa	doss toombonass roнass
a red deckchair	two red deckchairs

Comparatives

The comparative is formed by placing **más** (more) or **menos** (less) before the adjective or adverb and **que** (than) after it:

bonito	**más bonito**
boneeto	mass boneeto
beautiful	more beautiful
tranquilo	**menos tranquilo**
trankeelo	maynoss trankeelo
quiet	less quiet

este hotel es más/menos caro que el otro
estay otel es mass/maynoss karo kay el otro
this hotel is more/less expensive than the other one

¿tiene una habitación más soleada?
t-yaynay oona abeetath-yon mass solay-ada
do you have a sunnier room?

¿podría conducir más deprisa, por favor?
podree-a kondootheer mass depreesa por fabor
could you drive faster please?

Superlatives

Superlatives are formed by placing one of the following before the adjective: **el más, la más, los más** or **las más** (depending on the noun's gender and number):

¿cuál es el más divertido?
kwal ess el mass deebairteedo
which is the most entertaining?

el día más caluroso
el dee-a mass kalooroso
the hottest day

el coche más rápido
el kochay mass rapido
the fastest car

The following adjectives have irregular comparatives and superlatives:

bueno	**mejor**	**el mejor**
bwayno	meнor	el meнor
good	better	the best
grande	**mayor**	**el mayor**
granday	mī-or	el mī-or
big	bigger	the biggest
	older	the oldest
malo	**peor**	**el peor**
malo	pay-or	el pay-or
bad	worse	the worst

pequeño	menor	el menor
peken-yo	menor	el menor
small	younger	the youngest

Note that **más pequeño** means 'smaller'.

As ... as ... is translated as follows:

Madrid está tan bonita como siempre!
madree esta tan boneeta komo s-yempray
Madrid is as beautiful as ever!

The superlative form ending in **-ísimo** indicates that something is 'very/extremely ... ' without actually comparing it to something else:

guapo	guapísimo
gwapo	gwapisimo
attractive	very attractive

Adverbs

There are two ways to form an adverb. If the adjective ends in **-o**, take the feminine and add **-mente** to form the corresponding adverb:

exacto	exactamente
esakto	esaktamente
accurate	accurately

If the adjective ends in any other letter, add **-mente** to the basic form:

feliz	felizmente
feleeth	feleethmentay
happy	happily

Possessive Adjectives

Possessive adjectives, like other Spanish adjectives, agree with the noun in gender and number:

	singular		plural	
	masc	fem	masc	fem
my	**mi**	**mi**	**mis**	**mis**
	mee	mee	meess	meess
your (sing, fam)	**tu**	**tu**	**tus**	**tus**
	too	too	tooss	tooss
his/her/its/your (sing, pol)	**su**	**su**	**sus**	**sus**
	soo	soo	sooss	sooss
our	**nuestro**	**nuestra**	**nuestros**	**nuestras**
	nwestro	nwestra	nwestross	nwestrass
your (pl, fam)	**vuestro**	**vuestra**	**vuestros**	**vuestras**
	bwestro	bwestra	bwestross	bwestrass
their/your (pl, pol)	**su**	**su**	**sus**	**sus**
	soo	soo	sooss	sooss

tu bolsa
too b**o**lsa
your bag

sus pastillas
sooss past**ee**-yass
his/her/your tablets

vuestra maleta
bw**e**stra mal**ay**ta
your suitcase

nuestros trajes de baño
nw**e**stross tra**н**ess day b**a**n-yo
our swimming costumes

If when using **su/sus**, it is unclear whether you mean 'his', 'her', 'your' or 'their', you can use the following after the noun instead:

de él	day el	his
de ella	day **ay**-ya	her
de Usted	day oost**ay**	your (sing, pol)
de ellos	day **ay**-yoss	their (masculine)
de ellas	day **ay**-yass	their (feminine)
de Ustedes	day oost**ay**dess	your (pl, pol)

el dinero de usted
el deen**ai**ro day oost**ay**
your money

el dinero de ella
el deen**ai**ro day **ay**-ya
her money

el dinero de él
el deen**ai**ro day el
his money

Possessive Pronouns

To translate 'mine', 'yours' 'theirs' etc, use one of the following forms. Like possessive adjectives, possessive pronouns must agree in gender and number with the object or objects referred to:

	singular		plural	
	masculine	feminine	masculine	feminine
mine	el mío	la mía	los míos	las mías
	el **mee**-o	la **mee**-a	los **mee**-oss	las **mee**-ass
yours (sing, fam)	el tuyo	la tuya	los tuyos	las tuyas
	el **too**-yo	la **too**-ya	loss **too**-yoss	lass **too**-yass
his/hers	el suyo	la suya	los suyos	las suyas
	el **soo**-yo	la **soo**-ya	loss **soo**-yoss	lass **soo**-yass
yours (sing, pol)	el suyo	la suya	los suyos	las suyas
	el **soo**-yo	la **soo**-ya	loss **soo**-yoss	lass **soo**-yass
ours	el nuestro	la nuestra	los nuestros	las nuestras
	el **nwes**tro	la **nwes**tra	loss **nwes**tross	lass **nwes**trass
yours (pl, fam)	el vuestro	la vuestra	los vuestros	las vuestras
	el **bwes**tro	la **bwes**tra	loss **bwes**tross	lass **bwes**trass
theirs	el suyo	la suya	los suyos	las suyas
	el **soo**-yo	la **soo**-ya	loss **soo**-yoss	lass **soo**-yass
yours (pl, pol)	el suyo	la suya	los suyos	las suyas
	el **soo**-yo	la **soo**-ya	loss **soo**-yoss	lass **soo**-yass

ésta es su llave y ésta la mía
esta ess soo ya**bay** ee **e**sta la **mee**-a
this is your key and this is mine

no es la suya, es de sus amigos
no ess la **soo**-ya ess day sooss am**ee**goss
it's not his, it's his friends'

Personal Pronouns

Subject Pronouns

yo	yo	I
tú	too	you (sing, fam)
él	el	he/it
ella	**ay**-ya	she/it
ello	**ay**-yo	it
usted	oost**ay**	you (sing, pol)
nosotros	nos**o**tross	we (masculine)
nosotras	nos**o**trass	we (feminine)
vosotros	bos**o**tross	you (pl, fam, masculine)
vosotras	bos**o**trass	you (pl, fam, feminine)
ellos	**ay**-yoss	they (masculine)
ellas	**ay**-yass	they (feminine)
ustedes	oost**ay**dess	you (pl, pol)

Tú is used when speaking to one person and is the familiar form generally used when speaking to family, friends and children. **Vosotros/vosotras** is the plural form of **tú**.

Usted and **Ustedes** are the polite forms of address to be used when talking to someone you don't know. They take the third person forms of verbs: **Usted** takes the same form as 'he/she/it'; **Ustedes** takes the same form as 'they'.

In Spanish the subject pronoun is usually omitted:

no saben	**está cansado**
no s**a**ben	est**a** kans**a**do
they don't know	he is tired

although it may be retained for emphasis or to avoid confusion:

¡soy yo!	**¡somos nosotros!**
soy yo	s**o**moss nos**o**tross
it's me!	it's us!

yo pagaré los bocadillos, tú pagas las cervezas
yo pagar**ay** loss bokad**ee**-yoss too p**a**gass lass thairb**ay**thass
I'll pay for the sandwiches, you pay for the beers

él es inglés y ella es americana
el ess eengl**ay**ss ee **ay**-ya ess amaireek**a**na
he's English and she's American

The pronouns as listed above are also used after prepositions:

para usted	**con él**
para oost**ay**	kon el
for you	with him

sin ella	**después de usted**
seen **ay**-ya	despw**ay**ss day oost**ay**
without her	after you

The exceptions are **yo**, which is replaced by **mí**, and **tú** which is replaced by **ti**:

eso es para mí/ti
eso es p**a**ra mee/tee
that's for me/you

After **con** (with) **mí** and **ti** change as follows:

conmigo/contigo
konm**ee**go/kont**ee**go
with me/you

Object Pronouns

me	[may]	me
te	[tay]	you (sing, fam)
le	[lay]	him, you (pl, pol)
lo	[lo]	it
la	[la]	her/it, you (sing, pol)
nos	[noss]	us
os	[oss]	you (pl, fam)
les/los	[less/loss]	them, you (pl, pol, masculine)
las	[lass]	them, you (pl, pol, feminine)

Object pronouns generally precede the verb:

me la dio ayer
may la d**ee**-o a-y**air**
she gave it to me yesterday

las compré para ella
lass k**o**mpray p**a**ra **ay**-ya
I bought them for her

When used with infinitives, pronouns are added to the end of the infinitive:

¿puede llevarme al aeropuerto?
pw**ay**day yeb**a**rmay al airopw**ai**rto
can you take me to the airport?

intentaré recordarlo
eententar**ay** rekord**a**rlo
I'll try and remember it

When used with commands, pronouns are added to the end of the imperative form. See **Imperative** page 33.

If you are using an indirect pronoun to mean 'to me', 'to you' etc (although 'to' might not always be necessarily said in English), you generally use the following:

me	[may]	to me
te	[tay]	to you (sing, fam)
le	[lay]	to him/to her, to you (sing, pol)
nos	[noss]	to us
os	[oss]	to you (pl, fam)
les	[less]	to them, to you (pl, pol)

le compré flores
lay k**o**mpray fl**o**ress
I bought flowers for her

le pedí su dirección
lay ped**ee** soo deerekth-y**o**n
I asked him for his address

Reflexive Pronouns

These are used with reflexive verbs like **lavarse** 'to wash (oneself)', that is where the subject and the object are one and the same person:

me	[may]	myself (used with I)
te	[tay]	yourself (used with singular, familiar 'you')
se	[say]	him/her/itself (used with singular, polite 'you')
nos	[noss]	ourselves (used with 'we')
os	[oss]	yourselves (used with plural, familiar 'you')
se	[say]	themselves (used with 'they' and plural, polite 'you')

presentarse to introduce oneself
me presento: me llamo Richard
may presento: may yamo Richard
may I introduce myself? my name's Richard

divertirse to enjoy oneself
nos divertimos mucho en la fiesta
noss deebairteemoss moocho en la f-yesta
we enjoyed ourselves a lot at the party

Demonstratives

The English demonstrative adjective 'this' is translated by the Spanish **este**. 'That' is translated by **ese** and 'that (over there/further away)' is translated by **aquel**.

Ese refers to something near to the person being spoken to. **Aquel** refers to something further away.

Like other adjectives, they agree with the noun they qualify in gender and number but they come in front of the noun. Their forms are:

masculine singular			feminine singular		
este	ese	aquel	esta	esa	aquella
estay	aysay	akel	esta	aysa	akay-ya

masculine plural			feminine plural		
estos	esos	aquellos	estas	esas	aquellas
estoss	aysoss	akay-yoss	estass	aysass	akay-yass

este restaurante	ese camarero	aquella playa
estay restow**ra**ntay	**ay**say kamar**ai**ro	ak**ay**-ya pl**a**-ya
this restaurant	that waiter	that beach (**in the distance**)

'This one', 'that one', 'those', 'these' etc (as pronouns) are translated by the same words as above only they are spelt with an **é**:

éste	ése	aquél
estay	**ay**say	ak**e**l
this one	that one	that one (**over there**)

quisiera éstos/ésos/aquéllos
kees-y**ai**ra **e**stoss/**ay**soss/ak**ay**-yoss
I'd like these/those/those (**over there**)

The neuter forms **esto/eso/aquello** are used when no particular noun is being referred to:

esto	eso	aquello
esto	**ay**so	ak**ay**-yo

eso no es justo	**¿qué es esto?**
ayso no ess **н**oo**sto**	kay ess **e**sto
that's not fair	what is this?

Verbs

The basic form of the verb given in the English-Spanish and Spanish-English sections is the infinitive (e.g. to drive, to go etc). There are three verb types in Spanish which can be recognized by their infinitive endings: **-ar**, **-er**, **-ir**. For example:

hablar	[ablar]	to talk
comer	[kom**ai**r]	to eat
abrir	[abr**i**r]	to open

Present Tense

The present tense corresponds to 'I leave' and 'I am leaving' in English. To form the present tense for the three main types of verb in Spanish, remove the **-ar**, **-er** or **-ir** and add the following endings:

hablar to speak

habl-o	[**a**blo]	I speak
habl-as	[**a**blass]	you speak (sing, fam)
habl-a	[**a**bla]	he/she speaks, you speak (sing, pol)
habl-amos	[abl**a**moss]	we speak
habl-áis	[abla-**ee**ss]	you speak (pl, fam)
habl-an	[**a**blan]	they speak, you speak (pl, pol)

comer to eat

com-o	[**ko**mo]	I eat
com-es	[**ko**mess]	you eat (sing, fam)
com-e	[**ko**may]	he/she eats, you eat (sing, pol)
com-emos	[kom**ay**moss]	we eat
com-éis	[kom**ay**-eess]	you eat (pl, fam)
com-en	[**ko**men]	they eat, you eat (pl, pol)

abrir to open

abr-o	[**a**bro]	I open
abr-es	[**a**bress]	you open (sing, fam)
abr-e	[**a**bray]	he/she opens, you open (sing, pol)
abr-imos	[abr**ee**moss]	we open
abr-ís	[abr**ee**ss]	you open (pl, fam)
abr-en	[**a**bren]	they open, you open (pl, pol)

Some common verbs are irregular:

haber to have

he	[ay]	I have
has	[ass]	you have (sing, fam)
ha	[a]	he/she/it has, you have (sing, pol)

23

hemos	[**ay**moss]	we have
habéis	[a**bay**-eess]	you have (pl, fam)
han	[an]	they have, you have (pl, pol)

tener to have

tengo	[**te**ngo]
tienes	[t-**yay**ness]
tiene	[t-**yay**nay]
tenemos	[te**nay**moss]
tenéis	[te**nay**-eess]
tienen	[t-**yay**nen]

venir to come

vengo	[**be**ngo]
vienes	[b-**yay**ness]
viene	[b-**yay**nay]
venimos	[ben**ee**moss]
venís	[ben**ee**ss]
vienen	[b-**yay**nen]

ir to go

voy	[boy]
vas	[bass]
va	[ba]
vamos	[**ba**moss]
vais	[**ba**-eess]
van	[ban]

dar to give

doy	[doy]
das	[dass]
da	[da]
damos	[**da**moss]
dais	[**da**-eess]
dan	[dan]

poder to be able

puedo	[**pway**do]
puedes	[**pway**dess]
puede	[**pway**day]
podemos	[po**day**mos]
podéis	[po**day**-eess]
pueden	[**pway**den]

querer to want

quiero	[k-**yai**ro]
quieres	[k-**yai**ress]
quiere	[k-**yai**ray]
queremos	[kai**ray**moss]
queréis	[kai**ray**-eess]
quieren	[k-**yai**ren]

The first person singular (the 'I' form) of the following verbs is irregular:

decir to say	digo	[**dee**go]
hacer to do, to make	hago	[**a**-go]
poner to put	pongo	[**po**ngo]
saber to know	sé	[say]
salir to go out	salgo	[**sa**lgo]

See page 30 for the present tense of the verbs **ser** and **estar** 'to be'.

Past Tense:

Perfect Tense

The perfect tense is used to express an action that has taken place in the past. It is formed with the present tense of **haber** (see page 23) and the past participle of the verb.

To form the past participles, make the following changes to the infinitive forms:

infinitive	past participle	
hablar	hablado	[ablado]
comer	comido	[komeedo]
abrir	abrido	[abreedo]

hemos dado una propina
ay**moss** da**do oo**na propee**na**
we have given a tip

hemos comido bien
ay**moss** komee**do** b-yen
we've eaten well,
we've had a good meal

he encendido la luz
ay enthendee**do** la looth
I (have) put the light on

Some verbs have irregular past participles:

hacer to do/make	hecho	[**ay**cho]
abrir to open	abierto	[ab-y**air**to]
decir to say	dicho	[**dee**cho]
volver to return	vuelto	[bwelto]
poner to put	puesto	[pwesto]
ver to see	visto	[bee**sto**]
satisfacer to satisfy	satisfecho	[satees**fecho**]

Past Historic

The Past Historic is used to express what happened or what somebody did at a particular time in the past.

habl-é	[ablay]	I spoke
habl-aste	[ablastay]	you spoke (sing, fam)
habl-ó	[ablo]	he/she spoke, you spoke (sing, pol)
habl-amos	[ablamoss]	we spoke
habl-asteis	[ablastay-eess]	you spoke (pl, fam)
habl-aron	[ablaron]	they spoke, you spoke (pl, pol)

com-í	[komee]	I ate
com-iste	[komeestay]	you ate (sing, fam)
com-ió	[komi-o]	he/she ate, you ate (sing, pol)
com-imos	[komeemoss]	we ate
com-isteis	[komeestay-eess]	you ate (pl, fam)
com-ieron	[kom-yairon]	they ate, you ate (pl, pol)

abr-í	[abree]	I opened
abr-iste	[abreestay]	you opened (sing, fam)
abr-ió	[abri-o]	he/she opened, you opened (sing, pol)
abr-imos	[abreemoss]	we opened
abr-isteis	[abreestay-eess]	you opened (pl, fam)
abr-ieron	[abr-yairon]	they opened, you opened (pl, pol)

¿quién te dijo eso?	nos conocimos en Málaga
k-yen tay deeнo ayso	noss konotheemoss en malaga
who told you that?	we met each other in Málaga

lo compramos el año pasado
lo kompramoss el an-yo pasado
we bought it last year

Imperfect Tense

This tense is used to express what was going on regularly over an indefinite period of time and is sometimes translated by 'used to + infinitive'. It it is formed as follows:

hablar to speak

habl-**aba**	[abl**aba**]	I was speaking
habl-**abas**	[abl**abass**]	you were speaking (sing, fam)
habl-**aba**	[abl**aba**]	he/she/it was speaking, you were speaking (sing, pol)
habl-**ábamos**	[abl**abamoss**]	we were speaking
habl-**abais**	[abl**aba-eess**]	you were speaking (pl, fam)
habl-**aban**	[abl**aban**]	they were speaking, you were speaking (pl, polite)

comer to eat

com-**ía**	[kom**ee-a**]	I was eating
com-**ías**	[kom**ee-ass**]	you were eating (sing, fam)
com-**ía**	[kom**ee-a**]	he/she/it was eating, you were eating (sing, pol)
com-**íamos**	[kom**ee-amoss**]	we were eating
com-**íais**	[kom**ee-a-eess**]	you were eating (pl, fam)
com-**ían**	[kom**ee-an**]	they were eating, you were eating (pl, pol)

abrir to open

abr-**ía**	[abr**ee-a**]	I was opening
abr-**ías**	[abr**ee-ass**]	you were opening (sing, fam)
abr-**ía**	[abr**ee-a**]	he/she/it was opening, you were opening (sing, pol)
abr-**íamos**	[abr**ee-amoss**]	we were opening
abr-**íais**	[abr**ee-a-eess**]	you were opening (pl, fam)
abr-**ían**	[abr**ee-an**]	they were opening, you were opening (pl, pol)

Two other useful regular verbs in the imperfect tense are:

tener to have

tenía	[ten**ee**-a]	I had
tenías	[ten**ee**-ass]	you had (sing, fam)
tenía	[ten**ee**-a]	he/she/it had, you had (sing, pol)
teníamos	[ten**ee**-amoss]	we had
teníais	[ten**ee**-a-eess]	you had (pl, fam)
tenían	[ten**ee**-an]	they had, you had (pl, pol)

estar to be

estaba	[estaba]	I was
estabas	[estabass]	you were (sing, fam)
estaba	[estaba]	he/she/it was, you were (sing, pol)
estábamos	[estabamoss]	we were
estabais	[estaba-eess]	you were (pl, fam)
estaban	[estaban]	they were, you were (pl, pol)

The following are irregular in the imperfect tense:

ir to go

iba	[**ee**ba]	I was going
ibas	[**ee**bass]	you were going (sing, fam)
iba	[**ee**ba]	he/she/it was going, you were going (sing, pol)
íbamos	[**ee**bamoss]	we were going
ibais	[**ee**ba-eess]	you were going (pl, fam)
iban	[**ee**ban]	they were going, you were going (pl, pol)

ser to be (see page 30 for more on this)

era	[**ai**ra]	I was
eras	[**ai**rass]	you were (sing, fam)
era	[**ai**ra]	he/she/it was, you were (sing, pol)
éramos	[**ai**ramoss]	we were
erais	[**ai**ra-eess]	you were (pl, fam)
eran	[**ai**ran]	they were, you were (pl, pol)

todos los viernes salíamos a dar un paseo

todos loss b-**yai**rness sal**ee**-amoss a dar oon pass**ay**-o

every Friday we used to go for a walk, every Friday we
went for a walk

Future Tense

To form the future tense in Spanish (I will do, you will do
etc) add the following endings to the infinitive. The same
endings are used whether verbs end in **-ar**, **-er** or **-ir**:

hablar-**é**	[ablar**ay**]	I will speak
hablar-**ás**	[ablar**ass**]	you will speak
hablar-**á**	[**ablara**]	he/she/you will speak
hablar-**emos**	[ablar**ay**moss]	we will speak
hablar-**éis**	[ablar**ay**-eess]	you will speak
hablar-**án**	[ablar**an**]	they/you will speak

volveré más tarde

bolbair**ay** mass **tar**day

I'll come back later

The immediate future can also be translated by **ir** + **a** +
infinitive:

vamos a comprar una botella de vino tinto

b**a**moss a komprar **oo**na bot**ay**-ya day b**ee**no **tee**nto

we're going to buy a bottle of red wine

iré a recogerle

eer**ay** a raукон**air**lay

I'll fetch him, I'll go and fetch him

Sometimes the future tense in Spanish indicates probability:

será verdad

s**ai**ra bair**da**

it might be true

In Spanish, as in English, the future can sometimes be
expressed by the present tense:

tu avión sale a la una
too aby-**o**n s**a**lay a la **oo**na
your plane takes off at one o'clock

However, Spanish often uses the present tense where the future would be used in English:

le doy ochocientas pesetas
lay doy ochoth-y**e**ntass pes**a**ytass
I'll give you 800 pesetas

The following verbs are irregular in the future tense:

decir	to say	diré
		I will say
hacer	to do	haré
poder	to be able	podré
poner	to put	pondré
querer	to want	querré
saber	to know	sabré
salir	to leave	saldré
tener	to have	tendré
venir	to come	vendré

The Verb 'To Be'

There are two verbs 'to be' in Spanish: **ser** and **estar**. The present tense is as follows:

ser

soy	[soy]	I am
eres	[**ai**ress]	you are (sing, fam)
es	[ess]	he/she/it is, you are (sing, pol)
somos	[**so**moss]	we are
sois	[**so**yss]	you are (pl, fam)
son	[son]	they are, you are (pl, pol)

estar

estar		
estoy	[estoy]	I am
estás	[estass]	you are (sing, fam)
está	[esta]	he/she/it is, you are (sing, pol)
estamos	[estamoss]	we are
estáis	[esta-eess]	you are (pl, fam)
están	[estan]	they are, you are (pl, pol)

Ser

Ser indicates an inherent quality, a permanent state or characteristic, something which is unlikely to change:

la nieve es blanca
la n-yaybay ess blanka
snow is white

Ser is also used with occupations, nationalities, the time and to indicate possession:

somos escoceses
somoss eskothaysess
we are Scottish

mi madre es profesora
mi madray ess profesora
my mum is a teacher

éste es nuestro coche
estay ess nwestro kochay
this is our car

son las cinco de la tarde
son lass theenko day la tarday
it's five o'clock in the afternoon

Estar, on the other hand, is used for temporary qualities, for things which could change:

estoy enfadado contigo
estoy enfadado konteego
I'm angry with you

estoy cansado
estoy kansado
I'm tired

este filete está frío
estay feelaytay esta free-o
this steak is cold

Notice the difference between the following two phrases:

Isabel es muy guapa
Isabel ess mwee gwapa
Isabel is very pretty

Isabel está muy guapa (esta noche)
Isabel esta mwee gwapa esta nochay
Isabel looks very pretty (tonight)

Estar is also used to indicate position and situation:

Barcelona está en Cataluña
barthelona esta en kataloon-ya
Barcelona is in Catalonia

Negatives

To express a negative in Spanish, to say 'I don't want', 'it's not here' etc, place the word **no** in front of the verb:

comprendo
komprendo
I understand

no comprendo
no komprendo
I don't understand

me gusta este helado
may goosta aystay elado
I like this ice cream

no me gusta este helado
no may goosta aystay elado
I don't like this ice cream

lo alquilé aquí
lo alkeelay akee
I rented it here

no lo alquilé aquí
no lo alkeelay akee
I didn't rent it here

van a cantar
ban a kantar
they're going to sing

no van a cantar
no ban a kantar
they're not going to sing

Unlike English, Spanish makes use of double negatives with words like nothing/anything or nobody/anybody:

no hay nadie ahí
no ī nad-yay a-ee
there's nobody there

no compramos nada
no kompramoss nada
we didn't buy anything

no sabemos nada de ella
no sabaymoss nada day ay-ya
we don't know anything about her

To say 'there's no ...', 'I've no ...' etc, make the accompanying verb negative:

no hay vino
no ī **bee**no
there's no wine

no tengo cerillas
no **te**ngo thai**ree**-yass
I've no matches

To say 'not him', 'not her' etc just use the personal pronoun followed by **no**:

nosotros, no
nos**o**tross no
not us

ella, no
ay-ya no
not her

yo, no
yo no
not me

Imperative

When speaking to people using the **Usted** or **Ustedes** forms, you make commands by removing the **-ar**, **-er** or **-ir** from the infinitive and adding these endings:

	singular		plural	
hablar to speak	**habl-e**	a**blay**	**habl-en**	a**blen**
comer to eat	**com-a**	**ko**ma	**com-an**	**ko**man
abrir to open	**abr-a**	**a**bra	**abr-an**	**a**bran

coma despacio
koma despa**th**-yo
eat slowly

When you are telling someone not to do something, use the forms above and place **no** in front of the verb:

no me moleste, por favor
no may mole**stay** por fa**bor**
don't disturb me, please

¡no beba alcohol!
no **bay**ba alko**hol**
don't drink alcohol!

¡no venga esta noche!
no **ben**ga **e**sta **no**chay
don't come tonight

To form the imperative used to give commands to people you would normally address as **tú** and **vosotros**, remove the endings -ar, -er, and -ir from the verb and add these endings:

	tú		vosotros	
hablar (to speak)	habl-a	[abla]	habl-ad	[ablad]
comer (to eat)	com-e	[komay]	com-ed	[komayd]
abrir (to open)	abr-e	[abray]	abr-id	[abreed]

To form a negative imperative to people addressed as **tú** and **vosotros**, no is placed in front of the verb and the endings change:

tú		vosotros	
habla	no habl-es [no abless]	hablad	no habl-éis [no ablay-eess]
come	no com-as [no komass]	comed	no com-áis [no koma-eess]
abre	no abras [no abrass]	abrid	no abr-áis [no abra-eess]

> **por favor, no hables tan rápido** (to one person)
> por fabor no abless tan rapeedo
> please don't speak so fast

> **por favor, no habléis tan rápido** (to several people)
> por fabor no ablay-eess tan rapeedo
> please don't speak so fast

Pronouns are added to the end of the imperative form:

> **despiérteme a las ocho, por favor**
> desp-yairtemay a lass ocho por fabor
> wake me up at eight o'clock, please

> **bébelo**
> baybelo
> drink it

> **ciérralas**
> th-yairalass
> close them

> **ayúdeme, por favor**
> a-yoodemay por fabor
> help me please

34

but when the imperative is negative, they are placed in front of it:

no lo bebas
no lo **bay**bass
don't drink it

no las cierres
no lass th-**yai**ress
don't close them

Questions

Often the word order remains the same in a question, but the intonation changes, the voice rising at the end of the question:

quiero bailar
k-**yai**ro ba-eelar
I want to dance

¿no quieres bailar?
no k-**yai**ress ba-eelar
don't you want to dance?

Dates

Use the numbers on page 37 to express the date. In formal Spanish, the ordinal number may be used for 'the first', but not for other dates:

el uno/el primero de septiembre [**oo**no/el preem**ai**ro day sept-**yem**bray] the first of September

el dos de diciembre [doss day deeth-**yem**bray] the second of December

el treinta de mayo [tray-**een**ta day ma-yo] the thirtieth of May

el treinta y uno de mayo [tray-**een**tī **oo**no day ma-yo] the thirty-first of May

Time

what time is it? ¿qué hora es? [kay **o**ra ess]
one o'clock la una [la **oo**na]
two o'clock las dos [lass doss]
it's one o'clock es la una [ess la **oo**na]

it's two o'clock son las dos [son lass doss]

it's ten o'clock son las diez [son lass d-yeth]

five past one la una y cinco [la **oo**na ee th**ee**nko]

ten past two las dos y diez [lass doss ee d-yeth]

quarter past one la una y cuarto [la **oo**na ee kw**a**rto]

quarter past two las dos y cuarto [lass doss ee kw**a**rto]

half past ten las diez y media [lass d-yeth ee m**ay**d-ya]

twenty to ten las diez menos veinte [lass d-yeth m**ay**noss bay-**ee**ntay]

quarter to ten las diez menos cuarto [lass d-yeth m**ay**noss kw**a**rto]

at eight o'clock a las ocho [a lass **o**cho]

at half past four a las cuatro y media [a lass kw**a**tro ee m**ay**d-ya]

2 a.m. las dos de la mañana [lass doss day la man-y**a**na]

2 p.m. las dos de la tarde [lass doss day la t**a**rday]

6 a.m. las seis de la mañana [lass say-**ee**ss day la man-y**a**na]

6 p.m. las seis de la tarde [lass say-**ee**ss day la t**a**rday]

noon mediodía [m**ay**d-yo d**ee**-a]

midnight medianoche [m**ay**d-ya n**o**chay]

an hour una hora [**oo**na **o**ra]

a minute un minuto [oon meen**oo**to]

two minutes dos minutos [doss meen**oo**toss]

a second un segundo [oon seg**oo**ndo]

a quarter of an hour un cuarto de hora [kw**a**rto day **o**ra]

half an hour media hora [m**ay**d-ya **o**ra]

three quarters of an hour tres cuartos de hora [tress kw**a**rtoss day **o**ra]

Numbers

0	cero [thairo]	100	cien [th-yen]
1	uno, una [oono, oona]	120	ciento veinte [th-yento bay-eentay]
2	dos [doss]	200	doscientos, doscientas [dosth-yentoss, dosth-yentass]
3	tres [tress]	300	trescientos, trescientas [tresth-yentoss, tresth-yentass]
4	cuatro [kwatro]	400	cuatrocientos, cuatrocientas [kwatroth-yentoss, kwatroth-yentass]
5	cinco [theenko]	500	quinientos, quinientas [keen-yentoss, keen-yentass]
6	seis [say-eess]	600	seiscientos, seiscientas [say-eesth-yentoss, say-eesth-yentass]
7	siete [s-yaytay]	700	setecientos, setecientas [seteth-yentoss, seteth-yentass]
8	ocho [ocho]	800	ochocientos, ochocientas [ochoth-yentoss, ochoth-yentass]
9	nueve [nwaybay]	900	novecientos, novecientas [nobeth-yentoss, nobeth-yentass]
10	diez [d-yeth]	1,000	mil [meel]
11	once [onthay]	2,000	dos mil [doss meel]
12	doce [dothay]	5,000	cinco mil [theenko meel]
13	trece [traythay]	10,000	diez mil [d-yeth meel]
14	catorce [katorthay]	1,000,000	un millón [meel-yon]
15	quince [keenthay]		
16	dieciséis [d-yetheesay-eess]		
17	diecisiete [d-yethees-yaytay]		
18	dieciocho [d-yethee-ocho]		
19	diecinueve [d-yetheenwaybay]		
20	veinte [bay-eentay]		
21	veintiuno [bay-eentee-oono]		
22	veintidós [bay-eenteedoss]		
23	veintitrés [bay-eenteetress]		
30	treinta [tray-eenta]		
31	treinta y uno [tray-eenti oono]		
40	cuarenta [kwarenta]		
50	cincuenta [theenkwenta]		
60	sesenta [sesenta]		
70	setenta [setenta]		
80	ochenta [ochenta]		
90	noventa [nobenta]		

37

When **uno** is used with a masculine noun, the final **-o** is dropped:

> **un coche**
> oon kochay
> one car

una is used with feminine nouns:

> **una bicicleta**
> oona beetheeklayta
> one bike

With multiples of a hundred, the **-as** ending is used with feminine nouns:

trescientos hombres	**quinientas mujeres**
tresth-yentoss ombress	keen-yentass mooнairess
300 men	500 women

Ordinals

1st	primero	[preemairo]
2nd	segundo	[segoondo]
3rd	tercero	[tairthairo]
4th	cuarto	[kwarto]
5th	quinto	[keento]
6th	sexto	[sesto]
7th	séptimo	[septeemo]
8th	octavo	[oktabo]
9th	noveno	[nobayno]
10th	décimo	[detheemo]

Conversion Tables

1 centimetre = 0.39 inches

1 metre = 39.37 inches = 1.09 yards

1 kilometre = 0.62 miles = 5/8 mile

1 inch = 2.54 cm

1 foot = 30.48 cm

1 yard = 0.91 m

1 mile = 1.61 km

km	1	2	3	4	5	10	20	30	40	50	100
miles	0.6	1.2	1.9	2.5	3.1	6.2	12.4	18.6	24.8	31.0	62.1

miles	1	2	3	4	5	10	20	30	40	50	100
km	1.6	3.2	4.8	6.4	8.0	16.1	32.2	48.3	64.4	80.5	161

1 gram = 0.035 ounces   1 kilo = 1000 g = 2.2 pounds

g	100	250	500
oz	3.5	8.75	17.5

1 oz = 28.35 g

1 lb = 0.45 kg

kg	0.5	1	2	3	4	5	6	7	8	9	10
lb	1.1	2.2	4.4	6.6	8.8	11.0	13.2	15.4	17.6	19.8	22.0

kg	20	30	40	50	60	70	80	90	100
lb	44	66	88	110	132	154	176	198	220

lb	0.5	1	2	3	4	5	6	7	8	9	10	20
kg	0.2	0.5	0.9	1.4	1.8	2.3	2.7	3.2	3.6	4.1	4.5	9.0

1 litre = 1.75 UK pints / 2.13 US pints

1 UK pint = 0.57 l

1 US pint = 0.47 l

1 UK gallon = 4.55 l

1 US gallon = 3.79 l

centigrade / Celsius $C = (F - 32) \times 5/9$

C	-5	0	5	10	15	18	20	25	30	36.8	38
F	23	32	41	50	59	64	68	77	86	98.4	100.4

Fahrenheit $F = (C \times 9/5) + 32$

F	23	32	40	50	60	65	70	80	85	98.4	101
C	-5	0	4	10	16	18	21	27	29	36.8	38.3

English

→

Spanish

A

a, an* un, una [oon, **oo**na]

about: about 20 unos v**ei**nte

it's about 5 o'clock son
aproximadamente las cinco
[aproxeem**a**damentay]

a film about Spain una
película sobre España
[s**o**bray]

above ... encima de ...
[enth**ee**ma day]

abroad en el extranjero
[estranH**ai**ro]

absolutely (I agree) ¡desde
luego! [**des**day lw**ay**go]

accelerator el acelerador
[athelairad**o**r]

accept aceptar [atheptar]

accident el accidente
[aktheed**e**ntay]

there's been an accident ha
habido un accidente [a
ab**ee**do]

accommodation alojamiento
[aloHam-yento]

see **room** and **hotel**

accurate exacto

ache el dol**o**r

my back aches me duele la
espalda [may dw**ay**lay]

across: across the road al
otro l**a**do de la calle [k**a**-yay]

adapter el adaptad**o**r

address la dirección
[deerekth-y**o**n]

what's your address? ¿cuál
es su dirección? [kwal]

Addresses in Spain are
written as follows:
**Don José García
c/Picasso 2, 4 izda.
14600 Madrid**
– which means Picasso street
(**calle**) no. 2, fourth floor, left-hand
(**izquierda**) flat or office; **dcha**,
(**derecha**) means right and **cto.**
(**centro**) means centre. Other
confusions in Spanish addresses
result from the different spellings,
and sometimes words, used in
Catalan, Basque and Gallego – all of
which are to some extent replacing
their Castilian counterparts.

address book la libreta de
direcciones [leebr**ay**ta day
deerekth-y**o**ness]

admission charge la entrada

adult el ad**u**lto

advance: in advance por
adelant**a**do

aeroplane el avión [ab-yon]

after después (de) [despw**e**ss
day]

after you usted primero
[oost**ay** preem**ai**ro]

after lunch después del
alm**u**erzo

afternoon la tarde [**tar**day]

in the afternoon por la tarde

this afternoon **e**sta tarde

aftershave el 'aftershave'

aftersun cream la crema para
después del sol [kr**ay**ma para
despw**e**ss]

afterwards después [despw**e**ss]

again otra vez [beth]
against contra
age la edad [aydath]
ago: a week ago hace una
  semana [athay]
  an hour ago hace una hora
agree: I agree estoy de
  acuerdo [day akwairdo]
AIDS el SIDA [seeda]
air el aire [a-eeray]
  by air en avión [ab-yon]
air-conditioning el aire
  acondicionado [a-eeray
  akondeeth-yonado]
airmail: by airmail por avión
  [ab-yon]
airmail envelope el sobre
  aéreo [sobray a-airay-o]
airport el aeropuerto
  [a-airopwairto]
  to the airport, please al
  aeropuerto, por favor
airport bus el autobús del
  aeropuerto [owtobooss]
aisle seat asiento de pasillo
  [as-yento day pasee-yo]
alarm clock el despertador
alcohol el alcohol [alkol]
alcoholic alcohólico
Algeria Argelia [arHaylee-a]
all: all the boys todos los
  chicos
  all the girls todas las chicas
  all of it todo
  all of them todos ellos
  [ay-yoss]
  that's all, thanks eso es todo,
  gracias [ayso]
allergic: I'm allergic to ... soy

alérgico/alérgica a ...
  [alairHeeko]
allowed: is it allowed? ¿está
  permitido?
all right ¡bien! [b-yen]
  I'm all right estoy bien
  are you all right? (fam) ¿estás
  bien?
  (pol) ¿se encuentra bien?
  [say enkwayntra]
almond la almendra
almost casi
alone solo
alphabet el alfabeto

a a	j Hota	s aysay
b bay	k ka	t tay
c thay	l aylay	u oo
ch chay	m aymay	v oobay
d day	n aynay	w oobay doblay
e ay	ñ ayn-yay	x aykeess
f ayfay	o o	y ee gr-yayga
g Hay	p pay	z thayta
h achay	q koo	
i ee	r airray	

already ya
also también [tamb-yen]
although aunque [a-oonkay]
altogether del todo
always siempre [s-yempray]
am*: I am soy, estoy
a.m.: at seven a.m. a las siete
  de la mañana [day la man-
  yana]
amazing (surprising) increíble
  [eenkray-eeblay]
  (very good) estupendo
ambulance la ambulancia

[amboolanth-ya]
call an ambulance! ¡llame a
una ambulancia! [yamay]

Dial 061 for the
ambulance service
(**emergencias
sanitarias**).

America América
American (adj) americano
  I'm American (man/woman) soy
  americano/americana
among entre [entray]
amount la cantidad [kanteeda]
  (money) la suma
amp: a 13-amp fuse el fusible
  de trece amperios [fooseeblay
  day – ampairee-oss]
amphitheatre el anfiteatro
  [anfeetay-atro]
and y [ee]
angry enfadado
animal el animal
ankle el tobillo [tobee-yo]
anniversary (wedding) el
  aniversario de boda
  [aneebairsar-yo day]
**annoy: this man's annoying
  me** este hombre me está
  molestando [estay ombray may]
annoying molesto
another otro
  can we have another room?
  ¿puede darnos otra
  habitación? [pwayday –
  abeetath-yon]
  another beer, please otra
  cerveza, por favor

[thairbaytha]
antibiotics los antibióticos
  [anteeb-yoteekoss]
antifreeze el anticongelante
  [anteekonнelantay]
antihistamine el
  antihistamínico [antee-
  eestameeneeko]
antique: is it an antique? ¿es
  antiguo? [anteegwo]
antique shop la tienda de
  antigüedades [t-yenda day
  anteegway-dadess]
antiseptic el antiséptico
**any: have you got any
  bread/tomatoes?** ¿tiene
  pan/tomates? [t-yaynay]
  do you have any change?
  ¿tiene cambio? [kamb-yo]
  sorry, I don't have any lo
  siento, no tengo [s-yento]
anybody cualquiera [kwalk-
  yaira]
  **does anybody speak
  English?** ¿habla alguien
  inglés? [abla alg-yen eenglayss]
  there wasn't anybody there
  allí no había nadie [a-yee no
  abee-a nad-yay]
anything algo

dialogues

anything else? ¿algo más?
nothing else, thanks nada
más, gracias

**would you like anything to
drink?** ¿le apetece beber

algo? [lay apetethay bebair]
**I don't want anything,
thanks** no quiero nada,
gracias [no k-yairo nada]

apart from aparte de [apartay
day]
apartment el apartamento, el
piso
appendicitis la apendicitis
[apendeetheeteess]
appetizer la entrada
aperitif el aperitivo
[apereeteebo]
apology la disculpa
apple la manzana [manthana]
appointment la cita [theeta]

dialogue

good afternoon, sir, how
can I help you? buenas
tardes, señor, ¿en qué
puedo servirle? [bwenass
tardess, sen-yor en kay pwaydo
sairbeerlay]
I'd like to make an
appointment quisiera
pedir hora [kees-yaira
pedeer ora]
what time would you like?
¿a qué hora le viene
bien? [a kay ora lay b-yaynay
b-yen]
three o'clock a las tres
I'm afraid that's not
possible, is four o'clock all
right? me temo que no
será posible, está bien a

las cuatro? [may taymo kay
no saira poseeblay]
yes, that will be fine sí, está
bien
the name was ...? ¿su
nombre era ...? [nombray
aira]

apricot el albaricoque
[albarikokay]
April abril
are*: **we are** somos; estamos
you are (fam) eres [airess];
estás
(pol) es; está
they are son; están
area la zona [thona]
area code el prefijo [prefeeHo]
arm el brazo [bratho]
**arrange: will you arrange it for
us?** ¿nos lo organiza usted?
[organeetha oostay]
arrival la llegada [yegada]
arrive llegar [yegar]
when do we arrive? ¿cuándo
llegamos? [kwando yegamoss]
has my fax arrived yet? ¿ha
llegado ya mi fax? [a yegado]
we arrived today llegamos
hoy [yegamoss oy]
art el arte [artay]
art gallery el museo de bellas
artes [moosay-o day bay-yass
artess]
(smaller) la galería de arte
[galairee-a]
artist (man/woman) el pintor/la
pintora
as: as big as tan grande

como [**gran**day]
as soon as possible lo antes
posible [**antess** poseeblay]
ashtray el cenicero
[thayneeth**ai**ro]
ask preguntar [pregoon**tar**]
I didn't ask for this no había
pedido eso [a**bee**-a – **ay**so]
could you ask him to ...?
¿puede decirle que ...?
[**pway**day deth**eer**lay kay]
asleep: she's asleep está
dormida
aspirin la aspirina
asthma el asma
astonishing increíble [eenkray-
eeblay]
at: at the hotel en el hotel
at the station en la estación
at six o'clock a las seis
at Pedro's en la casa de
Pedro
athletics el atletismo
Atlantic Ocean el Océano
Atlántico [oth**ay**-ano]
attractive guapo, atractivo
[atrak**tee**bo]
aubergine la berenjena
[beren**hay**na]
August agosto
aunt la tía [**tee**-a]
Australia Australia [**ows**tral-ya]
Australian (adj) australiano
I'm Australian (man/woman)
soy australiano/australiana
automatic (car) automático
[owtoma**tee**ko]
automatic teller el cajero
automático [ka**Hai**ro]

autumn el otoño [o**ton**-yo]
in the autumn en otoño
avenue la avenida [abe**nee**da]
average (not good) regular
[rego**olar**]
on average por término
medio [**tair**meeno **mayd**-yo]
awake: is he awake? ¿está
despierto? [desp-**yair**to]
away: go away! ¡lárguese!
[**lar**gaysay]
is it far away? ¿está lejos?
[lay**Hoss**]
awful terrible [ter**ree**blay]
axle el eje [**ay**Hay]

B

baby el bebé [bay**bay**]
baby food la comida de bebé
[day]
baby's bottle el biberón
[beebai**ron**]
baby-sitter la niñera [neen-
yaira]
back (of body) la espalda
(back part) la parte de atrás
[**par**tay day]
at the back en la parte de
atrás
can I have my money back?
¿puede devolverme el
dinero? [**pway**day daybolb**air**may
el dee**nai**ro]
to come/go back volver
[bol**bair**]
backache el dolor de espalda
[day]

bacon el bacon [**bay**kon], la panceta [pan**theta**]
bad malo
  a bad headache un fuerte dolor de cabeza [**fwair**tay – day ka**bay**tha]
badly mal
  (injured) gravemente [grabe**mayn**tay]
bag la bolsa
  (handbag) el bolso
  (suitcase) la maleta [ma**lay**ta]
baggage el equipaje [ekeepa**Hay**]
baggage check la consigna [kon**see**gna]
baggage claim la recogida de equipajes [reko**Hee**da day ekeepa**Hess**]
bakery la panadería [panadai**ree**-a]
balcony el balcón
  a room with a balcony una habitación con balcón [abeetath-**yon**]
bald calvo [**kal**bo]
Balearic Islands las Baleares [balay-**ar**ess]
ball (large) la pelota
  (small) la bola
ballet el ballet
banana el plátano
band (musical) la orquesta [or**kesta**]
  (pop) el grupo
bandage la venda [**benda**]
Bandaid® la tirita
bank (money) el banco

In winter, banking hours are 9 a.m. to 2 p.m. Monday to Friday and 9 a.m. to 1 p.m. on Saturdays. In summer, banks don't open on Saturdays.

bank account la cuenta bancaria [**kwenta**]
bar el bar

In many bars in Spain – especially the traditional ones – you do not have to pay when ordering. You can wait until just before you leave. In others, you may have to pay right after you have been served or pay first at the cash desk then show your receipt (**el ticket**) at the bar when ordering. It's usually cheaper if you stand at the bar to drink.

  a bar of chocolate una barra de chocolate [day choko**lat**ay]
barber's el barbero [bar**bair**o]
Barcelona Barcelona [bartha**y**lona]
basket el cesto [**thesto**]
  (in shop) la cesta
bath el baño [**ban**-yo]
  can I have a bath? ¿puedo bañarme? [**pway**do ban-**yar**may]
bathroom el cuarto de baño [**kwarto**]
  with a private bathroom con baño privado [pree**bado**]
bath towel la toalla de baño [to-**a**-ya day]

battery la pila
(car) la batería [batai**ree**-a]
bay la bahía [ba-**ee**-a]
Bay of Biscay el Golfo de
Vizcaya [day beeth**kaya**]
be* ser [**sair**]; estar [ay**star**]
beach la playa [**pla**-ya]
beach mat la esterilla de
playa [estai**ree**-ya]
beach umbrella la sombrilla
[som**bree**-ya]
beans las judías [Hoo**dee**-ass]
runner beans las judías
verdes [**bair**dess]
broad beans las habas [**abass**]
beard la barba
beautiful bonito
because porque [**porkay**]
because of ... debido a ...
[deb**eedo**]
bed la cama
I'm going to bed now me
voy a acostar ya [**may boy**]
bed and breakfast habitación
y desayuno [abeetath-**yon** ee
desa-**yoono**]
see hotel
bedroom el dormitorio
[dormee**tor**-yo]
beef la carne de vaca [**karnay**
day baka]
beer la cerveza [thair**baytha**]
two beers, please dos
cervezas, por favor

In Spain if you order
'**cerveza**' you will be
served lager-type beer.
Other terms are:

cerveza negra [**naygra**] stout
clara or **shandy** lager and
lemonade
de grifo [**greefo**] on tap
de barril [**barreel**] on draught
una caña [**kan**-ya] a small
glass of draught lager
un tubo [**toobo**] a long tumbler
of draught lager
un botellín [botay-**yeen**]
1/5-litre bottle
un tercio [**tairth**-yo] 1/3-litre
bottle

before antes [**antess**]
begin empezar [empe**thar**]
when does it begin? ¿cuándo
empieza? [**kwando** emp-**yetha**]
beginner el/la principiante
[preentheep-**yantay**]
beginning: at the beginning al
principio [preent**heep**-yo]
behind detrás
behind me detrás de mí
beige beige [**bay**-eess]
Belgium Bélgica [**bayl**Heeka]
believe creer [kray-**air**]
below abajo [aba**Ho**]
belt el cinturón [theentoo**ron**]
bend (in road) la curva [**koor**ba]
berth (on ship) el camarote
[kama**ro**tay]
beside: beside the ... al lado
de la ...
best el mejor [me**Hor**]
better mejor
are you feeling better? ¿se
siente mejor? [say s-**yentay**]
between entre [**entray**]

beyond más allá [a-ya]
bicycle la bicicleta [beetheeklayta]
big grande [granday]
  too big demasiado grande [demass-yado]
  it's not big enough no es suficientemente grande [soofeeth-yentemayntay]
bike la bicicleta [beetheeklayta]
  (motorbike) la motocicleta [mototheeklayta]
bikini el bikini [beekeenee]
bill la cuenta [kwenta]
  (US: banknote) el billete [bee-yaytay]
  could I have the bill, please? la cuenta, por favor

 If you go out informally with a group, it is usual to share the bill equally. When somebody invites other people out, say, for his/her birthday, he or she is expected to treat you.

bin el cubo de la basura [koobo day]
bin liners las bolsas de basura
binding (ski) la atadura
bird el pájaro [paHaro]
biro® el bolígrafo
birthday el cumpleaños [koomplayan-yoss]
  happy birthday! ¡feliz cumpleaños! [feleeth]
biscuit la galleta [ga-yeta]
bit: a little bit un poquito [pokeeto]

a big bit un pedazo grande [pedatho granday]
a bit of ... un pedazo de ...
a bit expensive un poco caro
bite (by insect) la picadura
  (by dog) la mordedura
bitter (taste etc) amargo
black negro [naygro]
blanket la manta
bleach (for toilet) la lejía [leHee-a]
bless you! ¡Jesús! [HaysOOss]
blind ciego [th-yaygo]
blinds las persianas [pers-yanass]
blister la ampolla [ampo-ya]
blocked (road, pipe) obstruido [obstrweedo]
  (sink) atascado
block of flats el bloque de apartamentos [blokay day]
blond rubio [roob-yo]
blood la sangre [sangray]
  high blood pressure la tensión alta [tenss-yon]
blouse la blusa [bloosa]
blow-dry (verb) secar a mano
  I'd like a cut and blow-dry quisiera un corte y un marcado [kees-yaira oon kortay ee]
blue azul [athool]
blusher el colorete [koloraytay]
boarding house la casa de huéspedes [wespaydess]
boarding pass la tarjeta de embarque [tarHayta day embarkay]
boat el barco

body el cuerpo [kwairpo]
boil (water) hervir [airbeer]
boiled egg el huevo pasado por agua [waybo – agwa]
boiler la caldera [kaldaira]
bone el hueso [wayso]
bonnet (of car) el capó
book el libro [leebro]
  (verb) reservar [resairbar]
  can I book a seat? ¿puedo reservar un asiento? [pwaydo – as-yento]

dialogue

I'd like to book a table for two quisiera reservar una mesa para dos personas [kees-yaira resairbar oona maysa]
what time would you like it booked for? ¿para qué hora le gustaría reservarla? [kay ora lay goostaree-a resairbarla]
half past seven las siete y media
that's fine de acuerdo [day akwairdo]
and your name? ¿y su nombre es ...? [ee soo nombray]

bookshop, bookstore la librería [leebrairee-a]
boot (footwear) la bota
  (of car) el maletero [maletairo]
border (of country) la frontera [frontaira]

bored: I'm bored estoy aburrido
boring aburrido
born: I was born in Manchester nací en Manchester [nathee]
  I was born in 1960 nací en mil novecientos sesenta
borrow pedir prestado
  may I borrow ...? ¿puede prestarme ...? [pwayday prestarmay]
both los dos
bother: sorry to bother you lamento molestarle [molestarlay]
bottle la botella [botay-ya]
  a bottle of house red una botella de tinto de la casa [day]
bottle-opener el abrebotellas [abraybotay-yass]
bottom (of person) el trasero [trassairo]
  at the bottom of the ... (hill/road) al pie del/de la ... [p-yay del/day]
box la caja [kaHa]
box office la taquilla [takee-ya]
boy el chico
boyfriend el amigo
bra el sujetador [sooHetador]
bracelet la pulsera [poolsaira]
brake el freno [frayno]
brandy el coñac [kon-yak]
bread el pan
  white bread el pan blanco
  brown bread el pan moreno

[mor**ay**no]
wholemeal bread el pan integral
break (verb) romper [romp**air**]
I've broken the ... he roto el ... [ay]
I think I've broken my ... creo que me he roto el ... [kr**ay**-o kay may]
break down averiarse [abairee-**ar**say]
I've broken down he tenido una avería [ay – abair**ee**-a]
breakdown la avería

 If you break down, phone the **Ayuda en Carretera** (National Road Assistance Organization) on 91-7421213 at the nearest phone. For peace of mind, it might be worth taking out an insurance policy like the AA Five-Star scheme or AA Europe cover, which will pay for any on-the-spot repairs, and in the case of emergencies, ship you and all your passengers back home free of charge.

breakdown service el servicio de grúa [serb**eeth**-yo day gr**oo**-a]
breakfast el desayuno [desa-**yoo**no]
break-in: I've had a break-in han entrado los ladrones en mi casa [an – ladr**o**ness]
breast el pecho [**pay**cho]
breathe respirar
breeze la brisa [br**ee**sa]

bridge (over river) el puente [pw**en**tay]
brief breve [br**ay**bay]
briefcase el portafolios [portaf**ol**-yoss]
bright (light etc) brillante [bree-**yan**tay]
bright red rojo vivo [r**o**Ho b**ee**bo]
brilliant (idea, person) brillante [bree-**yan**tay]
bring traer [tra-**air**]
I'll bring it back later lo devolveré después [lo daybolbair**ay** despw**ess**]
Britain Gran Bretaña [bretan-ya]
British británico
I'm British (man/woman) soy británico/británica
brochure el folleto [fo-**yet**o]
broken roto
bronchitis la bronquitis [bronk**eet**eess]
brooch el broche [br**o**chay]
broom la escoba
brother el hermano [air**man**o]
brother-in-law el cuñado [koon-y**a**do]
brown marrón
brown hair el pelo castaño [cast**an**-yo]
brown eyes los ojos castaños [**o**Hoss]
bruise el cardenal
brush (for hair, cleaning) el cepillo [the**pee**-yo]
(artist's) el pincel [peenth**el**]
bucket el cubo [k**oo**bo]

buffet car el vagón restaurante [bag**on** restowr**an**tay]

buggy (for child) el cochecito de niño [kochayth**ee**to day n**ee**n-yo]

building el edificio [edeef**eeth**-yo]

bulb (light bulb) la bombilla [bomb**ee**-ya]

bull el t**o**ro

bullfight la corrida de toros [day]

bullfighter el torero [tor**ai**ro]

bullring la plaza de toros [pl**a**tha day]

bumper el parachoques [parach**o**kess]

bunk la litera [leet**ai**ra]

bureau de change (oficina de) cambio [ofeeth**ee**na day kamb-yo]

burglary el r**o**bo con allanamiento de morada [a-yanam-y**en**to]

burn la quemadura [kemad**oo**ra]
(verb) quemar [kem**ar**]

burnt: this is burnt está quemado [kem**a**do]

burst: a burst pipe una cañería rota [kan-yair**ee**-a]

bus el autobús [owtob**oo**ss]
what number bus is it to ...? ¿qué número es para ...? [kay n**oo**mairo]

when is the next bus to ...? ¿cuándo sale el próximo autobús para ...? [kwando

salay]

what time is the last bus? ¿a qué hora es el último autobús? [kay **o**ra – **oo**lteemo]

could you let me know when we get there? ¿puede avisarme cuando lleguemos allí? [pw**ay**day abees**ar**may kwando yeg**ay**moss a-y**ee**]

 City bus tickets in Spain are purchased on the bus from the driver or in cards of ten from kiosks. Drivers cannot usually change large notes and in many cities from 9 a.m. onwards it is compulsory to have the exact change for your ticket. A **bono-bus** is a ten-ticket card that has to be validated in a ticket stamping machine inside the bus. It's always cheaper than buying individual tickets. In some cities a bono-bus ticket can be used for an hour from the time it was first validated, even if you change buses.

dialogue

does this bus go to ...? ¿este autobús va a ...? [estay owtob**oo**ss ba]

no, you need a number ... no, tiene que coger el ... [t-y**ay**nay kay koH**air**]

business el negocio [neg**oth**-yo]

bus station la estación de

BU

autobuses [estath-**yon** day owto**boo**sess]
bus stop la parada de autobús
bust el pecho [**pay**cho]
busy (restaurant etc) concurrido
I'm busy tomorrow estoy ocupado mañana [man-**yana**]
but pero [**pai**ro]
butcher's la carnicería [karneethai**ree**-a]
butter la mantequilla [mante**kee**-ya]
button el botón
buy (verb) comprar
where can I buy ...? ¿dónde puedo comprar ...? [**don**day **pway**do]
by: by bus/car en autobús/coche
written by ... escrito por ...
by the window junto a la ventana [**Hoon**to]
by the sea a orillas del mar [o**ree**-yass]
by Thursday para el jueves
bye ¡adiós! [ad-**yoss**]

Apart from coffee, tea and cakes, you can have alcoholic drinks in Spanish cafés. In many of them you can also get inexpensive light snacks and meals, normally called **platos combinados**, which usually include fish or meat and fries and salad.
see **bar**

cagoule el chubasquero [choobas**kai**ro]
cake el pastel [pas**tayl**]
cake shop la pastelería [pastelai**ree**-a]
call (verb) llamar [ya**mar**]
(to phone) llamar (por teléfono)
what's it called? cómo se llama esto? [say **y**ama]
he/she is called ... se llama ...
please call the doctor llame al médico, por favor [**y**amay]
please give me a call at 7.30 am tomorrow por favor, llámeme mañana a las siete y media de la mañana [**y**amamay man-**yana**]
please ask him to call me por favor, dígale que me llame [**dee**galay kay may **y**amay]
call back: I'll call back later volveré más tarde [bolbai**ray** mass **tar**day]
(phone back) volveré a llamar [ya**mar**]
call round: I'll call round

C

tomorrow me paso mañana
[may]
camcorder la videocámara
[beeday-o **ka**maira]
camera la máquina de fotos
[ma**kee**na]
camera shop la tienda de
cámaras fotográficas [t-**yen**da
day]
camp (verb) acampar
 can we camp here? ¿se
 puede acampar aquí? [say
 pway**day** – a**kee**]
camping gas canister la
bombona de butano
[boo**ta**no]

Camping gas canisters
can be bought either from
a **ferretería** (hardware
store) or from campsite shops.

campsite el camping

In Spain it is legal to
camp almost anywhere
unless there is a sign
prohibiting camping. The limitations
include urban areas, military
premises and the surroundings of
campsites and touristic zones.

can la lata
 a can of beer una lata de
 cerveza [thairb**ay**tha]
can*: can you ...? ¿puede ...?
[pway**day**]
 can I have ...? ¿me da ...?
[may]

I can't ... no puedo ...
Canada el Canadá
Canadian canadiense [kanad-
yensay]
 I'm Canadian soy canadiense
canal el canal
Canaries las Islas Canarias
[**ees**lass kanar-**yass**]
cancel anular [anoo**lar**]
candies los caramelos
[karama**y**loss]
candle la vela [**bay**la]
canoe la piragua [peer**agwa**]
canoeing el piragüismo
[peeragw**ee**smo]
can-opener el abrelatas
cap (hat) la gorra
 (of bottle) el tapón
car el coche [**ko**chay]
 by car en coche
carafe la garrafa
 a carafe of house white,
 please una garrafa de vino
 blanco de la casa, por favor
 [day **bee**no]
caravan la caravana [kara**ba**na]
caravan site el camping
carburettor el carburador
card (birthday etc) la tarjeta
[tar**Hay**ta]
 here's my (business) card
 aquí tiene mi tarjeta (de
 visita) [a**kee** t-**yay**nay – day
 bees**ee**ta]
cardigan la rebeca [re**bay**ka]
cardphone el teléfono de
tarjeta [tel**ay**fono day tar**He**ta]
careful prudente [proo**den**tay]
 be careful! ¡tenga cuidado!

[kweed**ado**]

caretaker el encargado

car ferry el ferry, el transbordador de coches [ko**chess**]

car hire el alquiler de coches [alkee**lair** day]

car park el aparcamiento [aparkam-**yento**]

carpet la moqueta [mo**kayta**]

carriage (of train) el vagón [bag**on**]

carrier bag la bolsa de plástico [day pl**asteeko**]

carrot la zanahoria [thana-**or**-ya]

carry llevar [ye**bar**]

carry-cot el capazo [ka**patho**]

carton el cartón

carwash el lavacoches [laba**kochess**]

case (suitcase) la maleta [mal**ayta**]

cash el dinero [deen**airo**] (verb) cobrar

will you cash this for me? ¿podría hacerme efectivo un cheque? [pod**ree**-a ath**airmay** efekt**eebo** oon ch**aykay**]

cash desk la caja [k**aHa**]

cash dispenser el cajero automático [ka**Hairo** owtom**ateeko**]

cashier (man/woman) el cajero/la cajera

cassette la cassette [kas**et**]

cassette recorder el cassette

castanets las castañuelas [kastan-yw**aylass**]

Castile Castilla [kast**ee**-ya]

Castilian castellano [kastay-**yano**]

castle el castillo [kast**ee**-yo]

casualty department las urgencias [oor**Henth**-yass]

cat el gato

Catalonia Cataluña [kata-**loon**-ya]

catch (verb) coger [ko**Hair**]

where do we catch the bus to ...? ¿dónde se coge el autobús a ...? [**donday** say ko**Hay**]

cathedral la catedral

Catholic (adj) católico

cauliflower la coliflor

cave la cueva [kw**ayba**]

ceiling el techo [**taycho**]

celery el apio [**ap**-yo]

cellar (for wine) la bodega [bod**ayga**]

cemetery el cementerio [themen**tair**-yo]

Centigrade* centígrado [thent**eegrado**]

centimetre* el centímetro [thent**eemetro**]

central central [thent**ral**]

central heating la calefacción central [kalayfakth-**yon**]

centre el centro [**thentro**]

how do we get to the city centre? ¿cómo se llega al centro? [say **yayga**]

cereal los cereales [theray-**aless**]

certainly desde luego [**desday** lw**aygo**]

certainly not desde luego
que no [kay]
chair la silla [**see**-ya]
champagne el champán
change (money) el cambio
[**kamb**-yo]
(verb) cambiar [kamb-**yar**]
can I change this for ...?
¿puedo cambiar esto
por ...? [**pway**do]
I don't have any change no
tengo nada suelto [**swel**to]
**can you give me change for a
1,000 peseta note?** ¿puede
cambiarme un billete de
mil pesetas? [**pway**day kamb-
yarmay oon bee-**yay**tay day meel
pes**ay**tass]

dialogue

> **do we have to change
> (trains)?** ¿tenemos que
> cambiar de tren?
> [ten**ay**moss kay kay kamb-**yar**]
> **yes, change at Córdoba/no
> it's a direct train** sí, cambie
> en Córdoba/no, es un
> tren directo [kamb-**yay**]

changed: to get changed
cambiarse [kamb-**yar**say]
chapel la capilla [kap**ee**-ya]
charge (verb) cobrar
charge card
see **credit card**
cheap barato
**do you have anything
cheaper?** tiene algo más

barato? [t-**yay**nay]
check (US) el cheque
[**chay**kay]
see **cheque**
(US: bill) la cuenta [**kway**nta]
see **bill**
(verb) revisar [rebee**sar**]
**could you check the ...,
please?** ¿puede revisar el ...,
por favor? [**pway**day]
check book el talonario de
cheques [**chay**kess]
check-in la facturación
[faktoorath-**yon**]
check in facturar
**where do we have to check
in?** ¿dónde se factura?
[**don**day say]
cheek la mejilla [meнee-ya]
cheerio! hasta luego [**a**sta
lw**ay**go]
cheers! (toast) ¡salud! [sal**oo**]
cheese el queso [**kay**so]
chemist's la farmacia [farm**ath**-
ya]

 Spanish pharmacies are
well-qualified to give you
advice on minor ailments.
There's generally one or more all-
night pharmacies in bigger towns
and cities. They work on a rota
system and you generally find the
address of the one on duty
(**farmacia de guardia**) on the door
of any pharmacist and in local
newspapers.

cheque el cheque [**chay**kay]

do you take cheques?
¿aceptan cheques? [atheptan]

With most Eurocheque cards and cashline/cheque cards you can get cash from the majority of banks in Spain, including many cash dispensers (with instructions in four languages). You may have to pay a service charge of a few pounds. Eurocheques are widely accepted by shops and hotels. Also Mastercard and Visa cards can be used in cash dispensers in Spain - but you'd better find out before you go about your bank's arrangements with Spanish banks.

cheque book el talonario de cheques [day]
cheque card la tarjeta de banco [tarHayta]
cherry la cereza [thairaytha]
chess el ajedrez [aHedreth]
chest el pecho [paycho]
chewing gum el chicle [cheeklay]
chicken el pollo [po-yo]
chickenpox la varicela [bareethela]
child (male/female) el niño [neen-yo]/la niña
 children los niños
child minder la niñera [neen-yaira]
children's pool la piscina infantil [peestheena eenfanteel]

children's portion la ración pequeña (para niños) [rath-yon pekayn-ya – neen-yoss]
chin la barbilla [barbee-ya]
china la porcelana [porthelana]
Chinese (adj) chino [cheeno]
chips las patatas fritas
chocolate el chocolate [chokolatay]
 milk chocolate el chocolate con leche [lechay]
 plain chocolate el chocolate negro [naygro]
 a hot chocolate la taza de chocolate [tatha]
choose elegir [eleHeer]
Christian name el nombre de pila [nombray day peela]
Christmas Navidad [nabeeda]
 Christmas Eve Nochebuena [nochay-bwayna]
 merry Christmas! ¡Feliz Navidad! [feleeth]
church la iglesia [eeglays-ya]
cider la sidra [seedra]
cigar el puro [pooro]
cigarette el cigarro [theegarro], el cigarrillo [theegarree-yo]
cigarette lighter el encendedor [enthendedor]
cinema el cine [theenay]
circle el círculo [theerkoolo] (in theatre) el anfiteatro [anfeetay-atro]
city la ciudad [thee-oo-da]
city centre el centro de la ciudad [thentro day]
clean (adj) limpio [leemp-yo]

can you clean these for me?
¿puede limpiarme estos?
[pwayday leemp-yarmay]

cleaning solution (for contact lenses) el líquido limpiador para las lentillas [leekeedo leemp-yador – lentee-yass]

cleansing lotion la crema limpiadora [krayma leemp-yadora]

clear claro

clever listo

cliff el acantilado

climbing el alpinismo

cling film el plástico de envolver [day embolbair]

clinic la clínica

cloakroom el guardarropa [gwardarropa]

clock el reloj [reloH]

close (verb) cerrar [therrar]

dialogue

> **what time do you close?**
> ¿a qué hora se cierra?
> [kay ora say th-yairra]
> **we close at 8 p.m. on weekdays and 1:30 p.m. on Saturdays** cerramos a las ocho de la tarde entre semana y a la una y media los sábados
> [therramoss – day la tarday entray]
> **do you close for lunch?**
> ¿cierra al mediodía?
> [th-yairra – med-yodee-a]
> **yes, between 1 and 3.30**

p.m. sí, entre una y tres y media de la tarde [entray – day la tarday]

closed cerrado [thairrado]

cloth (fabric) la tela [tayla]
(for cleaning etc) el trapo

clothes la ropa

clothes line la cuerda para tender [kwairda para tendair]

clothes peg la pinza de la ropa [peentha day]

cloud la nube [noobay]

cloudy nublado

clutch el embrague [embragay]

coach (bus) el autocar [owtokar]
(on train) el vagón [bagon]

coach station la estación de autobuses [estath-yon day owtoboosess]

coach trip la excursión (en autobús) [eskoorss-yon]

coast la costa

on the coast en la costa

coat (long coat) el abrigo
(jacket) la chaqueta [chakayta]

coathanger la percha [pairecha]

cockroach la cucaracha [kookaracha]

cocoa el cacao [kaka-o]

coconut el coco

code (for phoning) el prefijo [prefeeHo]

what's the (dialling) code for Málaga? ¿cuál es el prefijo de Málaga [kwal]

coffee el café [kafay]

two coffees, please dos

cafés, por favor

If you ask for 'un café' you will be given a café sólo which is strong black espresso-style coffee. If you want a large cup ask for a 'un café doble' [doblay]. Other types of coffee are:

un café con leche [lechay] very milky coffee
un cortado with a dash of milk
un carajillo [karaHee-yo] with a liqueur (brandy, cognac or whisky)
un café descafeinado [deskafay-eenado] decaffeinated coffee (made with hot milk rather than with hot water)
una leche manchada milk with a dash of coffee

coin la moneda [monayda]
Coke® la Coca-Cola
cold frío [free-o]
I'm cold tengo frío
I have a cold tengo catarro
collapse: he's collapsed se ha desmayado [say a desma-yado]
collar el cuello [kway-yo]
collect recoger [rekoHair]
I've come to collect ... he venido a recoger ... [ay beneedo]
collect call la llamada a cobro revertido [yamada – rebairteedo]
college la Universidad [ooneebairseeda]
colour el color

do you have this in other colours? ¿tiene otros colores? [t-yaynay]
colour film la película en color
comb el peine [pay-eenay]
come venir [bayneer]

dialogue

where do you come from? ¿de dónde es? [day donday]
I come from Edinburgh soy de Edimburgo

come back volver [bolbair]
I'll come back tomorrow volveré mañana [bolbairay]
come in entrar
comfortable cómodo
compact disc el compact disc
company (business) la compañía [kompan-yee-a]
compartment (on train) el compartimento
compass la brújula [brooHoola]
complain quejarse [kayHarsay]
complaint la queja [kayHa]
I have a complaint tengo una queja
completely completamente [komplaytamentay]
computer el ordenador
concert el concierto [konthyairto]
concussion la conmoción

cerebral [kommoth-yon thairebral]

conditioner (for hair) el acondicionador de pelo [akondeeth-yonador day paylo]

condom el condón

conference el congreso

confirm confirmar

congratulations! ¡enhorabuena! [enorabwayna]

connecting flight el vuelo de conexión [bwaylo day koneks-yon]

connection el enlace [enlathay]

conscious consciente [konth-yentay]

constipation el estreñimiento [estren-yeem-yento]

consulate el consulado [konsoolado]

contact (verb) ponerse en contacto con [ponairsay]

contact lenses las lentes de contacto, las lentillas [lentess – lentee-yass]

contraceptive el anticonceptivo [anteekonthepteebo]

convenient a mano

that's not convenient eso no viene bien [b-yaynay b-yen]

cook (verb) cocinar [kotheenar]

not cooked poco hecho [echo]

cooker la cocina [kotheena]

cookie la galleta [ga-yayta]

cooking utensils los utensilios de cocina [ootenseel-yoss day kotheena]

cool fresco [fraysko]

cork el corcho

corkscrew el sacacorchos

corner: on the corner en la esquina [eskeena]

in the corner en el rincón

cornflakes los cornflakes

correct (right) correcto

corridor el pasillo [pasee-yo]

cosmetics los cosméticos

cost (verb) costar

how much does it cost? ¿cuánto cuesta? [kwanto kwesta]

cot la cuna

cotton el algodón

cotton wool el algodón

couch (sofa) el sofá

couchette la litera [leetaira]

cough la tos

cough medicine la medicina para la tos [medeetheena]

could: could you ...? ¿podría ...?

could I have ...? quisiera ... [kees-yaira...]

I couldn't ... (wasn't able to) no podía ...

country (nation) el país [pa-eess]

(countryside) el campo

countryside el campo

couple (two people) la pareja [parayHa]

a couple of ... un par de ...

courgette el calabacín

[kalabath**ee**n]

courier el/la guía turístico [g**ee**-a]

course (main course etc) el plato

of course por supuesto [soopw**e**sto]

of course not ¡claro que no! [k**ay**]

cousin (male/female) el primo [pr**ee**mo]/la prima

cow la vaca [b**a**ka]

crab el cangrejo [kangr**ay**Ho]

cracker la galleta salada [ga-y**ay**ta]

craft shop la tienda de artesanía [t-y**e**nda day artesan**ee**-a]

crash el accidente [akth**ee**d**e**ntay]

I've had a crash he tenido un accidente [ay ten**ee**do]

crazy loco

cream (on milk, in cake) la nata (lotion) la crema [kr**ay**ma] (colour) color crema

creche la guardería infantil [gwardair**ee**-a]

credit card la tarjeta de crédito [tarH**ay**ta day]

Major credit cards and charge cards are accepted in many shops and also for cash advances at many banks and automatic tellers. They're not usually accepted in small shops, or inexpensive restaurants and hotels.

dialogue

can I pay by credit card? ¿puedo pagar con tarjeta? [pw**ay**do]

which card do you want to use? ¿qué tarjeta quiere usar? [kay – k-y**ai**ray oos**ar**]

yes, sir sí, señor [sen-y**or**]

what's the number? ¿qué número es? [n**oo**mairo]

and the expiry date? ¿y la fecha de caducidad? [f**e**cha day kadooth**ee**da]

crisps las patatas fritas (de bolsa)

crockery la loza [l**o**tha]

crossing (by sea) la travesía [trabes**ee**-a]

crossroads el cruce [kr**oo**thay]

crowd la muchedumbre [moochay-d**oo**mbray]

crowded lleno [y**ay**no]

crown (on tooth) la funda [f**oo**nda]

cruise el crucero [krooth**ai**ro]

crutches la muleta [mool**ay**ta]

cry (verb) llorar [yor**ar**]

cucumber el pepino

cup la taza [t**a**tha]

a cup of ..., please una taza de ..., por favor

cupboard el armario [arm**ar**-yo]

cure la cura [k**oo**ra]

curly rizado [reeth**a**do]

current la corriente [korr-y**e**ntay]

curtains las cortinas

cushion el cojín [koHeen]

custom la costumbre [kostoombray]

Customs la aduana [adwana]

cut el corte [kortay]
(verb) cortar
I've cut myself me he cortado [may ay]

cutlery los cubiertos [koobyairtoss]

cycling el ciclismo [theekleesmo]

cyclist el/la ciclista [theekleesta]

D

dad el papá

daily el periódico [pairyodeeko]

damage: damaged estropeado [estropay-ado]
I'm sorry, I've damaged this lo siento, he estropeado esto [s-yento – ay]

damn! ¡maldita sea! [say-a]

damp (adj) húmedo [oomaydo]

dance el baile [ba-eelay]
(verb) bailar [ba-eelar]
would you like to dance? ¿quiere bailar? [k-yairay]

dangerous peligroso

Danish el danés [danayss]

dark (adj: colour) oscuro [oskooro]
(hair) moreno [morayno]

it's getting dark está oscureciendo [oskoorethyendo]

date*: what's the date today? ¿qué día es hoy? [kay – oy]
let's make a date for next Monday vamos a quedar para el lunes que viene [bamoss a kedar – kay b-yaynay]

dates (fruit) los dátiles [dateeless]

daughter la hija [eeHa]

daughter-in-law la nuera [nwaira]

dawn el amanecer [amanethair]
at dawn al amanecer

day el día
the day after el día siguiente [seeg-yentay]
the day after tomorrow pasado mañana [man-yana]
the day before el día anterior [antair-yor]
the day before yesterday anteayer [antay-a-yair]
every day todos los días
all day todo el día
in two days' time dentro de dos días
have a nice day! ¡que pase un buen día! [kay pasay oon bwen]

day trip la excursión [exkoors-yon]

dead muerto [mwairto]

deaf sordo

deal (business) la transacción [transakth-yon]

it's a deal trato hecho
[**ay**cho]
death la muerte [mw**air**tay]
decaffeinated coffee el café
descafeinado [kaf**ay** deskafay-
een**a**do]
December diciembre [deeth-
yembray]
decide decidir [detheed**eer**]
we haven't decided yet
todavía no hemos decidido
[todab**ee**-a no **ay**moss
detheed**ee**do]
decision la decisión [detheess-
yon]
deck (on ship) la cubierta
[koob-y**air**ta]
deckchair la tumbona
deduct descontar
deep profundo
definitely claramente, ¡desde
luego! [klaram**en**tay d**es**day
lw**ay**go]
definitely not desde luego
que no [kay]
degree (qualification) la carrera
[karr**air**a]
delay el retraso
deliberately a propósito
delicatessen la charcutería
[charkootair**ee**-a]
delicious delicioso [deleeth-
yoso]
deliver repartir
delivery (of mail) el reparto
Denmark Dinamarca
dental floss el hilo dental
[**ee**lo]
dentist el/la dentista

dialogue

it's this one here es ésta de
aquí [day ak**ee**]
this one? ¿ésta?
no, that one no, esa [**ay**sa]
here? ¿aquí?
yes sí

dentures la dentadura postiza
[post**ee**tha]
deodorant el desodorante
[desodor**an**tay]
department el departamento
department store los grandes
almacenes [gr**an**dess
almath**ay**ness]
departure la salida
departure lounge la sala de
embarque [day emb**ar**kay]
depend: it depends depende
[dep**en**day]
it depends on ... depende
de ... [day]
deposit (as security) la fianza
[fee-**an**tha]
(as part payment) el depósito
description la descripción
[deskreepth-y**on**]
dessert el postre [p**os**tray]
destination el destino
develop (photos) revelar
[rebel**ar**]

dialogue

could you develop these
films? ¿puede revelar
estos carretes? [pw**ay**day –

karr**ay**tess]
when will they be ready?
¿cuándo estarán listos?
[kw**a**ndo]
tomorrow afternoon
mañana por la tarde [man-
y**a**na por la t**a**rday]
**how much is the four-hour
service?** ¿cuánto es el
servicio de cuatro horas?
[kw**a**nto ess el sairb**ee**th-yo day
kw**a**tro **o**rass]

diabetic (man/woman) el
diabético [dee-ab**ay**teeko]/la
diabética
diabetic foods la comida
para diabéticos
dial marcar
dialling code el prefijo
[pref**ee**Ho]

 The dialling code for
international calls is 00.
When you hear a high-
pitched tone dial the country codes
as follows:

UK	44
US/Canada	1
New Zealand	64
Australia	61
Ireland	353

then dial the area code and number,
omitting the inital zero.

diamond el diamante
[d-yam**a**ntay]
diaper el pañal [pan-y**a**l]
diarrhoea la diarrea

[d-yarr**ay**-a]
diary (business etc) la agenda
[aH**e**nda]
(for personal experiences) el
diario [d-y**a**r-yo]
dictionary el diccionario
[deekth-yon**a**r-yo]
didn't
see **not**
die morir
diesel el gasoil
diet la dieta [d-y**a**yta]
I'm on a diet estoy a dieta
I have to follow a special diet
tengo que seguir una dieta
especial [kay seg**ee**r – espeth-
y**a**l]
difference la diferencia
[deefair**e**nth-ya]
what's the difference? ¿cuál
es la diferencia? [kw**a**l]
different diferente
[deefair**e**ntay]
this one is different éste es
diferente [**e**stay]
a different table otra mesa
[m**a**ysa]
difficult difícil [deef**ee**theel]
difficulty la dificultad
[deefeekoolt**a**]
dinghy el bote [b**o**tay]
dining room el comedor
[komayd**o**r]
dinner (evening meal) la cena
[th**a**yna]
to have dinner cenar
direct (adj) directo
is there a direct train? ¿hay
un tren directo? [ī]

direction la dirección
[deerekth-yon]
which direction is it? ¿en qué
dirección está? [kay]
is it in this direction? ¿es por
aquí? [akee]
directory enquiries
información [eenformath-
yon]

 The number for directory
enquiries is 003 for
Spain; 008 for Europe,
and 005 for the rest of the world.

dirt la suciedad [sooth-yayda]
dirty sucio [sooth-yo]
disabled minusválido
[meenoosbaleedo]
**is there access for the
disabled?** ¿hay acceso
para minusválidos? [ī
akthayso]
disappear desaparecer
[dessaparethair]
it's disappeared ha
desaparecido [a
dessaparetheedo]
disappointed desilusionado
[deseelooss-yonado]
disappointing
decepcionante [dethepth-
yonantay]
disaster el desastre
[desastray]
disco la discoteca
discount el descuento
[deskwento]
is there a discount? ¿hacen

descuento? [athen]
disease la enfermedad
[enfairmeda]
disgusting repugnante
[repoognantay]
dish (meal) el plato
dishcloth el paño de cocina
[pan-yo day kotheena]
disinfectant el desinfectante
[deseenfektantay]
disk (for computer) diskette
[deeskaytay]
disposable diapers los
pañales (braguita) [pan-yaless
brageeta]
disposable nappies los
pañales (braguita)
distance la distancia
[deestanth-ya]
in the distance a lo lejos
[layHoss]
distilled water el agua
destilada [agwa]
district el distrito
disturb molestar
diversion (detour) el desvío
[desbee-o]
diving board el trampolín
divorced divorciado [deeborth-
yado]
dizzy: I feel dizzy estoy
mareado [maray-ado]
do hacer [athair]
what shall we do? ¿qué
hacemos? [kay athaymoss]
how do you do it? ¿cómo se
hace? [say athay]
will you do it for me? ¿me lo
puede hacer usted? [pwayday

athair oostay]

dialogues

how do you do? ¿qué tal?
[kay]
nice to meet you
encantado de conocerle
[day konothairlay]
what do you do? (work) ¿a
qué se dedica? [say]
I'm a teacher, and you?
soy profesor, ¿y usted? [ee
oostay]
I'm a student soy
estudiante [estood-yantay]
what are you doing this
evening? ¿qué hace esta
tarde? [athay]
we're going out for a drink;
do you want to join us?
vamos a salir a tomar una
copa; ¿nos acompaña?
[bamoss – akompan-ya]

do you want cream?
¿quiere crema? [k-yairay
krayma]
I do, but she doesn't yo
sí, pero ella no [pairo
ay-ya]

doctor el/la médico
we need a doctor
necesitamos un médico
[naytheseetamoss]
please call a doctor por
favor, llame a un médico
[yamay]

British citizens should
take form E111 with them.
This is obtainable from
post offices before you leave and
should enable you to get free
treatment and pay for prescriptions
at the local rate.

dialogue

where does it hurt?
¿dónde le duele? [donday
lay dwaylay]
right here justo aquí
[Hoosto akee]
does that hurt now? ¿le
duele ahora? [lay dwaylay a-
ora]
yes sí
take this to the chemist's
lleve esto a la farmacia
[yaybay – farmath-ya]

document el documento
[dokoomento]
dog el perro [pairro]
doll la muñeca [moon-yayka]
domestic flight el vuelo
nacional [bwaylo nath-yonal]
donkey el burro [boorro]
don't! ¡no lo haga! [aga]
don't do that! ¡no haga eso!
[ayso]
see not
door la puerta [pwairta]
doorman el portero [portairo]
double doble [doblay]
double bed la cama de
matrimonio [matreemon-yo]

double room la habitación doble [abeetath-yon doblay]

doughnut el dónut [donoot]

down: down here aquí abajo [akee abaнo]

put it down over there póngalo ahí [a-ee]

it's down there on the right está ahí a la derecha [dairecha]

it's further down the road está bajando la calle [baнando la ka-yay]

downhill skiing el esquí alpino [ayskee alpeeno]

downmarket (restaurant etc) barato

downstairs abajo [abaнo]

dozen la docena [dothayna]

half a dozen media docena [mayd-ya]

drain el desagüe [desagway]

draught beer la cerveza de grifo [thairbaytha day]

draughty: it's draughty hay corriente [ī korr-yentay]

drawer el cajón [kaнon]

drawing el dibujo [deebooнo]

dreadful horrible [orreeblay]

dream el sueño [swayn-yo]

dress el vestido [besteedo]

dressed: to get dressed vestirse [besteersay]

dressing (for cut) el vendaje [bendaнay]

salad dressing el aliño [aleen-yo]

dressing gown la bata

drink (alcoholic) la copa (non-alcoholic) la bebida (verb) beber [bebair]

a cold drink una bebida fría

can I get you a drink? ¿quiere beber algo? [k-yairay]

what would you like (to drink)? ¿qué le apetece beber? [kay lay apetaythay]

no thanks, I don't drink no gracias, no bebo [grath-yass no baybo]

I'll just have a drink of water voy a beber sólo agua [boy – agwa]

In Spain it is usual to have water and table wine (very often with **gaseosa** [gasay-osa] (lemonade) with your meal. It is also customary to have a drink (**aperitivo**) and a snack (**tapa**) just before the lunchtime meal either at home or in a bar. see **bar**

drinking water agua potable [agwa potablay]

is this drinking water? ¿esto es agua potable?

drive (verb) conducir [kondootheer]

we drove here vinimos en coche [beenemoss en kochay]

I'll drive you home te llevaré a casa en el coche [tay

yebar**ay** – k**o**chay]

Most foreign driving licences are honoured in Spain – including all EC, US and Canadian ones – but an international Driver's Licence is an easy way to set your mind at rest. If you're bringing your own car, you must have a green card from your insurers, and a bail bond or extra coverage for legal costs is also worth having, since if you do have an accident, it'll be your fault, as a foreigner, regardless of the circumstances. Without a bail bond, both you and the car could be locked up pending investigation. Away from main roads, you yield to vehicles approaching from the right. Speed limits are posted – maximum on urban roads is 60kph, other roads 90kph, motorways 120kph – and (on the main highways at least) speed traps are common. If you're stopped for any violation, the Spanish police can and usually will levy a stiff on-the-spot fine before letting you go on your way, especially since as a foreigner you're unlikely to want, or be able to appear in court. The legal alcohol limit when driving is infinitesimally small, so do not drink and drive.

driver (man/woman) el conductor [kond**oo**ktor]/la conduct**o**ra
driving licence el permiso de conducir [pairm**ee**so day kond**oo**th**eer**]
drop: just a drop, please (of drink) un poqu**i**to [pok**ee**to]
drug la medic**i**na [maydeeth**ee**na]
drugs (narcotics) la dr**o**ga
drunk (adj) borr**a**cho
drunken driving conducir en est**a**do de embriaguez [kond**oo**th**eer** – embr-yag**eth**]
dry (adj) seco [s**ay**ko]
(sherry) fino
dry-cleaner la tintorer**í**a [teentorair**ee**-a]
duck el pato
due: he was due to arrive yesterday ten**í**a que llegar ayer [ten**ee**-a kay yegar a-y**air**]
when is the train due? ¿cu**á**ndo tiene el tren la llegada? [kw**a**ndo t-y**ay**nay – yeg**a**da]
dull (pain) s**o**rdo
(weather) gris [greess]
dummy (baby's) el chupete [choop**ay**tay]
during durante [door**a**ntay]
dust el polvo [p**o**lbo]
dusty polvoriento [polbor-y**e**nto]
dustbin el cubo de la basura [k**oo**bo day]
duty-free (goods) (los productos) duty free
duty-free shop la tienda de duty free [t-y**e**nda day]
duvet el edred**ó**n

E

each cada

 how much are they each?
 ¿cuánto es cada uno?
 [kwanto]

ear la oreja [orayHa]

earache: I have earache tengo
 dolor de oídos [o-eedoss]

early temprano

 early in the morning por la
 mañana temprano [man-
 yana]

 I called by earlier vine antes
 [beenay antess]

earring el pendiente [pend-
 yentay]

east este [estay]

 in the east en el este

Easter la Semana Santa

easy fácil [fatheel]

eat comer [komair]

 we've already eaten, thanks
 ya hemos comido, gracias
 [aymoss]

eating habits
 Eating times in Spain are
 different from the rest of
Europe. Spaniards usually have a
very light breakfast, **desayuno**
[desa-yoono], consisting of coffee
and biscuits or a cake or bread and
butter and jam. The main meal, **la
comida** or **el almuerzo** [al-
mwairtho], is taken sometime in
between 1.30 and 3.30. It usually
consists of three courses: a hot soup

or stew; a second course of fish or
meat, followed by fruit and coffee.
La cena [thayna] (dinner),
sometime between 8 and 10.30 p.m.
or even later, is not as substantial
and very often it's just an informal
snack. Some people have a mid-
morning snack, an afternoon snack
(around 6 p.m.) called a **merienda**,
and an **aperitivo** just before the
afternoon meal. .

eau de toilette el agua de
 baño [agwa day ban-yo]

EC la CE [thay-ay]

economy class la clase turista
 [klassay]

Edinburgh Edimburgo
 [edeemboorgo]

egg el huevo [waybo]

eggplant la berenjena
 [berenHayna]

either: either ... or ... o ... o ...

 either of them cualquiera de
 ellos [kwalk-yaira day ay-yoss]

elastic el elástico

elastic band la goma elástica

elbow el codo

electric eléctrico

electrical appliances los
 electrodomésticos

electric fire la estufa eléctrica

electrician el electricista
 [elektreeth**ee**sta]

electricity la electricidad
 [elektreeth**ee**da]

 see **voltage**

elevator el ascensor [asthensor]

else: something else algo más

somewhere else en otra
parte [partay]

dialogue

would you like anything
else? ¿quiere algo más?
[k-yairay]
no, nothing else, thanks
nada más, gracias

embassy la embajada
[embaHada]
emergency la emergencia
[emairHenth-ya]
this is an emergency! ¡es una
emergencia!
emergency exit la salida de
emergencia
empty vacío [bathee-o]
end el final [feenal]
(verb) terminar [tairmeenar]
at the end of the street al
final de la calle [day la ka-yay]
when does it end? ¿cuándo
termina? [kwando tairmeena]
engaged (toilet) ocupado
(telephone) comunicando
(to be married) prometido
engine (car) el motor
England Inglaterra
[eenglatairra]
English inglés [eenglayss]
I'm English (man/woman) soy
inglés/inglesa
do you speak English?
¿habla inglés? [abla]
enjoy: to enjoy oneself
divertirse [deebairteersay]

dialogue

how did you like the film?
¿le gustó la película? [lay
goosto]
I enjoyed it very much, did
you enjoy it? me gustó
mucho, ¿le gustó a usted?
[may – moocho – lay – oostay]

enjoyable entretenido
enlargement (of photo) la
ampliación [ampl-yath-yon]
enormous enorme [enormay]
enough suficiente [soofeeth-
yentay]
there's not enough no hay
bastante [ī bastantay]
it's not big enough no es
suficientemente grande
[soofeeth-yentementay]
that's enough es suficiente
entrance la entrada
envelope el sobre [sobray]
epileptic epiléptico
equipment el equipo
[ekeepo]
especially especialmente
[espeth-yalmentay]
essential imprescindible
[eemprestheendeeblay]
it is essential that ... es
imprescindible que ... [kay]
EU UE [oo-ay]
euro el euro [ay-ooro]
Eurocheque el eurocheque
[ay-oorochekay]
Eurocheque card la tarjeta
eurocheque [tarHayta]

Europe Europa [ay-ooropa]
European europeo [ay-ooropay-o]
European Union la Unión Europea [oon-yon]
even (including) incluso [eenklooso]
even if ... incluso si ...
evening (early evening) la tarde [tarday]
(after nightfall) la noche [nochay]
this evening esta tarde/noche
in the evening por la tarde/noche
evening meal la cena [thayna]
eventually finalmente [feenalmentay]
ever alguna vez [beth]

dialogue

> have you ever been to Barcelona? ¿ha estado alguna vez en Barcelona? [a]
> yes, I was there two years ago sí, estuve allí hace dos años [estoobay a-yee athay – an-yoss]

every cada
every day todos los días
everyone todos
everything todo
everywhere en todas partes [partess]

exactly! ¡exactamente! [exactamentay]
exam el examen
example el ejemplo [eHaymplo]
for example por ejemplo
excellent excelente [esthelentay]
excellent! ¡estupendo!
except excepto [esthepto]
excess baggage el exceso de equipaje [esthayso day ekeepaHay]
exchange rate el cambio [kamb-yo]
exciting emocionante [emoth-yonantay]
excuse me (to get past) con permiso
(to get attention) ¡por favor! [fabor]
(to say sorry) perdone [pairdonay]
exhaust (pipe) el tubo de escape [toobo day eskapay]
exhausted (tired) agotado
exhibition la exposición [exposeeth-yon]
exit la salida
where's the nearest exit? ¿cuál es la salida más próxima? [kwal]
expect esperar [espairar]
expensive caro
experienced con experiencia [espair-yenth-ya]
explain explicar [espleekar]
can you explain that? ¿puede explicármelo?

[pway day]

express (mail) urgente
[oorHentay]

(train) expreso [esprayso]

extension (phone) extensión
[estens-yon]

extension 221, please
extensión doscientos
veintiuno, por favor

extension lead el alargador

**extra: can we have an extra
one?** ¿nos puede dar otro?
[pwayday]

do you charge extra for that?
¿esto tiene recargo?
[t-yaynay]

extraordinary
extraordinario [estra-ordeenar-
yo]

extremely extremadamente
[estremadamentay]

eye el ojo [oHo]

**will you keep an eye on my
suitcase for me?** ¿puede
cuidarme la maleta?
[pwayday kweedarmay la
malayta]

eyebrow pencil el lápiz de
cejas [lapeeth day thayHass]

eye drops el colirio
[koleer-yo]

eyeglasses las gafas

eyeliner el lápiz de ojos
[lapeeth day oHoss]

eye make-up remover el
desmaquillador de ojos
[desmakee-yador]

eye shadow la sombra de
ojos

F
---

face la cara

factory la fábrica

Fahrenheit* Fahrenheit

faint (verb) desmayarse [desma-
yarsay]

she's fainted se ha
desmayado [say a desma-yado]

I feel faint estoy mareado
[maray-ado]

fair la feria [fair-ya]

(adj) justo [Hoosto]

fairly bastante [bastantay]

fake la falsificación
[falseefeekath-yon]

Fall el otoño [oton-yo]
see autumn

fall caerse [ka-airsay]

she's had a fall se ha caído
[say a ka-eedo]

false falso [fal-so]

family la familia [fameel-ya]

famous famoso

fan (electrical) el ventilador
[benteelador]

(hand held) el abanico

(sports) el/la hincha [eencha]

fan belt la correa del
ventilador [korray-a del
benteelador]

fantastic fantástico

far lejos [layHoss]

dialogue

is it far from here? ¿está
lejos de aquí? [day akee]

no, not very far no, no muy lejos [mwee]
well how far? bueno, ¿cuánto? [bwayno kwanto]
it's about 20 kilometres unos veinte kilómetros

fare el precio [prayth-yo]
farm la granja [granHa]
fashionable de moda
fast rápido
fat (person) gordo
(on meat) la grasa
father el padre [padray]
father-in-law el suegro [swaygro]
faucet el grifo [greefo]
fault el defecto
sorry, it was my fault lo siento, fue culpa mía [s-yento fway koolpa mee-a]
it's not my fault no es culpa mía
faulty defectuoso [dayfektwoso]
favourite favorito [faboreeto]
fax el fax
(verb: person) mandar un fax a
(document) mandar por fax
February febrero [febrairo]
feel sentir
I feel hot tengo calor
I feel unwell no me siento bien [may s-yento b-yen]
I feel like going for a walk me apetece dar un paseo [apetaythay – pasay-o]
how are you feeling today? ¿qué tal se encuentra hoy? [kay tal say enkwentra oy]

I'm feeling better me siento mejor [mayHor]
felt-tip (pen) el rotulador
fence la valla [ba-ya]
fender el parachoques [parachokess]
ferry el ferry
festival el festival [festeebal]
fetch: I'll fetch him yo iré a recogerle [eeray a raykoHairlay]
will you come and fetch me later? ¿quiere venir a buscarme más tarde? [k-yairay beneer a booskarmay mass tarday]
feverish con fiebre [f-yaybray]
few: a few unos pocos
a few days unos pocos días
fiancé el novio [nob-yo]
fiancée la novia [nob-ya]
field el campo
fight la pelea [pelay-a]
figs los higos [eegoss]
fill (verb) llenar [yenar]
fill in rellenar [ray-yenar]
do I have to fill this in? ¿tengo que rellenar esto? [kay]
fill up llenar [yenar]
fill it up, please lleno, por favor [yayno]
filling (in cake, sandwich) el relleno [ray-yeno]
(in tooth) el empaste [empastay]
film (movie, for camera) la película

dialogue

do you have this kind of film? ¿tiene películas de este tipo? [t-**yay**nay – day e**stay**]
yes, how many exposures? sí, ¿de cuántas fotos? [**kwan**tass]
36 treinta y seis

film processing el revelado [rebe**la**do]
filter coffee el café de filtro [ka**fay** day **feel**tro]
filter papers los filtros
filthy sucísimo [sooth**ee**seemo]
find (verb) encontrar
I can't find it no lo encuentro [enk**wen**tro]
I've found it lo he encontrado [ay]
find out enterarse [ente**rar**say]
could you find out for me? ¿me lo puede preguntar? [may lo p**way**day pregoon**tar**]
fine (weather) bueno [b**way**no]
(noun) la multa [**mool**ta]

dialogues

how are you? ¿cómo estás?
I'm fine, thanks bien, gracias [b-yen **grath**-yass]

is that OK? ¿va bien así? [ba]

that's fine, thanks está bien, gracias

finger el dedo [**day**do]
finish (verb) terminar [tairmee**nar**], acabar
I haven't finished yet no he terminado todavía [ay tairmee**na**do todabee-a]
when does it finish? ¿cuándo termina? [**kwan**do ter**mee**na]
fire: fire! ¡fuego! [f**way**go]
can we light a fire here? ¿se puede encender fuego aquí? [say p**way**day enthen**dair** – a**kee**]
it's on fire está ardiendo [ard-**yen**do]
fire alarm la alarma de incendios [day eenth**end**-yoss]
fire brigade los bomberos [bomb**air**oss]

 In the event of a fire, the number to ring is 080.

fire escape la salida de incendios [day eenth**end**-yoss]
fire extinguisher el extintor [estee**ntor**]
first primero [pree**mair**o]
I was first fui el primero [fwoo-ee]
at first al principio [preen**theep**-yo]
the first time la primera vez [beth]
first on the left la primera a

la izquierda [eethk-yairda]
first aid primeros auxilios [owkseel-yoss]
first aid kit el botiquín [boteekeen]
first class (travel etc) de primera (clase) [preemaira klasay]
first floor la primera planta (US) la planta baja [baHa]
first name el nombre de pila [nombray day]
fish el pez [peth]
(food) el pescado
fishing village el pueblo de pescadores [pweblo day peskadoress]
fishmonger's la pescadería [peskadairee-a]
fit (attack) el ataque [atakay]
fit: it doesn't fit me no me viene bien [b-yaynay b-yen]
fitting room el probador
fix (verb) arreglar
(arrange) fijar [feeHar]
can you fix this? ¿puede arreglar esto? [pwayday]
fizzy con gas
flag la bandera [bandaira]
flannel la manopla
flash (for camera) el flash
flat (noun: apartment) el piso
(adj) llano [yano]
I've got a flat tyre tengo un pinchazo [peenchatho]
flavour el sabor
flea la pulga
flight el vuelo [bwaylo]
flight number el número de

vuelo [noomairo day]
flippers las aletas [alaytass]
flood la inundación [eenoondath-yon]
floor (of room) el suelo [swaylo]
(of building) el piso
on the floor en el suelo
florist la floristería [floreestairee-a]
flour la harina [areena]
flower la flor
flu la gripe [greepay]
fluent: he speaks fluent Spanish domina el castellano [kastay-yano]
fly la mosca
(verb) volar [bolar]
can we fly there? ¿podemos ir en avión allí? [podaymoss eer en ab-yon a-yee]
fly in llegar en avión [yegar]
fly out irse en avión [eersay]
fog la niebla [n-yebla]
foggy: it's foggy hay niebla [i]
folk dancing el baile tradicional [ba-eelay tradeeth-yonal]
folk music la música popular [mooseeka popoolar]
follow seguir [segeer]
follow me sígame [seegamay]
food la comida
food poisoning la intoxicación alimenticia [eentoxeekath-yon aleementeeth-ya]
food shop/store la tienda de comestibles [t-yenda day komesteebless]

76

foot* el pie [p-yay]
 on foot a pie
football (game) el fútbol
 (ball) el balón
football match el partido de
 fútbol
for para, por
 do you have something
 for ...? (headache/diarrhoea etc)
 ¿tiene algo para ...?
 [t-yaynay]

dialogues

who's the chicken paella
for? ¿para quién es la
paella con pollo? [k-yen
ess la pa-ay-ya con po-yo]
that's for me es para mí
and this one? ¿y ésta? [ee]
that's for her ésa es para
ella [aysa – ay-ya]

where do I get the bus for
Granada? ¿dónde se coge
el autobús para Granada?
[donday say koHay]
the bus for Granada leaves
from Plaza de España el
autobús para Granada
sale de la Plaza de España
[salay day]

how long have you been
here for? ¿cuánto tiempo
lleva aquí? [kwanto t-yempo
yayba akee]
I've been here for two
days, how about you?

llevo aquí dos días, ¿y
usted? [yaybo – ee oostay]
I've been here for a week
llevo aquí una semana

forehead la frente [frentay]
foreign extranjero [estranHairo]
foreigner (man/woman) el
 extranjero/la extranjera
forest el bosque [boskay]
forget olvidar [olbeedar]
 I forget no me acuerdo [no
 may akwairdo]
 I've forgotten me he
 olvidado [ay olbeedado]
fork el tenedor
 (in road) la bifurcación
 [beefoorkath-yon]
form (document) el impreso
 [eemprayso]
formal (dress) de etiqueta [day
 eteekayta]
fortnight quince días
 [keenthay]
fortunately afortunadamente
 [afortoonadamentay]
forward: could you forward my
 mail? ¿puede enviarme el
 correo? [pwayday emb-yarmay el
 korray-o]
forwarding address la nueva
 dirección [nwayba deerekth-
 yon]
foundation (make-up) la crema
 base [krayma basay]
fountain la fuente [fwentay]
foyer (of hotel, theatre) el hall
 [Hol]
fracture la fractura [fraktoora]

Fr

77

Fr

France Francia [franth-ya]
free libre [leebray]
(no charge) gratuito [gratweeto]
is it free (of charge)? ¿es
gratis?
freeway la autopista
[owtopeesta]
freezer el congelador
[konHaylador]
French francés [franthess]
French fries las patatas fritas
frequent frecuente
[frekwentay]
how frequent is the bus to
Seville? ¿cada cuánto
tiempo hay autobús a
Sevilla? [kwanto t-yempo ī]
fresh fresco
fresh orange el zumo de
naranja natural [thoomo de
naranHa natooral]
Friday viernes [b-yairness]
fridge el frigorífico
fried frito
fried egg el huevo frito
[waybo]
friend (male/female) el
amigo/la amiga
friendly simpático
from de, desde [day, desday]
when does the next train
from Tarragona arrive?
¿cuándo llega el próximo
tren de Tarragona? [kwando
yayga]
from Monday to Friday de
lunes a viernes [day]
from next Thursday desde el
próximo jueves

dialogue

where are you from? ¿de
dónde es usted? [day
donday ess oostay]
I'm from Slough soy de
Slough [soy day]

front la parte delantera [partay
delantaira]
in front delante [delantay]
in front of the hotel delante
del hotel
at the front delante
frost la escarcha
frozen congelado [konHaylado]
frozen food los congelados
fruit la fruta
fruit juice el zumo de frutas
[thoomo]
fry freír [fray-eer]
frying pan la sartén
full lleno [yayno]
it's full of ... está lleno de ...
[day]
I'm full estoy lleno/llena
full board pensión completa
[pens-yon komplayta]
fun: it was fun fue muy
divertido [fway mwee
deebairteedo]
funeral el funeral [foonairal]
funny (strange) raro
(amusing) gracioso [grath-yoso]
furniture los muebles
[mwaybless]
further más allá [a-ya]
it's further down the road está
más adelante [adelantay]

dialogue

how much further is it to Cáceres? ¿cuánto queda para Cáceres? [kwanto kayda]
about 5 kilometres unos cinco kilómetros

fuse el fusible [fooseeblay]
 the lights have fused se han fundido los plomos [say an]
fuse box la caja de fusibles [kaHa day fooseebless]
fuse wire el plomo
future el futuro [footooro]
 in the future en lo sucesivo [sootheseebo]

G

gallon* el galón
game (cards etc) el juego [Hwaygo]
 (match) el partido
 (meat) la caza [catha]
garage (for fuel) la gasolinera [gasoleenaira]
 (for repairs) el taller (de reparaciones) [ta-yair day reparath-yoness]
 (for parking) el garaje [garaHay]
garden el jardín [Hardeen]
garlic el ajo [aHo]
gas el gas
 (US) la gasolina
 see **petrol**
gas cylinder (camping gas) la

bombona de gas
gasoline la gasolina
 see **petrol**
gas permeable lenses las lentillas porosas [lentee-yass]
gas station la gasolinera [gasoleenaira]
gate la puerta [pwairta]
 (at airport) la puerta de embarque [embarkay]
gay el gay
gay bar el bar gay
gears la marcha
gearbox la caja de cambios [kaHa day kamb-yoss]
gear lever la palanca de velocidades [belotheedadess]
general general [Heneral]
gents (toilet) el aseo de caballeros [asay-o day kaba-yaiross]
genuine (antique etc) genuino [Henweeno]
German alemán
German measles la rubéola [roobay-ola]
Germany Alemania [aleman-ya]
Gerona Gerona [Herona]
get (fetch) traer [tra-air]
 will you get me another one, please? me quiere traer otro, por favor [may keeairay]
 how do I get to ...? ¿cómo se va a ...? [say ba]
 do you know where I can get them? ¿sabe dónde las puedo comprar? [sabay donday lass pwaydo]

dialogue

can I get you a drink?
¿puedo ofrecerle algo de beber? [pway do ofrethair-lay – day bebair]
no, I'll get this one; what would you like? no, ésta la pago yo; ¿qué le apetece? [kay lay apaytaythay]
a glass of red wine un vaso de vino tinto [baso day beeno teento]

get back (return) volver [bolbair]
get in (arrive) llegar [yegar]
get off bajarse [baHarsay]
where do I get off? ¿dónde tengo que bajarme? [donday – kay baHarmay]
get on (to train etc) subirse [soobeersay]
get out (of car etc) bajarse [baHarsay]
get up (in the morning) levantarse [lebantarsay]
gift el regalo

 Some Spaniards give presents at Christmas, but they all exchange presents on the sixth of January, on **la noche de los Reyes Magos** (Night of The Three Wise Men – Twelfth Night).

gift shop la tienda de regalos [t-yenda]

gin la ginebra [Heenaybra]
a gin and tonic, please un gintónic, por favor [Heentoneek]
girl la chica [cheeka]
girlfriend la novia [nob-ya]
give dar
can you give me some change? ¿me puede dar cambio? [may pwayday – kamb-yo]
I gave it to him se lo dí a él [say]
will you give this to ...? ¿podría entregarle esto a ...? [entregarlay]

dialogue

how much do you want for this? ¿cuánto quiere por esto? [kwanto k-yairay]
1,000 pesetas mil pesetas [pesaytass]
I'll give you 800 pesetas le doy ochocientas pesetas [lay]

give back devolver [debolbair]
glad alegre [alegray]
glass (material) el cristal [kreestal]
(tumbler) el vaso [baso]
(wine glass) la copa
glasses las gafas
gloves los guantes [gwantess]
glue el pegamento
go (verb) ir [eer]
we'd like to go to the

swimming-pool nos gustaría ir a la piscina [pees**tee**na]

where are you going? ¿adónde va? [a**don**day ba]

where does this bus go? ¿adónde va este autobús? [e**stay**]

let's go! ¡vamos! [**ba**moss]

she's gone (left) se ha marchado [say a]

where has he gone? ¿dónde se ha ido? [**don**day – **ee**do]

I went there last week fui allí la semana pasada [fwee a-**yee**]

go away irse [**eer**say]

go away! ¡váyase! [ba**ya**say]

go back (return) volver [bolb**air**]

go down (the stairs etc) bajar [ba**Har**]

go in entrar

go out salir

do you want to go out tonight? ¿quiere salir esta noche? [k-y**air**ay – **no**chay]

go through pasar por

go up (the stairs etc) subir

goat la cabra

God Dios [d-y**oss**]

goggles las gafas protectoras

gold el oro

golf el golf

golf course el campo de golf

good bueno [**bway**no]

good! ¡muy bien! [mwee b-yen]

it's no good es inútil

[een**oo**teel]

goodbye adiós [ad-y**oss**]

good evening buenas tardes [bwen**ass tar**dess]

Good Friday el Viernes Santo [b-y**air**ness]

 Good Friday is a public holiday in Spain. All over the country, but especially in the south, there are religious processions that will make it almost impossible to drive in large towns and cities.

good morning buenos días [bway**noss**]

good night buenas noches [**no**chess]

goose el ganso

got: we've got to ... tenemos que ... [tay**nay**moss kay]

have you got any apples? ¿tiene manzanas? [t-y**ay**nay]

government el gobierno [gob-y**air**no]

gradually gradualmente [gradwal**men**tay]

grammar la gramática

gram(me) el gramo

granddaughter la nieta [n-y**ayta**]

grandfather el abuelo [ab**way**lo]

grandmother la abuela [ab**way**la]

grandson el nieto [n-y**ay**to]

grapefruit el pomelo [pom**ay**lo]

grapefruit juice el zumo de

pomelo [th**oo**mo]
grapes las uvas [**oo**bass]
grass la hierba [y**ai**rba]
grateful agradecido
[agrade**thee**do]
gravy la salsa
great (excellent) muy bueno
[mwee bw**ay**no]
that's great! ¡estupendo!
[estoop**e**ndo]
a great success un gran
éxito
Great Britain Gran Bretaña
[bret**a**nya]
Greece Grecia [gr**ay**th-ya]
greedy comilón
Greek (adj) griego [gr-y**ay**go]
green verde [b**ai**rday]
green card (car insurance) la
carta verde
greengrocer's la frutería
[froot**ai**re-a]
grey gris
grill la parrilla [parr**ee**-ya]
grilled a la parrilla
grocer's (la tienda de)
comestibles [t-y**e**nda day
komest**ee**bless]
ground el suelo [sw**ay**lo]
on the ground en el suelo
ground floor la planta baja
[b**a**Ha]
group el grupo
guarantee la garantía
is it guaranteed? ¿está
garantizado? [garante**tha**do]
guest (man/woman) el invitado
[eembeet**a**do]/la invitada
guesthouse la casa de

huéspedes [day w**e**spedess]
see hotel
guide el/la guía [g**ee**-a]
guidebook la guía
guided tour la visita con guía
[bees**ee**ta]
guitar la guitarra [gee**ta**rra]
gum (in mouth) la encía
[enth**ee**-a]
gun la pistola
gym el gimnasio [H**ee**mn**a**s-yo]

H

hair el pelo [p**ay**lo]
hairbrush el cepillo para el
pelo [thep**ee**-yo]
haircut el corte de pelo
[k**o**rtay]
hairdresser's (men's) la
barbería
(women's) la peluquería
[pelookair**ee**-a]
hairdryer el secador de pelo
[day p**ay**lo]
hair gel el fijador (para el
pelo) [feeh**a**dor]
hairgrips la horquilla [ork**ee**-
ya]
hair spray la laca
half* la mitad [la me**e**ta]
half an hour media hora
[m**ay**d-ya **o**ra]
half a litre medio litro
about half that
aproximadamente la mitad
de eso [aproximadam**e**ntay – day
ayso]

half board la media pensión [pens-yon]
half-bottle la botella pequeña [botay-ya pekayn-ya]
half fare el medio billete [mayd-yo bee-yaytay]
half price la mitad del precio [meeta del preth-yo]
ham el jamón [Hamon]

Jamón serrano is cured ham, similar to Parma ham. **Jamón de York** or **jamón cocido** is similar to British ham. Both kinds of jamón are sold in **charcuterías** in thin slices and are used in sandwiches, starters and a variety of dishes. **Jamón serrano** is also sold as a whole leg and is often seen hanging in charcuterías and bars. The best kind of jamón serrano is called **pata negra**.

hamburger la hamburguesa [amboorgaysa]
hammer el martillo [martee-yo]
hand la mano
handbag el bolso
handbrake el freno de mano [frayno day]
handkerchief el pañuelo [pan-ywaylo]
handle (on door) la manilla [manee-ya]
(on suitcase etc) el asa
hand luggage el equipaje de mano [ekeepahay]
hang-gliding el ala delta

hangover la resaca
I've got a hangover tengo resaca
happen suceder [soothedair]
what's happening? ¿qué pasa? [kay]
what has happened? ¿qué ha pasado? [a]
happy contento
I'm not happy about this esto no me agrada [may]
harbour el puerto [pwairto]
hard duro [dooro]
(difficult) difícil [deefeetheel]
hard-boiled egg el huevo duro [waybo]
hard lenses las lentillas duras [lentee-yass]
hardly apenas [apaynass]
hardly ever casi nunca
hardware shop la ferretería [fairretairee-a]
hat el sombrero
hate (verb) odiar
have* tener [tenair]
can I have a ...? ¿me da ...? [may]
do you have ...? ¿tiene ...? [t-yaynay]
what'll you have? ¿qué va a tomar? [kay ba]
I have to leave now tengo que dejarle ahora [dayHarlay a-ora]
do I have to ...? ¿tengo que ...?
can we have some ...? ¿nos pone ...? [ponay]
hayfever la alergia al polen

[alairHee-a al polayn]

hazelnut la avellana [abay-yana]

he* él

head la cabeza [kabaytha]

headache el dolor de cabeza

headlights el faro

headphones los auriculares [owreekoolaress]

health food shop la tienda naturista [t-yenda natooreesta]

healthy sano

hear oir [o-eer]

dialogue

can you hear me? ¿me oye? [may oy-ay]
I can't hear you, could you repeat that? no le oigo, podría repetirlo [lay oygo podree-a]

hearing aid el aparato del oído [o-eedo]

heart el corazón [korathon]

heart attack el infarto

heat el calor

heater (in room) el calefactor (in car) la calefacción [kalayfakth-yon]

heating la calefacción

heavy pesado

heel (of foot) el talón (of shoe) el tacón

could you heel these? ¿podría cambiarles los tacones? [kamb-yarless – takoness]

heelbar el zapatero [thapatairo]

height la altura

helicopter el helicóptero

hello ¡hola! [ola]
(answer on phone) ¡dígame! [deegamay]

helmet el casco

help la ayuda [a-yooda]
(verb) ayudar [a-yoodar]
help! ¡socorro!
can you help me? ¿puede ayudarme? [pwayday a-yoodarmay]
thank you very much for your help gracias por su ayuda

helpful amable [amablay]

hepatitis la hepatitis [epateeteess]

her*: I haven't seen her no la he visto [ay]
to her a ella [ay-ya]
with her con ella
for her para ella
that's her ésa es (ella) [aysa]
that's her towel ésa es su toalla

herbal tea el té de hierbas [tay day yairbass]

herbs las hierbas

here aquí [akee]
here is/are ... aquí está/están ...
here you are (offering) tenga

hers* (el) suyo [soo-yo], (la) suya
that's hers es de ella [day ay-ya], es suyo/suya

hey! ¡oiga!

hi! (hello) ¡hola! [ola]

hide (verb) esconder
[eskondair]
high alto
highchair la silla alta para
bebés [see-ya – baybayss]
highway (US) la autopista
[owtopeeesta]
hill la colina
him*: I haven't seen him no le
he visto [lay ay]
to him a él
with him con él
for him para él
that's him ése es (él) [aysay]
hip la cadera [kadaira]
hire: (verb) alquilar [alkeelar]
for hire de alquiler [alkeelair]
where can I hire a bike?
¿dónde puedo alquilar una
bicicleta? [donday pwaydo]
see rent
his*: it's his car es su coche
that's his eso de él [ayso day],
eso es suyo [soo-yo]
hit (verb) golpear [golpay-ar]
hitch-hike hacer autostop
[athair owtostop]
hobby el pasatiempo [pasat-
yempo]
hold (verb) sostener [sostaynair]
hole el agujero [agooнairo]
holiday las vacaciones [bakath-
yoness]
on holiday de vacaciones
home la casa
at home (in my house) en casa
(in my country) en mi país [pa-
eess]
we go home tomorrow

volvemos a casa mañana
[bolbaymoss]
honest honrado [onrado]
honey la miel [m-yel]
honeymoon la luna de miel
[loona day]
hood (US) el capó
hope la esperanza [espairantha]
I hope so espero que sí
[espairo kay]
I hope not espero que no
hopefully it won't rain no
lloverá, eso espero [no yobaira
ayso]
horn (of car) la bocina
[botheena]
horrible horrible [orreeblay]
horse el caballo [kaba-yo]
horse riding la equitación
[ekeetath-yon]
hospital el hospital [ospeetal]
hospitality la hospitalidad
[ospeetaleeda]
thank you for your hospitality
gracias por su hospitalidad
[soo]
hot caliente [kal-yentay]
(spicy) picante [peekantay]
I'm hot tengo calor
it's hot today hoy hace calor
[oy athay]
hotel el hotel [otel]

 The one thing all
travellers need to master
is the elaborate variety of
accommodation. Least expensive of
all are **fondas** (identifiable by a
square blue sign with a white **F** on

it, and often positioned above a bar), closely followed by **casas de huéspedes** (**CH** on a similar sign), **pensiones** (**P**) and, less commonly, **hospedajes**. Distinctions between all of these are rather blurred, but in general you'll find food served at both fondas and pensiones (some of which may offer rooms only on a meals-inclusive basis). Casas de huéspedes – literally 'guest houses' – were traditionally for longer stays, and to some extent, particularly in the older family seaside resorts, they still are. Slightly more expensive but far more common are **hostales** (marked **Hs**) and **hostal-residencias** (**H&R**). These are categorized from one star to three stars, but even so prices vary enormously according to location – in general the more remote, the less expensive. Most hostales offer good functional rooms, usually with private shower, and, for doubles at least, they can be excellent value. The residencia designation means that no meals other than perhaps breakfast are served. Moving up the scale you finally reach fully-fledged **hoteles** (**H**), again star-graded by the authorities (from one to five). Near the top end of this scale there are also state-run **paradores**: beautiful places, often converted from castles, monasteries and other minor Spanish monuments.

hotel room: in my hotel room

en mi habitación del hotel [abeetath-yon]
hour la hora [ora]
house la casa
house wine el vino de la casa [beeno day]
hovercraft el aerodeslizador [a-airodesleethador]
how como
　how many? ¿cuántos? [kwantoss]
　how do you do? ¡mucho gusto! [moocho]

dialogues

how are you? ¿cómo está?
fine, thanks, and you? bien gracias, y usted [b-yen – ee oostay]

how much is it? ¿cuánto es? [kwanto]
1,000 pesetas mil pesetas [pesaytass]
I'll take it me lo quedo [may lo kaydo]

humid húmedo [oomedo]
humour el humor [oomor]
hungry hámbriento [ambr-yento]
　I'm hungry tengo hambre [ambray]
　are you hungry? ¿tiene hambre? [t-yaynay]
hurry (verb) darse prisa [darsay preesa]
　I'm in a hurry tengo prisa

there's no hurry no hay prisa
[i]

hurry up! ¡dese prisa! [**day**say]

hurt doler [dol**air**]

it really hurts me duele
mucho [may dw**ay**lay m**oo**cho]

husband mi marido

hydrofoil la hidroala [eedro-
ala]

hypermarket el
hipermercado
[eepairmair**ka**do]

I

I yo

ice el hielo [**yay**lo]
with ice con hielo
no ice, thanks sin hielo,
gracias [seen]

ice cream el helado [e**la**do]

ice-cream cone el cucurucho
de helado [kookoor**oo**choo]

iced coffee el café helado

ice lolly el polo

idea la idea [eed**ay**-a]

idiot el/la idiota [eed-y**ota**]

if si

ignition el encendido
[enthend**ee**do]

ill enfermo [en**fair**mo]
I feel ill me encuentro mal
[may enkw**en**tro]

illness la enfermedad
[enfair**may**da]

imitation (leather etc) de
imitación [day eemeetath-y**on**]

immediately ahora mismo

[a-**ora** m**ee**smo]

important importante
[eemportan**tay**]
it's very important es muy
importante [mwee]
it's not important no tiene
importancia [t-**yay**nay
eemportanth-ya]

impossible imposible
[eempos**ee**blay]

impressive impresionante
[eempres-yon**an**tay]

improve mejorar [mayHor**ar**]
I want to improve my Spanish
quiero mejorar mi español
[k-y**ai**ro – espan-y**ol**]

in: it's in the centre está en el
centro
in my car en mi coche
in Córdoba en Córdoba
in two days from now dentro
de dos días [day]
in five minutes dentro de
cinco minutos
in May en mayo
in English en inglés
in Spanish en español?
is he in? ¿está?

inch* la pulgada [pool**ga**da]

include incluir [eenkl**weer**]
does that include meals?
¿eso incluye las comidas?
[**ay**so eenkl**oo**-yay]
is that included? ¿está eso
incluido en el precio?
[eenkl**wee**do en el pr**ay**th-yo]

inconvenient inoportuno
[eenoport**oo**no]

incredible increíble [eenkray-eeblay]

Indian (adj) indio [**eend**-yo]

indicator el intermitente [eentairmee**ten**tay]

indigestion la indigestión [eendee**Hest**-yon]

indoor pool la piscina cubierta [peest**hee**na koob-**yair**ta]

indoors dentro

inexpensive barato
see cheap

infection la infección [eenfekth-**yon**]

infectious infeccioso [eenfekth-**yoso**]

inflammation la inflamación [eenflamath-**yon**]

informal (occasion, meeting) informal [eenfor**mal**]
(dress) de sport [day]

information la información [eenformath-**yon**]
do you have any information about ...? ¿tiene información sobre ... ? [t-**yay**nay – **so**bray]

information desk la información

injection la inyección [een-yekth-**yon**]

injured herido [e**reedo**]
she's been injured está herida

in-laws mi familia política [fa**meel**-ya]

inner tube (for tyre) la cámara de aire [a-**ee**ray]

innocent inocente

[eenothentay]

insect el insecto

insect bite la picadura de insecto [day]
do you have anything for insect bites? ¿tiene algo para la picadura de insectos? [t-**yay**nay]

insect repellent el repelente de insectos [repe**len**tay day]

inside dentro de [day]
inside the hotel dentro del hotel
let's sit inside vamos a sentarnos adentro [ba**moss**]

insist insistir [eensee**steer**]
I insist insisto

insomnia el insomnio [een**somn**-yo]

instant coffee el café instantáneo [ka**fay** eenstanta**nay**-o]

instead: give me that one instead deme ese otro [**day**may **ay**say]
instead of ... en lugar de ... [day]

intersection el cruce [**kroo**thay]

insulin la insulina [eensoo**lee**na]

insurance el seguro [se**goo**ro]

intelligent inteligente [eentelee**Hen**tay]

interested: I'm interested in ... estoy interesado en ...

interesting interesante [eenteresantay]
that's very interesting eso es

muy interesante [**ay**so ess mwee]

international internacional [internath-**yon**al]

interpret actuar de intérprete [actoo-**ar** day een**tair**pretay]

interpreter el/la intérprete

interval (at theatre) el descanso

into en

I'm not into ... no me gusta ... [may **goo**sta]

introduce presentar

may I introduce ...? le presento a ...

invitation la invitación [eembeetath-**yon**]

invite invitar [eembee**tar**]

Ireland Irlanda [ee**rlan**da]

Irish irlandés [eerland**ayss**]

I'm Irish (man/woman) soy irlandés/irland**e**sa

iron (for ironing) la plancha

can you iron these for me? ¿puede planchármelos? [**pway**day]

is* es, está

island la isla [**ee**ssla]

it ello, lo [**ay**-yo]

it is ... es ...; está ...

is it ...? ¿es ...?; ¿está ... ?

where is it? ¿dónde está? [**don**day]

it's him es él

it was ... era ...; estaba ... [**ai**ra]

Italian (adj) italiano [eetal-**ya**no]

Italy Italia

itch: it itches me pica [may]

J

jack (for car) el gato

jacket la chaqueta [chak**ay**ta]

jar el tarro

jam la mermelada [mairmay**la**da]

jammed: it's jammed está atascado

January enero [e**nai**ro]

jaw la mandíbula [mand**ee**boola]

jazz el jazz

jealous celoso [thel**o**so]

jeans los vaqueros [bak**ai**ross]

jellyfish la medusa [med**oo**sa]

jersey el jersey [**Hair**say]

jetty el muelle [**mway**-yay]

Jewish judío [Hoodee-o]

jeweller's la joyería [Ho-yer**ee**-a]

jewellery las joyas [**Ho**yass]

job el trabajo [tra**ba**Ho]

jogging el footing

to go jogging hacer footing [a**thair**]

joke el chiste [**chee**stay]

journey el viaje [b-ya**Hay**]

have a good journey! ¡buen viaje! [bwen b-ya**Hay**]

jug la jarra [**Ha**rra]

a jug of water una jarra de agua [**ag**wa]

juice el zumo [**thoo**mo]

July julio [**Hool**-yo]

jump (verb) saltar

jumper el jersey [**Hair**say]

jump leads las pinzas (para la

batería) [**peenthass** – **batairee**-a]
junction el cruce [**kroothay**]
June junio [**Hoon**-yo]
just (only) solamente
[**solamentay**]
just two sólo dos
just for me sólo para mí
just here aquí mismo [a**kee**
meesmo]
not just now ahora no [a-**ora**]
we've just arrived acabamos
de llegar [**yegar**]

K

keep quedarse [ke**dar**say]
keep the change quédese
con el cambio [**kay**-daysay –
kamb-yo]
can I keep it? ¿puedo
quedármelo? [**pway**do
ke**dar**melo]
please keep it por favor,
quédeselo [**kay**dayselo]
ketchup el ketchup
kettle el hervidor [airbee**dor**]
key la llave [**ya**bay]
the key for room 201, please
la llave de la habitacion
doscientos uno, por favor
[**day** la abeetath-**yon**]
key ring el llavero [ya**bairo**]
kidneys los riñones [reen-
yoness]
kill matar
kilo* el kilo
kilometre* el kilómetro
how many kilometres is it

to ...? ¿cuántos kilómetros
hay a ...? [**kwantoss** – ī]
kind (nice) amable [a**mab**lay]
that's very kind es muy
amable [mwee]

dialogue

which kind do you want?
¿qué tipo quiere? [kay
teepo k-**yairay**]
I want this/that kind
quiero este/aquel tipo
[k-**yairo estay**/a**kel**]

king el rey [ray]
kiosk el quiosco [kee-**osko**]
kiss el beso [**bayso**]
(verb) besarse [bay**sar**say]

kissing
It is customary to greet
friends and relatives by
kissing them on both cheeks, apart
from men who shake hands with
each other on meeting – except if
they are close relatives. Foreign
visitors are expected to do the same.

kitchen la cocina [ko**theena**]
kitchenette la cocina
pequeña [pek**wayn**-ya]
Kleenex® el kleenex®
knee la rodilla [ro**dee**-ya]
knickers las bragas
knife el cuchillo [koo**chee**-yo]
knitwear los géneros de
punto [**Henai**ross]
knock (verb: on door) llamar

[yamar]

knock down atropellar [atropay-yar]

he's been knocked down le han atropellado [lay an atropay-yado]

knock over (object) volcar [bolkar]

(pedestrian) atropellar [atropay-yar]

know (somebody, a place) conocer [konothair]

(something) saber [sabair]

I don't know no sé [say]

I didn't know that no lo sabía

do you know where I can find ...? ¿sabe dónde puedo encontrar ...? [sabay donday pwaydo]

dialogue

> **do you know how this works?** ¿sabe cómo funciona esto? [foonth-yona]
>
> **sorry, I don't know** lo siento, no sé [s-yento – say]

L

label la etiqueta [eteekayta]

ladies' (toilets) el aseo de señoras [asay-o day sen-yorass]

ladies' wear la ropa de señoras

lady la señora [sen-yora]

lager la cerveza [thairbaytha]
see **beer**

lake el lago

lamb (meat) el cordero [kordairo]

lamp la lámpara

lane (motorway) el carril [karreel]

(small road) la callejuela [ka-yay-Hwayla]

language el idioma [eed-yoma]

language course el curso de idiomas [koorso day]

large grande [granday]

last último [oolteemo]

last week la semana pasada

last Friday el viernes pasado

last night anoche [anochay]

what time is the last train to Toledo? ¿a qué hora es el último tren a Toledo? [kay ora]

late tarde [tarday]

sorry I'm late siento llegar tarde [s-yaynto yegar]

the train was late el tren llegó con retraso [yaygo]

we must go – we'll be late debemos irnos – llegaremos tarde [debaymoss eernoss – yegaraymoss]

it's getting late se hace tarde [say athay]

later más tarde

I'll come back later volveré más tarde [bolbairay]

see you later hasta luego [asta lwaygo]

later on más tarde

latest lo último [**oo**lteemo]
  by Wednesday at the latest para el miércoles lo más tarde
laugh (verb) reírse [**ray-ee**rsay]
launderette/laundromat la lavandería [labanda**ree**-a]
laundry (clothes) la ropa sucia [**soo**th-ya]
  (place) la lavandería
lavatory el lavabo [la**ba**bo]
law la ley [lay]
lawn el césped [**thes**ped]
lawyer (man/woman) el abogado/la abogada
laxative el laxante [la**xan**tay]
lazy perezoso [paire**tho**so]
lead (electrical) el cable [**kab**lay]
lead (verb) conducir [kondoo**theer**]
  where does this lead to? ¿adónde va esta carretera? [a**don**day ba – karray**tai**ra]
leaf la hoja [**o**Ha]
leaflet el folleto [fo-**yay**to]
leak (in roof) la gotera [go**tai**ra]
  (gas, water) el escape [es**ka**pay]
  (verb) filtrar [feel**trar**]
  the roof leaks el tejado tiene goteras [te**Ha**do t-**yay**nay go**tai**rass]
learn aprender [apren**dair**]
least: not in the least de ninguna manera [day neen**goo**na ma**nai**ra]
  at least por lo menos [**may**noss]
leather (fine) la piel [p-yel]
  (heavy) el cuero [**kwai**ro]

leave (verb) irse [**eer**say]
  I am leaving tomorrow me marcho mañana [may]
  he left yesterday se marchó ayer [say]
  may I leave this here? ¿puedo dejar esto aquí? [**pway**do day**Har** – a**kee**]
  I left my coat in the bar me he dejado el abrigo en el bar [ay day**Ha**do]

dialogue

when does the bus for Montoro leave? ¿cuándo sale el autobús para Montoro? [**kwan**do sa**lay**]
it leaves at 9 o'clock sale a las nueve

leek el puerro [**pwai**rro]
left izquierda [eethk-**yair**da]
  on the left a la izquierda
  to the left a la izquierda
  turn left gire a la izquierda [**Hee**ray]
  there's none left no queda ninguno [**kay**da]
left-handed zurdo [**thoor**do]
left luggage (office) la consigna [kon**see**gna]
leg la pierna [p-**yair**na]
lemon el limón [lee**mon**]
lemonade la limonada
lemon tea el té con limón [tay]
lend prestar
  will you lend me your ... ?

¿podría prestarme su ...?
[prestar**may**]

lens (of camera) el objetivo
[obHet**ee**bo]

lesbian la lesbiana

less menos [**may**noss]

  less expensive menos caro

  less than 10 menos de diez

  less than you menos que tú
[kay too]

lesson la lección [lekth-**y**on]

let (allow) dejar [day**H**ar]

  will you let me know? ¿me lo
dirá? [may]

  I'll let you know se lo diré
[say lo deer**ay**]

  let's go for something to eat
vamos a comer algo [b**amoss**
a kom**air**]

let off: will you let me off at ...?
¿me para en ...? [may]

letter la carta

  **do you have any letters for
me?** ¿tiene cartas para mí?
[t-y**ay**nay]

letterbox el buzón [booth**on**]

 Letterboxes in Spain are
yellow.

lettuce la lechuga [lech**oo**ga]

lever la palanca

library la biblioteca [beebl-
yot**ay**ka]

licence el permiso

lid la tapa

lie (verb: tell untruth) mentir

lie down acostarse [akost**ar**say],

echarse [**ay**charsay]

life la vida [b**ee**da]

lifebelt el salvavidas
[salbab**ee**dass]

lifeguard el/la socorrista

life jacket el chaleco
salvavidas [chal**ay**ko
salbab**ee**dass]

lift (in building) el ascensor
[asthens**or**]

  could you give me a lift?
¿podría llevarme en su
coche? [yebar**may** – **ko**chay]

  would you like a lift? ¿quiere
que le lleve? [k-y**air**ay kay lay
y**ay**bay]

lift pass el forfait [forfa-**ee**]

  a daily/weekly lift pass un
forfait de un día/una
semana

light la luz [looth]

  (not heavy) ligero [leeH**ai**ro]

  do you have a light? (for
cigarette) ¿tiene fuego?
[t-y**ay**nay fw**ay**go]

light green verde claro
[b**air**day]

light bulb la bombilla
[bomb**ee**-ya]

  I need a new light bulb
necesito una bombilla
nueva [netheth**ee**to – nw**ay**ba]

lighter (cigarette) el
encendedor [enthended**or**]

lightning el relámpago

like (verb) gustar [g**oo**star]

  I like it me gusta [may]

  I like going for walks me
gusta pasear [pasay-**ar**]

I like you me gustas
I don't like it no me gusta
do you like ...? ¿le gusta ...? [lay]
I'd like a beer quisiera una cerveza [kees-yaira oona thairbaytha]
I'd like to go swimming me gustaría ir a nadar
would you like a drink? ¿le apetece beber algo? [apaytaythay bebair]
would you like to go for a walk? ¿le apetece dar un paseo? [lay – pasay-o]
what's it like? ¿cómo es?
I want one like this quiero uno como éste [k-yairo – estay]
lime la lima [leema]
lime cordial el zumo de lima [thoomo day]
line la línea [leenay-a]
could you give me an outside line? ¿puede darme línea? [pwayday darmay]
lips el labio [lab-yo]
lip salve la crema de labios [krayma]
lipstick el lápiz de labios [lapeeth]
liqueur el licor
listen escuchar [eskoochar]
litre* el litro
a litre of white wine un litro de vino blanco [day beeno]
little pequeño [paykayn-yo]
just a little, thanks sólo un poco, gracias

a little milk un poco de leche [lechay]
a little bit more un poquito más [pokeeto]
live (verb) vivir [beebeer]
we live together vivimos juntos [beebeemoss Hoontoss]

dialogue

> where do you live? ¿dónde vive? [donday beebay]
> I live in London vivo en Londres [beebo]

lively alegre [alaygray]
liver el hígado [eegado]
loaf el pan
lobby (in hotel) el vestíbulo [besteeboolo]
lobster la langosta
local local
can you recommend a local wine/restaurant? puede recomendarme un vino/un restaurante local [pwayday rekomendarmay oon beeno/oon restowrantay]

Every region in Spain has its own distinctive wines. If you want to try the local wine ask for vino del país or vino de la casa. It is usually quite cheap although the quality varies.

lock la cerradura [thairradoora] (verb) cerrar [thairrar]
it's locked está cerrado con

llave [thairrado kon yabay]

lock in dejar encerrado [day-Har enthairrado]

lock out: I've locked myself out he cerrado la puerta con las llaves dentro [ay – la pwairta – yabayss]

locker (for luggage etc) la consigna automática [konseegna owtomateeka]

lollipop el chupa-chups® [choopa-choopss]

London Londres [londress]

long largo

how long will it take to fix it? ¿cuánto tiempo llevará arreglarlo? [kwanto t-yempo yaybara]

how long does it take? ¿cuánto tiempo se tarda? [say]

a long time mucho tiempo [moocho]

one day/two days longer un día/dos días más

long distance call la conferencia [konfairenth-ya]

look: I'm just looking, thanks sólo estoy mirando, gracias

you don't look well no tienes buen aspecto [t-yayness bwen]

look out! ¡cuidado! [kweedado]

can I have a look? ¿puedo mirar? [pwaydo]

look after cuidar [kweedar]

look at mirar

look for buscar

I'm looking for ... estoy

buscando ...

look forward to: I'm looking forward to it: tengo muchas ganas [moochass]

loose (handle etc) suelto [swelto]

lorry el camión [kam-yon]

lose perder [pairdair]

I've lost my way me he perdido [may ay pairdeedo]

I'm lost, I want to get to ... estoy perdido/perdida, quiero ir a ... [k-yairo]

I've lost my bag he perdido el bolso [ay]

lost property (office) (la oficina de) objetos perdidos [ofeetheena day obHaytoss pairdeedoss]

lot: a lot, lots mucho, muchos [moocho]

not a lot no mucho

a lot of people mucha gente [Hentay]

a lot bigger mucho mayor

I like it a lot me gusta mucho [may goosta]

lotion la loción [loth-yon]

loud fuerte [fwairtay]

lounge (in house, hotel) el salón (in airport) la sala de espera [day espaira]

love el amor

(verb) querer [kairair]

I love Spain me encanta España [may]

lovely encantador

low bajo [baHo]

luck la suerte [swairtay]

good luck! ¡buena suerte! [bwayna]

luggage el equipaje [ekeepaHay]

luggage trolley el carrito portaequipaje [porta-ekeepaHay]

lump (on body) la hinchazón [eenchathon]

lunch el almuerzo [almwairtho]

lungs los pulmones [poolmoness]

luxurious (hotel, furnishings) de lujo [looHo]

luxury el lujo

M

machine la máquina [makeena]

mad (insane) loco
(angry) furioso [foor-yoso]

Madrid Madrid [madree]

magazine la revista [rebeesta]

maid (in hotel) la camarera [kamaraira]

maiden name el nombre de soltera [nombray day soltaira]

mail el correo [korray-o]
is there any mail for me? ¿hay correspondencia para mí? [ī korrespondenth-ya]
see post

mailbox el buzón [boothon]
see letterbox

main principal [preentheepal]

main course el plato principal

main post office la oficina central de correos [ofeetheena thentral day korray-oss]

main road (in town) la calle principal [ka-yay preentheepal]
(in country) la carretera principal [karretaira]

mains (for water) la llave de paso [yabay day]

mains switch (for electricity) el interruptor de la red eléctrica [eentairrooptor day]

Majorca Mallorca [ma-yorka]

make (brand name) la marca
(verb) hacer [athair]
I make it 500 pesetas creo que son quinientas pesetas [krayo kay – pesaytass]
what is it made of? ¿de qué está hecho? [day kay – aycho]

make-up el maquillaje [makee-yaHay]

man el hombre [ombray]

manager el gerente [Hairentay]
can I see the manager? ¿puedo ver al gerente? [pwaydo bair]

manageress la gerente

manual (car with manual gears) el coche de marchas [kochay]

many muchos [moochoss]
not many no muchos

map (city plan) el plano
(road map, geographical) el mapa

March marzo [martho]

margarine la margarina

market el mercado [mairkado]

marmalade la mermelada de

naranja [mairmelada day naranHa]

married: I'm married (said by a man/woman) estoy casado/casada

are you married? (said to a man/woman) ¿está casado/casada?

mascara el rímel

match (football etc) el partido

matches las cerillas [thairee-yass]

material (fabric) el tejido [teHeedo]

matter: it doesn't matter no importa

what's the matter? ¿qué pasa? [kay]

mattress el colchón

May mayo [ma-yo]

may: may I have another one? ¿me da otro? [may]

may I come in? ¿se puede entrar? [say pwayday]

may I see it? ¿puedo verlo? [pwaydo bairlo]

may I sit here? ¿puedo sentarme aquí? [sentarmay akee]

maybe tal vez [beth]

mayonnaise la mayonesa [ma-yonaysa]

me*: that's for me eso es para mí [ayso]

send it to me envíemelo [embee-aymelo]

me too yo también [tamb-yen]

meal la comida

dialogue

did you enjoy your meal? ¿te ha gustado la comida? [tay a goostado]

it was excellent, thank you estaba riquísima, gracias [reekeeseema]

mean (verb) querer decir [kairair detheer]

what do you mean? ¿qué quiere decir? [kay k-yairay]

dialogue

what does this word mean? ¿qué significa esta palabra? [kay]

it means ... in English significa ... en inglés [eenglayss]

measles el sarampión [saramp-yon]

meat la carne [karnay]

mechanic el mecánico

medicine la medicina [medeetheena]

Mediterranean el Mediterráneo [medeetairranay-o]

medium (adj: size) medio [mayd-yo]

medium-dry semi-seco [sayko]

(sherry) amontillado [amontee-yado]

medium-rare poco hecho

[**ay**cho]

medium-sized de tamaño medio [tamañ-yo **mayd**-yo]

meet encontrar

(for the first time) conocer [kono**thair**]

nice to meet you encantado de conocerle [day kono**thair**lay]

where shall I meet you? ¿dónde nos vemos? [**don**day noss **bay**moss]

meeting la reunión [ray-oon-**yon**]

meeting place el lugar de reunión [**loo**gar]

melon el melón

men los hombres [**om**bress]

mend arreglar

could you mend this for me? ¿puede arreglarme esto? [**pway**day arreglar**may**]

men's room el servicio de caballeros [sair**beeth**-yo day kaba-**yair**oss]

menswear la ropa de caballero

mention (verb) mencionar [menth-**yonar**]

don't mention it de nada [day]

menu el menú [men**oo**]

may I see the menu, please? ¿puede traerme el menú? [**pway**day tra-air**may**]

see menu reader page 229

message: are there any messages for me? ¿hay algún recado para mí? [i]

I want to leave a message

for ... quisiera dejar un recado para ... [kees-**yai**ra day-**Har**]

metal el metal

metre* el metro

microwave (oven) el (horno) microondas [**or**no meekro-**on**dass]

midday el mediodía [**mayd**-yo**dee**-a]

at midday al mediodía

middle: in the middle en el medio [**mayd**-yo]

in the middle of the night a mitad de la noche [**mee**ta day la **no**chay]

the middle one el del medio

midnight la medianoche [**mayd**-ya-**no**chay]

at midnight a medianoche

might: I might es posible [po**see**blay]

I might not puede que no [**pway**day kay]

I might want to stay another day quizás decida quedarme otro día [**keet**hass deth**ee**da ke**dar**may]

migraine la jaqueca [Ha**kay**ka]

mild (taste) suave [**swa**bay]

(weather) templado

mile* la milla [**mee**-ya]

milk la leche [**le**chay]

milkshake el batido

millimetre* el milímetro

minced meat la carne picada [**kar**nay]

mind: never mind ¡qué más da! [kay]

98

I've changed my mind he cambiado de idea [ay kamb-yado day eeday-a]

dialogue

do you mind if I open the window? ¿le importa si abro la ventana? [lay eemporta – bentana]

no, I don't mind no, no me importa [may]

mine*: it's mine es mío

mineral water el agua mineral [agwa meenairal]

mint-flavoured con sabor a menta

mints los caramelos de menta [karamayloss day]

minute el minuto [meenooto]
 in a minute en seguida [segeeda]
 just a minute un momento

mirror el espejo [espayHo]

Miss Señorita [sen-yoreeta]

miss: I missed the bus he perdido el autobús [ay pairdeedo]

missing: one of my ... is missing me falta uno de mis ... [may – day]
 there's a suitcase missing falta una maleta

mist la niebla [n-yaybla]

mistake el error
 I think there's a mistake me parece que hay una equivocación [may parethay kay ī oona ekeebokath-yon]

sorry, I've made a mistake perdón, me he equivocado [may ay ekeebokado]

misunderstanding el malentendido

mix-up: sorry, there's been a mix-up perdón ha habido una confusión [a abeedo oona konfoos-yon]

modern moderno [modairno]

modern art gallery la galería de arte moderno [galairee-a day artay]

moisturizer la crema hidratante [krayma eedratantay]

moment: I won't be a moment vuelvo enseguida [bwelbo ensegeeda]

monastery el monasterio [monastair-yo]

Monday lunes [looness]

money el dinero [deenairo]

month el mes

monument el monumento [monoomento]
 (statue) la estatua [estatwa]

moon la luna

moped el ciclomotor [theeklomotor]

more* más
 can I have some more water, please? más agua, por favor
 more expensive/interesting más caro/interesante
 more than 50 más de cincuenta
 more than that más que eso [kay ayso]

a lot more mucho más
[**moo**cho]

dialogue

would you like some
more? ¿quiere más?
[k-ya**ir**ay]
no, no more for me, thanks
no, para mí no, gracias
how about you? ¿y usted?
[ee oos**tay**]
I don't want any more,
thanks no quiero más,
gracias [k-**yair**o]

morning la mañana [man-**ya**na]
this morning esta mañana
in the morning por la
mañana
Morocco Marruecos
[marr**way**koss]
mosquito el mosquito
mosquito repellent el
repelente de mosquitos
[repe**len**tay]
most: I like this one most of all
éste es el que más me gusta
[**es**tay – kay mass may **goo**sta]
most of the time la mayor
parte del tiempo [ma-**yor**
partay del t-**yem**po]
most tourists la mayoría de
los turistas [ma-yor**ee**-a day]
mostly generalmente
[Haynairal**men**tay]
mother la madre [**ma**dray]
motorbike la moto
motorboat la (lancha) motora

motorway la autopista
[owtop**ee**sta]
mountain la montaña [montan-
ya]
in the mountains en las
montañas
mountaineering el
montañismo [montan-**yee**smo]
mouse el ratón
moustache el bigote
[beeg**o**tay]
mouth la boca
mouth ulcer la llaga [**ya**ga]
move: he's moved to another
room se ha cambiado a otra
habitación [say a kamb-**ya**do –
abeetath-**yon**]
could you move your car?
¿podría cambiar de sitio su
coche? [podr**ee**-a kamb-**yar** day
seet-yo]
could you move up a little?
¿puede correrse un poco?
[**pway**day corr**air**say]
where has it moved to?
¿adónde se ha trasladado?
[ad**on**day say a]
movie la película [pel**ee**koola]
movie theater el cine [**thee**nay]
Mr Señor [sen-**yor**]
Mrs Señora [sen-**yor**a]
Ms Señorita [sen-yor**ee**ta]
much mucho [**moo**cho]
much better/worse mucho
mejor/peor [ma-**yor**/pay-**or**]
much hotter mucho más
caliente [kal-**yen**tay]
not (very) much no mucho
I don't want very much no

quiero mucho [k-yairo]

mud el barro

mug (for drinking) la taza
[tatha]

I've been mugged me han
asaltado [may an]

mum la mamá

mumps las paperas [papairass]

museum el museo [moosay-o]

mushrooms los champiñones
[champeen-yoness]

music la música [mooseeka]

musician el/la músico

Muslim (adj) musulmán
[moosoolman]

mussels los mejillones
[meнeeyoness]

must*: I must tengo que
[kay]

I mustn't drink alcohol no
debo beber alcohol [daybo
bebair alko-ol]

mustard la mostaza
[mostatha]

my* mi; (pl) mis

myself: I'll do it myself lo haré
yo mismo [aray yo meesmo]

by myself yo solo

Spaniards have two
surnames (the father's
first surname + the
mother's first surname). Women
don't change their maiden name
when they get married. First names
are used in informal relationships,
for example, between friends and
relatives. In formal situations **don** or
doña (Mr or Mrs/Ms) + first name
are used.

my name's John me llamo
John [may yamo]

what's your name? ¿cómo se
llama usted? [say – oostay]

what is the name of this
street? ¿cómo se llama esta
calle?

napkin la servilleta [sairbee-
yayta]

nappy el pañal [pan-yal]

narrow (street) estrecho
[estraycho]

nasty (person) desagradable
[desagradablay]
(weather, accident) malo

national nacional [nath-yonal]

nationality la nacionalidad
[nath-yonaleeda]

natural natural [natooral]

nausea la nausea [nowsay-a]

navy (blue) azul marino
[athool mareeno]

near cerca [thairka]

is it near the city centre?
¿está cerca del centro?
[thentro]

do you go near Las Ramblas?

N

nail (finger) la uña [oon-ya]
(metal) el clavo [klabo]

nailbrush el cepillo para las
uñas [thepee-yo –oon-yass]

nail varnish el esmalte para
uñas [esmaltay]

name el nombre [nombray]

¿pasa usted cerca de Las Ramblas? [oostay – day]

where is the nearest ...?
¿dónde está el ... más cercano? [donday – thairkano]

nearby por aquí cerca [akee]

nearly casi

necessary necesario [nethesaryo]

neck el cuello [kway-yo]

necklace el collar [ko-yar]

necktie la corbata

need: I need ... necesito un ... [netheseeto]

do I need to pay? ¿necesito pagar?

needle la aguja [agooHa]

negative (film) el negativo [negateeebo]

neither: neither (one) of them ninguno (de ellos) [neengoono day ay-yoss]

neither ... nor ... ni ... ni ...

nephew el sobrino

Nerja Nerja [nairHa]

net (in sport) la red

Netherlands Los Países Bajos [pa-eesess baHoss]

network map el mapa

never nunca [noonka]

dialogue

have you ever been to Seville? ¿ha estado alguna vez en Sevilla? [a – beth]

no, never, I've never been there no, nunca, nunca he estado allí [ay – a-yee]

new nuevo [nwaybo]

news (radio, TV etc) las noticias [noteeth-yass]

newsagent's el kiosko de prensa [day]

newspaper el periódico [pair-yodeeko]

newspaper kiosk el kiosko de prensa [day]

New Year el Año Nuevo [an-yo nwaybo]

Spaniards celebrate New Year's Eve (**La Noche Vieja**) either in the streets or at parties. In many parts of Spain it is usual to have a special supper with relatives or friends. At twelve o'clock it is the custom to eat 12 grapes, one at each stroke of the clock. If you manage to eat them all in time you'll have a successful year.

Happy New Year! ¡Feliz Año Nuevo [feleeth]

New Year's Eve Nochevieja [nochay-b-yayHa]

New Zealand Nueva Zelanda [nwayba thelanda]

New Zealander: I'm a New Zealander (man/woman) soy neozelandés/neozelandesa [nayo-thelandayss]

next próximo

the next turning/street on the left la siguiente calle a la izquierda [seeg-yentay ka-yay a la eethk-yairda]

at the next stop en la

siguiente parada
next week la próxima
semana
next to al lado de [day]
nice (food) bueno [**bway**no]
(looks, view etc) bonito
(person) simpático
niece la sobrina
night la noche [**no**chay]
at night por la noche
good night buenas noches
[**bway**nass]

dialogue

**do you have a single room
for one night?** ¿tiene una
habitación individual
para una noche? [t-**yay**nay
oona abeetath-**yon**
eendeebeed**wal**]
yes, madam sí, señora
[sen-**yo**ra]
how much is it per night?
¿cuánto es la noche?
[**kwan**to]
**it's 3,000 pesetas for one
night** son tres mil pesetas
la noche [pes**ay**tass]
thank you, I'll take it
gracias, me la quedo [may
la **kay**do]

nightclub la discoteca
[deeskot**ay**ka]
nightdress el camisón
night porter el portero
[port**ai**ro]
no no

I've no change no tengo
cambio [**kamb**-yo]
there's no ... left no queda ...
[**kay**da]
no way! ¡ni hablar! [**ab**lar]
oh no! (upset, annoyed) ¡Dios
mío!
nobody nadie [**nad**-yay]
there's nobody there no hay
nadie ahí [ī – a-**ee**]
noise el ruido [**rwee**do]
noisy: it's too noisy hay
demasiado ruido [ī daymas-
yado]
non-alcoholic sin alcohol
[alko-**ol**]
none ninguno
non-smoking compartment
no fumadores [foomad**or**ess]
noon el mediodía [**mayd**-yo-
dee-a]
no-one nadie [**nad**-yay]
nor: nor do I yo tampoco
normal normal
north norte [**nor**tay]
in the north en el norte
north of Girona al norte de
Girona
northeast nordeste [nord**es**tay]
northern del norte [**nor**tay]
northwest noroeste [noro-
estay]
Northern Ireland Irlanda del
Norte [eer**lan**da del **nor**tay]
Norway Noruega [nor**way**ga]
Norwegian (adj) noruego
nose la nariz [nar**eeth**]
nosebleed la hemorragia
nasal [emorra**H**-ya]

103

not* no

no, I'm not hungry no, no tengo hambre [**am**bray]

I don't want any, thank you no quiero ninguno, gracias [k-**yai**ro]

it's not necessary no es necesario [naythe**sar**-yo]

I didn't know that no lo sabía

not that one – this one ése no – éste [**ay**say – **es**tay]

note (banknote) el billete [bee-**yay**tay]

notebook el cuaderno [kwa**dair**no]

notepaper (for letters) el papel de carta

nothing nada

nothing for me, thanks para mí nada, gracias

nothing else nada más

novel la novela [no**bay**la]

November noviembre [nob-**yem**bray]

now ahora [a-**o**ra]

number el número [**noo**mairo]

I've got the wrong number me he equivocado de número [may ay ekeebok**a**do day]

what is your phone number? ¿cuál es su número de teléfono? [kwal – te**lay**fono]

number plate la matrícula

nurse (man/woman) el enfermero [enfair**mai**ro]/la enfermera

nursery slope la pista de principiantes [day preentheep-

yantess]

nut (for bolt) la tuerca [**twair**ka]

nuts los frutos secos

O

o'clock* en punto [**poon**to]

occupied (toilet) ocupado [okoo**pa**do]

October octubre [ok**too**bray]

odd (strange) raro

of* de [day]

off (lights) apagado

it's just off calle Corredera está cerca de calle Corredera [**thair**ka day ka-**yay**]

we're off tomorrow nos vamos mañana [**ba**moss]

offensive (language, behaviour) insultante [eensool**tan**tay]

office (place of work) la oficina [ofee**thee**na]

officer (said to policeman) señor [sen-**yor**]

often a menudo

not often pocas veces [**bay**thess]

how often are the buses? ¿cada cuánto son los autobuses? [**kwan**to]

oil el aceite [a**thay**-eetay]

ointment la pomada

OK vale [**ba**lay]

are you OK? ¿está bien? [b-yen]

is that OK with you? ¿le parece bien? [lay pa**ray**thay]

is it OK to ...? ¿se puede ...?

[say pw**ay**day]
that's OK thanks (it doesn't
matter) está bien, gracias
I'm OK (nothing for me) yo no
quiero [k-y**ai**ro]
(I feel OK) me siento bien
[may s-y**en**to]
is this train OK for ...? ¿este
tren va a...? [est**ay** – ba]
I said I'm sorry, OK? he
dicho que lo siento, ¿vale?
[ay – kay – b**a**lay]
old viejo [b-y**ay**HO]

dialogue

how old are you? ¿cuántos
años tiene? [kwantoss an-
yoss t-y**ay**nay]
I'm twenty-five tengo
veinticinco
and you? ¿y usted? [ee
oost**ay**]

old-fashioned pasado de
moda [day]
old town (old part of town) el
casco antiguo [ant**ee**gwo]
in the old town en el casco
antiguo
olive la aceituna [athay-
eet**oo**na], la oliva
black/green olives las
aceitunas negras/verdes
[b**ai**rdess]
olive oil el aceite de oliva
[ath**ay**-e**e**tay day ol**ee**ba]
omelette la tortilla [tort**ee**-ya]
on* en

on the street/beach en la
calle/la playa
is it on this road? ¿está en
esta calle?
on the plane en el avión
[ab-y**on**]
on Saturday el sábado
on television en la tele
[t**ay**lay]
I haven't got it on me no lo
llevo encima [y**ay**bo enth**ee**ma]
this one's on me (drink) ésta
va de mi cuenta [ba day mee
kw**en**ta]
the light wasn't on la luz no
estaba encendida [looth –
enthend**ee**da]
what's on tonight? ¿qué
ponen esta noche? [kay]
once (one time) una vez [**oo**na
beth]
at once (immediately) en
seguida [seg**ee**da]
one* uno [**oo**no], una
the white one el blanco, la
blanca
**one-way: a one-way ticket
to ...** un billete de ida
para ... [bee-y**ay**tay day e**e**da]
onion la cebolla [theb**o**-ya]
only sólo
only one sólo uno
it's only 6 o'clock son sólo
las seis
I've only just got here acabo
de llegar [yeg**ar**]
on/off switch el interruptor
[eentairroopt**or**]
open (adjective) abierto

[ab-yairto]
(verb) abrir [abreer]
when do you open? ¿a qué
hora abre? [kay ora abray]
I can't get it open no puedo
abrirlo [pwaydo]
in the open air al aire libre
[a-eeray leebray]
opening times el horario
[orar-yo]
open ticket el billete abierto
[bee-yaytay ab-yairto]
opera la ópera
operation (medical) la
operación [opairath-yon]
operator (telephone:
man/woman) el operador/la
operadora
opposite: the opposite
direction la dirección
contraria [deerekth-yon kontrar-
ya]
the bar opposite el bar de
enfrente [day enfrentay]
opposite my hotel enfrente
de mi hotel
optician el óptico

or o
orange (fruit) la naranja
[naranHa]
(colour) (color) naranja
orange juice (fresh) el zumo
de naranja [thoomo day]
(fizzy, diluted) la naranjada
[naranHada]
orchestra la orquesta [orkesta]
order: can we order now? (in
restaurant) ¿podemos pedir
ya? [podaymoss]

I've already ordered, thanks
ya he pedido, gracias [ay]
I didn't order this no he
pedido eso [ayso]
out of order averiado, fuera
de servicio [abair-yado, fwaira
day sairbeeth-yo]
ordinary corriente [korr-yentay]
other otro
the other one el otro
the other day el otro día
I'm waiting for the others
estoy esperando a los demás
do you have any others?
¿tiene usted otros? [t-yaynay
oostay]
otherwise de otra manera
[manaira]
our* nuestro [nwestro],
nuestra; (pl) nuestros,
nuestras
ours* (el) nuestro, (la)
nuestra
out: he's out no está
three kilometres out of town
a tres kilómetros de la
ciudad
outdoors fuera de casa [fwaira
day]
outside ... fuera de ...
can we sit outside?
¿podemos sentarnos fuera?
[podaymoss]
oven el horno [orno]
over: over here por aquí
[akee]
over there por allí [a-yee]
over 500 más de quinientos
it's over se acabó [say]

overcharge: you've overcharged me me ha cobrado de más [may a – day]
overcoat el abrigo
overlook: I'd like a room overlooking the courtyard querría una habitación que dé al patio [kairree-a oona abeetyon kay day]
overnight (travel) de noche [day nochay]
overtake adelantar
owe: how much do I owe you? ¿cuánto le debo? [kwanto lay daybo]
own: my own ... mi propio ... [prop-yo]
are you on your own? (to a man/woman) ¿está solo/sola?
I'm on my own (man/woman) estoy solo/sola
owner (man/woman) el propietario [prop-yetar-yo]/la propietaria

P

pack: a pack of ... un paquete de ... [pakaytay day]
(verb) hacer las maletas [malaytass]
package el paquete [pakaytay]
package holiday el viaje organizado [b-yaHay organeethado]
packed lunch la bolsa con la comida
packet: a packet of cigarettes

un paquete de cigarrillos [pakaytay day theegaree-yoss]
padlock el candado
page (of book) la página [paHeena]
could you page Mr ...? ¿podría llamar al Señor (por altavoz) ...? [yamar]
pain el dolor
I have a pain here me duele aquí [may dwaylay akee]
painful doloroso
painkillers los analgésicos [analHayseekoss]
paint la pintura
painting el cuadro [kwadro]
pair: a pair of ... un par de ... [day]
Pakistani (adj) paquistaní [pakeestanee]
palace el palacio [palath-yo]
pale pálido
pale blue azul claro [athool]
pan la cazuela [kathwayla]
panties las bragas
pants (underwear: men's) los calzoncillos [kalthonthee-yoss]
(women's) las bragas
(US: trousers) los pantalones [pantaloness]
pantyhose los panties
paper el papel
(newspaper) el periódico [pair-yodeeko]
a piece of paper un trozo de papel [trotho day]
paper handkerchiefs los kleenex®

parcel el paquete [pak**ay**tay]
pardon (me)? (didn't understand/hear) ¿cómo?
parents: my parents mis padres [p**a**dress]
parents-in-law los suegros [sw**e**gross]
park el parque [p**a**rkay] (verb) aparcar
 can I park here? ¿puedo aparcar aquí? [pw**ay**do – ak**ee**]
parking lot el aparcamiento [aparcam-y**e**nto]
part la parte [p**a**rtay]
partner (boyfriend, girlfriend etc) el compañero [kompan-y**ai**ro]
party (group) el grupo (celebration) la fiesta
pass (in mountains) el puerto [pw**ai**rto]
passenger (man/woman) el pasajero [pasaH**ai**ro]/la pasajera
passport el pasaporte [pasap**o**rtay]
past*: in the past antiguamente [anteegwam**e**ntay]
 just past the information office justo después de la oficina de información [H**oo**sto despw**ay**ss day]
path el camino
pattern el dibujo [deeb**oo**Ho]
pavement la acera [ath**ai**ra]
 on the pavement en la acera
pavement café el café terraza [terr**a**tha]

pay (verb) pagar
 can I pay, please? la cuenta, por favor [kw**e**nta]
 it's already paid for ya está pagado

dialogue

> **who's paying?** ¿quién paga? [k-yen]
> **I'll pay** pago yo
> **no, you paid last time, I'll pay** no, usted pagó la última vez, yo pago [oost**ay** – **oo**lteema beth]

pay phone el teléfono público [tel**ay**fono p**oo**bleeko]
peaceful tranquilo [trank**ee**lo]
peach el melocotón
peanuts los cacahuetes [kakaw**ay**tess]
pear la pera [p**ai**ra]
peas los guisantes [gees**a**ntess]
peculiar (taste, custom) raro
pedestrian crossing el paso de peatones [pay-at**o**ness]
pedestrian precinct la calle peatonal [k**a**-yay pay-aton**a**l]
peg (for washing) la pinza [p**ee**ntha]
 (for tent) la estaca
pen la pluma [pl**oo**ma]
pencil el lápiz [l**a**peeth]
penfriend (male/female) el amigo/la amiga por correspondencia [korrespond**e**nth-ya]
penicillin la penicilina

[peneetheel**ee**na]

penknife la navaja [naba**Ha**]

pensioner el/la pensionista [pens-yon**ee**sta]

people la gente [**Hen**tay]

the other people in the hotel los otros huéspedes del hotel [**we**spedess]

too many people demasiada gente [daymas-**ya**da]

pepper (spice) la pimienta [peem-**yen**ta]

(vegetable) el pimiento

peppermint (sweet) el caramelo de menta [karam**ay**lo day]

per: per night por noche [**no**chay]

how much per day? ¿cuánto es por noche? [**kwan**to]

per cent por ciento [th-**yen**to]

perfect perfecto [pair**fek**to]

perfume el perfume [pair**foo**may]

perhaps quizás [keeth**ass**]

perhaps not quizás no

period (of time, menstruation) el período [pair**ee**-odo]

perm la permanente [pairman**en**tay]

permit el permiso [pair**mee**so]

person la persona [pair**so**na]

personal stereo el walkman® [**wol**man]

petrol la gasolina

The following types of petrol are available in Spain: **super** (4-star),

normal (lower grade), **sin plomo** (unleaded).

petrol can la lata de gasolina [day]

petrol station la gasolinera [gasoleen**ai**ra]

pharmacy la farmacia [far-**math**-ya]

see **chemist's**

phone el teléfono [tel**ay**fono]

(verb) llamar por teléfono [yam**ar**]

Most payphones in Spain take both coins (all except one-peseta coins can be used) and phonecards (**tarjetas telefónicas**) which you can buy in tobacconists (**estanco**). The more modern payphones enable you to select the instructions in English. Phoning abroad costs less from 10 p.m. onwards and calls within Spain cost less after 8 p.m.

see **speak**

phone book la guía telefónica [**gee**-a]

phone box la cabina telefónica [kab**ee**na]

phonecard la tarjeta de teléfono [tar**Hay**ta day tayl**ay**fono]

phone number el número de teléfono [**noo**mairo]

photo la foto

excuse me, could you take a photo of us? ¿le importaría

hacernos una foto? [lay – athairnoss]

phrasebook el libro de frases [day frasess]

piano el piano [p-yano]

pickpocket el/la carterista

pick up: will you be there to pick me up? ¿va a ir a recogerme? [ba – rekoHairmay]

picnic el picnic

picture el cuadro [kwadro]

pie (meat) la empanada (fruit) la tarta

piece el pedazo [pedatho] a piece of ... un pedazo de ... [day]

pill la píldora I'm on the pill estoy tomando la píldora

pillow la almohada [almo-ada]

pillow case la funda (de almohada) [foonda]

pin el alfiler [alfeelair]

pineapple la piña [peen-ya]

pineapple juice el zumo de piña [thoomo]

pink rosa

pipe (for smoking) la pipa [peepa] (for water) el tubo [toobo]

pipe cleaners los limpiapipas [leemp-yapeepass]

pity: it's a pity es una lástima

pizza la pizza

place el sitio [seet-yo] is this place taken? ¿está ocupado este sitio? [estay] at your place en tu casa

at his place en su casa

plain (not patterned) liso

plane el avión [ab-yon] by plane en avión

plant la planta

plaster cast la escayola [eska-yola]

plasters las tiritas

plastic plástico (credit cards) las tarjetas de crédito [tarHaytass day kraydeeto]

plastic bag la bolsa de plástico

plate el plato

platform el andén which platform is it for Saragossa, please? ¿qué andén para Zaragoza, por favor? [kay]

play (in theatre) la obra (verb) jugar [Hoogar]

playground el patio de recreo [pat-yo day rekray-o]

pleasant agradable [agradablay]

please por favor [fabor] yes please sí, por favor could you please ...? ¿podría hacer el favor de ...? [athair – day] please don't no, por favor pleased to meet you encantado de conocerle [day konothairlay]

pleasure: my pleasure es un placer [plathair]

plenty: plenty of ... mucho ... [moocho]

there's plenty of time
tenemos mucho tiempo
[taynaymoss – t-yempo]
that's plenty, thanks es
suficiente, gracias [soofeeth-yentay]
pliers los alicates [aleekatess]
plug (electrical) el enchufe
[enchoofay]
(for car) la bujía [booHee-a]
(in sink) el tapón
plumber el fontanero
[fontanairo]
p.m.* de la tarde [day la tarday]
poached egg el huevo
escalfado [waybo]
pocket el bolsillo [bolsee-yo]
point: two point five dos coma
cinco
there's no point no merece
la pena [mairaythay la payna]
points (in car) los platinos
poisonous venenoso
[benenoso]
police la policía [poleethee-a]
call the police! ¡llame a la
policía! [yamay]

 There are two basic types
of police that operate all
over the country: the
Guardia Civil (dressed in green) and
Policía Nacional (dressed in blue).
Each town has its own body of local
police (**Policía Municipal**). Some
regions have their own independent
police force. In The Basque Country
they are called **Ertzantza**, in
Catalonia **Mossos d'Esquadra** and

in Andalucía **Policía Autonómica**.
Dial 091 for the Policía Nacional or
062 for the Guardia Civil.

policeman el (agente de)
policía [aHentay day]
police station la comisaría de
policía
policewoman la policía
polish el betún [betoon]
polite educado [edookado]
polluted contaminado
pony el poney
pool (for swimming) la piscina
[peestheena]
poor (not rich) pobre [pobray]
(quality) de baja calidad [day
baHa kaleeda]
pop music la música pop
[mooseeka]
pop singer el/la cantante de
música pop [kantantay]
population la población
[poblath-yon]
pork la carne de cerdo
[karnay day thairdo]
port (for boats) el puerto
[pwairto]
(drink) el Oporto
porter (in hotel) el conserje
[konsairHay]
portrait el retrato
Portugal Portugal
Portuguese (adj) portugués
[portoogayss]
posh (restaurant) de lujo
[looHo]
(people) pijo [peeHo]
possible posible [poseeblay]

is it possible to ...? ¿es posible ...?

as ... as possible tan ... como sea posible [**say**-a]

post (mail) el correo [korr**ay**-o] (verb) echar al correo

could you post this for me? ¿podría enviarme esto por correo? [emb-y**armay**]

postal service
Post Offices (**Correos**) open Monday to Friday from 8.30 a.m. to 2 p.m. and in large towns and cities they open again from 4.30 p.m. to 8 p.m. although these times may vary depending on the season. It takes about two or three days for a letter to get to another area within Spain. If you want a quicker service tell the clerk you need **un sello urgente**. If you need to send a registered parcel or letter ask for **correo certificado**. If you need ordinary stamps you can buy them in an **estanco**. You should tell the assistant the destination of your letter.

postbox el buzón [booth**on**]
postcard la postal
poster el poster [**po**stair], el cartel
post office Correos [korr**ay**-oss]
poste restante la lista de Correos [**lee**sta]
potato la patata
potato chips las patatas fritas

(de bolsa)

pots and pans (ie cooking implements) los cacharros de cocina [day koth**ee**na]
pottery (objects) la cerámica [thair**amee**ka]
pound* (money, weight) la libra
power cut el apagón
power point la toma de corriente [day korr-y**entay**]
practise: I want to practise my Spanish quiero practicar el español [k-y**airo** – espan-y**ol**]
prawns las gambas
prefer: I prefer ... prefiero ... [pref-y**airo**]
pregnant embarazada [embarath**ada**]
prescription (for chemist) la receta [reth**ay**ta]
present (gift) el regalo
president (of country) el/la presidente [preseed**entay**]
pretty mono
it's pretty expensive es bastante caro [bast**antay**]
price el precio [**preth**-yo]
priest el sacerdote [sathaird**otay**]
prime minister (man/woman) el primer ministro [preem**air**]/la primera ministra
printed matter los impresos [eempr**aysoss**]
priority (in driving) la preferencia [prefairenth-ya]
prison la cárcel [**karthel**]
private privado [pree**bado**]
private bathroom el baño

privado [ban-yo]

probably probablemente [probablementay]

problem el problema [problayma]

  no problem! ¡con mucho gusto! [moocho goosto]

program(me) el programa

promise: I promise lo prometo [promayto]

pronounce: how is this pronounced? ¿cómo se pronuncia esto? [say pronoonth-ya]

properly (repaired, locked etc) bien [b-yen]

protection factor (of suntan lotion) el factor de protección [protekth-yon]

Protestant (adj) protestante [protestantay]

public convenience los aseos públicos [asay-oss poobleekoss]

public holiday el día de fiesta [day]

pudding (dessert) el postre [postray]

pull tirar

pullover el jersey [Hairsay]

puncture el pinchazo [peenchatho]

purple morado

purse (for money) el monedero [monedairo]

  (US: handbag) el bolso

push empujar [empooHar]

pushchair la sillita de ruedas [see-yeeta day rwaydass]

put poner [ponair]

where can I put ...? ¿dónde puedo poner ...? [donday pwaydo]

could you put us up for the night? ¿podría alojarnos esta noche? [aloHarnoss – nochay]

pyjamas el pijama [peeHama]

Pyrenees los Pirineos [peereenay-oss]

Q

quality la calidad [kaleeda]

quarantine la cuarentena [kwarentayna]

quarter la cuarta parte [kwarta partay]

quayside: on the quayside en el muelle [mway-yay]

question la pregunta [pregoonta]

queue la cola

quick rápido

  that was quick sí que ha sido rápido [kay a]

  what's the quickest way there? ¿cuál es el camino más rápido? [kwal]

  fancy a quick drink? ¿te apetece algo rápido de beber? [tay apetaythay – day bebair]

quickly rápidamente [rapeedamentay]

quiet (place, hotel) tranquilo [trankeelo]

quiet! ¡cállese! [ka-yaysay]

quite (fairly) bastante

[bastantay]
(very) muy [mwee]
that's quite right eso es
cierto [th-**yai**rto]
quite a lot bastante

R

rabbit el conejo [kon**ay**Ho]
race (for runners, cars) la carrera
[kar**rai**ra]
racket (tennis etc) la raqueta
[rak**ay**ta]
radiator (of car, in room) el
radiador [rad-yad**or**]
radio la radio [**r**ad-yo]
on the radio por la radio
rail: by rail en tren
railway el ferrocarril
rain la lluvia [**yoo**b-ya]
in the rain bajo la lluvia
[**ba**Ho]
it's raining está lloviendo
[yob-y**e**ndo]
raincoat el impermeable
[eempairmay-**a**blay]
rape la violación [b-yolath-**yon**]
rare (steak) (muy) poco
hecho [mwee – **ay**cho]
rash (on skin) la erupción
cutánea [airoopth-yon
koot**a**nay-a]
raspberry la frambuesa
[frambw**ay**sa]
rat la rata
rate (for changing money) el
cambio [**ka**mb-yo]
rather: it's rather good es

bastante bueno [bast**a**ntay
bw**ay**no]
I'd rather ... prefiero ... [pref-
yairo]
razor la maquinilla de afeitar
[makeen**ee**-ya day afay-eet**ar**]
(electric) la máquina de
afeitar eléctrica [mak**ee**na]
razor blades las hojas de
afeitar [**o**Hass]
read leer [lay-**air**]
ready preparado
are you ready? ¿estás listo?
[l**ee**sto]
I'm not ready yet aún no
estoy listo [a-**oo**n]

dialogue

when will it be ready?
¿cuándo estará listo?
[kw**a**ndo]
it should be ready in a
couple of days estará listo
dentro de un par de días
[day]

real verdadero [bairdad**ai**ro]
really realmente [ray-alm**e**ntay]
that's really great eso es
estupendo [**ay**so]
really? (doubt) ¿de verdad?
[day bair**da**]
(polite interest) ¿sí?
rearview mirror el (espejo)
retrovisor [esp**ay**Ho retrobees**or**]
reasonable (prices etc)
razonable [rathon**a**blay]
receipt el recibo [reth**ee**bo]

recently recientemente [reth-yentementay]

reception la recepción [rethepth-yon]

at reception en recepción

reception desk la recepción

receptionist el/la recepcionista [rethepth-yoneesta]

recognize reconocer [rekonothair]

recommend: could you recommend ...? ¿puede usted recomendar ...? [pwayday oostay]

record (music) el disco [deesko]

red rojo [roHo]

red wine el vino tinto [beeno teento]

refund el reembolso [ray-embolso]

can I have a refund? ¿puede devolverme el dinero? [pwayday debolbairmay el deenairo]

region la zona [thona], la región [reH-yon]

registered: by registered mail por correo certificado [korray-o thairteefeekado]

registration number el número de la matrícula [noomairo day]

relatives los parientes [par-yentess]

religion la religión [releeH-yon]

remember: I don't remember no recuerdo [rekwairdo]

I remember recuerdo

do you remember? ¿recuarda? [rekwairda]

rent (for apartment etc) el alquiler [alkeelair] (verb) alquilar

to/for rent de alquiler

dialogue

I'd like to rent a car quisiera alquilar un coche [kees-yaira]

for how long? ¿por cuánto tiempo? [kwanto t-yempo]

two days dos días

this is our range ésta es nuestra gama [nwestra]

I'll take the ... me quedo con el ... [may kaydo]

is that with unlimited mileage? ¿es con kilometraje ilimitado? [keelometraHay eeleemeetado]

it is es

can I see your licence please? ¿me deja ver su permiso, por favor? [may dayHa bair soo pairmeeso]

and your passport y su pasaporte [ee soo pasaportay]

is insurance included? ¿va incluido el seguro? [ba eenkloo-eedo]

yes, but you pay the first 50,000 pesetas sí, pero usted paga las primeras cincuenta mil pesetas

nochay]
yes madam, for how many people? sí, señora, ¿para cuántos? [sen-**yo**ra – **kwan**toss]
for two para dos
and for what time? ¿y para qué hora? [kay **o**ra]
for eight o'clock para las **o**cho
and could I have your name please? ¿me dice su nombre, por favor? [may **dee**thay soo **no**mbray]
see **alphabet** for spelling

[**pai**ro oos**tay** – preem**ai**rass – pe**say**tass]
can you leave a deposit of ...? ¿puede dejar un depósito de ...? [**pway**day day**Har** – day]

rented car el coche alquilado [**ko**chay alkee**la**do]
repair (verb) reparar
can you repair it? ¿puede arreglarlo? [**pway**day]
repeat repetir
could you repeat that? ¿puede repetir eso? [**pway**day – **ay**so]
reservation la reserva [re**sair**ba]
I'd like to make a reservation quisiera hacer una reserva [kees-**yai**ra a**thair**]

rest: I need a rest necesito un descanso [nethe**see**to]
the rest of the group el resto del grupo [**groo**po]
restaurant el restaurante [restow**ran**tay]

dialogue

I have a reservation tengo una reserva
yes sir, what name please? sí, señor, ¿a qué nombre, por favor? [sen-**yo**r a kay **no**mbray]

reserve reservar [re**sair**bar]

dialogue

can I reserve a table for tonight? ¿puedo reservar una mesa para esta noche? [**pway**do – **may**sa –

Spanish restaurants are categorized by a fork symbol (from 1 to 5 forks according to their quality). You can sit down and have a full meal in a **comedor**, a **cafetería**, a **restaurante** or a **marisquería** – all in addition to the more food-oriented bars, where tapas are available. Comedores are the places to seek out if your main criteria are price and quantity. Sometimes you will see them attached to a bar (often in a room behind); or as the dining room of a **pensión** or **fonda**, but as often as not they're virtually

unmarked and discovered only if you
pass an open door. Replacing
comedores to some extent are
cafeterías, which the local
authorities now grade from one to
three cups (the ratings, as with
restaurants, seem to be based on
facilities offered rather than quality
of food). Moving up the scale there
are **restaurantes** and
marisquerías, the latter serving
exclusively fish and seafood.

restaurant car el vagón-
cafetería [bagon kafetairee-a]
rest room los servicios
[sairbeeth-yoss]
see **toilet**
retired: I'm retired estoy
jubilado/jubilada
[Hoobeelado]
return (ticket) el billete de ida
y vuelta [bee-yaytay day eeda ee
bwelta]
see **ticket**
reverse charge call la llamada
a cobro revertido [yamada –
reberteedo]
reverse gear la marcha atrás
revolting asqueroso [askairoso]
rib la costilla [kostee-ya]
rice arroz [arroth]
rich (person) rico [reeko]
(food) sustancial [soostanth-yal]
ridiculous ridículo
[reedeekoolo]
right (correct) correcto
(not left) derecho
 you were right tenía razón

[rathon]
that's right eso es [ayso]
this can't be right esto no
puede ser así [pwayday sair]
right! ¡bien! [b-yen]
is this the right road for ...?
¿por aquí se va bien a ...?
[akee say ba b-yen]
on the right a la derecha
turn right gire a la derecha
[Heeray]
right-hand drive con el
volante a la derecha
[bolantay]
ring (on finger) la sortija
[sorteeHa]
I'll ring you te llamaré [tay
yamaray]
ring back volver a llamar
[bolbair a yamar]
ripe (fruit) maduro
rip-off: it's a rip-off es un timo
rip-off prices los precios
altísimos [prayth-yoss]
risky arriesgado [arr-yesgado]
river el río
road la carretera [karretaira]
 is this the road for ...? ¿es
ésta la carretera que va a ...?
[kay ba]
 down the road en esta calle
[ka-yay]
road accident el accidente
automovilístico [aktheedentay
owtomobeeleesteeko]
road map el mapa de
carreteras
roadsign la señal de tráfico
[sen-yal day]

rob: I've been robbed ¡me han robado! [may an]
rock la roca
(music) el rock
on the rocks (with ice) con hielo [yaylo]
roll (bread) el bollo [bo-yo]
roof el tejado [teHado]
roof rack la baca
room la habitación [abeetath-yon]
in my room en mi habitación

dialogue

do you have any rooms?
¿tiene habitaciones?
[t-yaynay abeetath-yoness]
for how many people?
¿para cuántos? [kwantoss]
for one/for two para uno/dos
yes, we have rooms free
sí, tenemos habitaciones libres [tenaymoss – leebress]
for how many nights will it be? ¿para cuántas noches? [kwantass nochess]
just for one night sólo para una noche [oona]
how much is it? ¿cuánto es? [kwanto]
... with bathroom and ... without bathroom ... con baño y ... sin baño [ban-yo – ee seen]
can I see a room with bathroom? ¿me enseña una habitación con baño? [may ensen-ya]
OK, I'll take it vale, me la quedo [balay may la kaydo]

room service el servicio de habitaciones [sairbeeth-yo day]
rope la cuerda [kwairda]
rosé (wine) vino rosado [beeno]
roughly (approximately) aproximadamente [–mentay]
round: it's my round es mi turno [toorno]
roundabout (for traffic) la rotonda
round trip ticket el billete de ida y vuelta [bee-yaytay day eeda ee bwelta]
see ticket
route la ruta [roota]
what's the best route? ¿cuál es la mejor ruta? [kwal ess la mayHor]
rubber (material) la goma
(eraser) la goma de borrar
rubber band la goma elástica
rubbish (waste) la basura
(poor quality goods) las porquerías [porkairee-ass]
rubbish! (nonsense) ¡tonterías! [tontairee-ass]
rucksack la mochila
rude grosero [grosairo]
ruins las ruinas [rweenass]
rum el ron
rum and coke el ron con coca-cola®

run (verb: person) correr
[korrair]
how often do the buses run?
¿cada cuánto pasan los
autobuses? [kwanto]
I've run out of money se me
ha acabado el dinero [say
may a – deenairo]
rush hour la hora punta [ora
poonta]

S

sad triste [treestay]
saddle (for horse) la silla de
montar [see-ya day]
(on bike) el sillín [see-yeen]
safe seguro [segooro]
safety pin el imperdible
[eempairdeeblay]
sail la vela [bayla]
sailboard el windsurf
sailboarding el windsurf
salad la ensalada
salad dressing el aliño para
la ensalada [aleen-yo]
sale: for sale en venta [em
baynta]
salmon el salmón [sal-mon]
salt la sal
same: the same mismo
[meesmo]
the same as this igual que
éste [eegwal kay estay]
the same again, please lo
mismo otra vez, por favor
[beth]
it's all the same to me me es

igual [may – eegwal]
sand la arena [arayna]
sandals las sandalias [sandal-
yass]
sandwich el sandwich
sanitary napkin la compresa
[kompraysa]
sanitary towel la compresa
Saragossa Zaragoza
[tharagotha]
sardines las sardinas
Saturday sábado
sauce la salsa
saucepan el cazo [katho]
saucer el platillo [platee-yo]
sauna la sauna [sowna]
sausage la salchicha
say: **how do you say ... in
Spanish?** ¿cómo se dice ...
en español? [say deethay en
espan-yol]
what did he say? ¿que ha
dicho? [kay a]
I said ... he dicho ... [ay]
he said ... ha dicho ... [ay]
could you say that again?
¿podría repetirlo?
scarf (for neck) la bufanda
(for head) el pañuelo [pan-
ywaylo]
scenery el paisaje [pa-eesaHay]
schedule (US) el horario
[orar-yo]
scheduled flight el vuelo
regular [bwaylo regoolar]
school la escuela [eskwayla]
scissors: **a pair of scissors** las
tijeras [teeHairass]
scotch el whisky

119

Scotch tape® la cinta adhesiva [**thee**nta adee**ee**ba]
Scotland Escocia [es**koth**-ya]
Scottish escocés [es**kothayss**]
 I'm Scottish (man/woman) soy escocés/escocesa
scrambled eggs los huevos revueltos [**way**boss reb**way**ltoss]
scratch el rasguño [rasg**oo**n-yo]
screw el tornillo [tor**nee**-yo]
screwdriver el destornillador [destornee-yad**or**]
sea el mar
 by the sea junto al mar [**Hoo**nto]
seafood los mariscos
seafood restaurant la marisquería [mareeskai**ree**-a]
seafront el paseo marítimo [pas**ay**-o mar**ee**teemo]
 on the seafront en línea de playa [**lee**nay-a day pla-ya]
seagull la gaviota [gab-y**o**ta]
search (verb) buscar
seashell la concha marina
seasick: I feel seasick estoy mareado [maray-**a**do]
 I get seasick me mareo [may maray-**o**]
seaside: by the seaside en la playa [pla-ya]
seat el asiento [as-y**e**nto]
 is this anyone's seat? ¿es de alguien este asiento? [day **a**lg-yen e**sta**y]
seat belt el cinturón de seguridad [theentoo**ro**n day segooree**da**]

sea urchin el erizo de mar [air**ee**tho]
seaweed el alga
secluded apartado
second (adjective) segundo [se**goo**ndo]
 (of time) el segundo
 just a second! ¡un momento!
second class (travel) en segunda clase [**kla**ssay]
secondhand de segunda mano [day]
see ver [bair]
 can I see? ¿puedo ver? [pw**ay**do]
 have you seen ...? ¿ha visto ...? [a b**ee**sto]
 I saw him this morning le vi esta mañana [lay bee]
 see you! ¡hasta luego! [**a**sta lw**ay**go]
 I see (I understand) ya comprendo
self-catering apartment el apartamento
self-service autoservicio [owtosairb**ee**th-yo]
sell vender [bend**ai**r]
 do you sell ...? ¿vende ...? [bend**ay**]
Sellotape® la cinta adhesiva [**thee**nta adee**ee**ba]
send enviar [emb-y**ar**]
 I want to send this to England quiero enviar esto a Inglaterra [k-y**ai**ro emb-y**ar**]
senior citizen el/la pensionista [pens-yon**ee**sta]

120

separate separado

separated: I'm separated estoy separado/separada

separately (pay, travel) por separado

September septiembre [septyembray]

septic séptico

serious serio [sair-yo]

service charge el servicio [sairbeeth-yo]

service station la estacion de servicio [estath-yon day]

serviette la servilleta [sairbeeyayta]

set menu el menu del día [menoo]

several varios [bar-yoss]

Seville Sevilla [sebee-ya]

sew coser [kosair]

could you sew this back on? ¿podría coserme esto? [kosairmay]

sex el sexo

sexy sexy

shade: in the shade a la sombra

shake: let's shake hands choque esa mano [chokay aysa]

shallow (water) poco profundo [profoondo]

shame: what a shame! ¡que lástima! [kay]

shampoo el champú

a shampoo and set un lavado y marcado [labado ee]

share (verb: room, table etc) compartir

sharp (knife) afilado

(taste) ácido [atheedo]

(pain) agudo

shattered (very tired) agotado

shaver la máquina de afeitar [makeena day afay-eetar]

shaving foam la espuma de afeitar

shaving point el enchufe (para la máquina de afeitar) [enchoofay – makeena]

she* ella [ay-ya]

is she here? ¿está (ella) aquí? [akee]

sheet (for bed) la sábana

shelf la estantería [estantairee-a]

shellfish los mariscos

sherry el jerez [Hereth]

The classic Andalucian wine is sherry – **vino de Jerez**. This is served chilled or at **bodega** temperature – a perfect drink to wash down **tapas** – and like everything Spanish, comes in a perplexing variety of forms. The main distinctions are between **fino** or **jerez seco** (dry sherry), **amontillado** [amonteeyado] (medium), and **oloroso** or **jerez dulce** (sweet), and these are the terms you should use to order. Similar – though not identical – are **montilla** [montee-ya] and **manzanilla** [manthanee-ya], dry, sherry-like wines from the provinces of Córdoba and Huelva. These too are excellent and widely available.

ship el barco
 by ship en barco
shirt el camisa
shit! ¡mierda! [m-yairda]
shock el susto [soosto]
 I got an electric shock me ha
 dado calambre [may a –
 kalambray]
shock-absorber el
 amortiguador [amorteegwador]
shocking escandaloso
shoes los zapatos [thapatoss]
 a pair of shoes un par de
 zapatos
shoelaces los cordones para
 zapatos [kordoness]
shoe polish la crema para los
 zapatos [krayma]
shoe repairer's la zapatería
 [thapatairee-a]
shop la tienda [t-yenda]

Business hours vary from
place to place and from
season to season. Shops
open some time between 9 and 10
a.m. and food shops open earlier
than other shops. In winter, they
generally close for lunch between
1.30 and 4 p.m. and in summer they
re-open later at 5 or 5.30 p.m. They
then stay open until 8 p.m. in winter
and 9 p.m. in summer. Department
stores and hypermarkets usually
open from 10 a.m to 9 p.m. and
don't close for lunch.

shopping: I'm going shopping
 voy de compras [boy]

shopping centre el centro
 comercial [thentro komairth-yal]
shop window el escaparate
 [eskaparatay]
shore la orilla [oree-ya]
short (time, journey) corto
 (person) bajo [baHo]
 it's only a short distance
 queda bastante cerca
 [kayda bastantay thairka]
shortcut el atajo [ataHo]
shorts los pantalones cortos
 [pantaloness]
should: what should I do?
 ¿que hago? [kay ago]
 he shouldn't be long no
 tardará mucho [moocho]
 you should have told me
 debiste habérmelo dicho
 [debeestay abairmelo]
shoulder el hombro [ombro]
shout (verb) gritar
show (in theatre) el
 espectáculo [espektakoolo]
 could you show me? ¿me lo
 enseña? [may lo ensen-ya]
shower (in bathroom) la ducha
 [doocha]
 with shower con ducha
shower gel el gel de ducha
 [Hel]
shut (verb) cerrar [thairrar]
 when do you shut? ¿a qué
 hora cierran? [a kay ora
 th-yairran]
 when do they shut? ¿a qué
 hora cierran?
 they're shut está cerrado
 [thairrado]

122

I've shut myself out he cerrado y he dejado la llave dentro [ay – ee ay dayнado la yabay]

shut up! ¡cállese! [ka-yesay]

shutter (on camera) el obturador

(on window) la contraventana [kontrabentana]

shy tímido [teemeedo]

sick (ill) enfermo [enfairmo]

I'm going to be sick (vomit) voy a vomitar [boy a bomeetar] see **ill**

side el lado

the other side of town al otro lado de la ciudad [day la th-yooda]

side lights las luces de posición [loothess day poseeth-yon]

side salad la ensalada aparte [apartay]

side street la callejuela [ka-yay-нwayla]

sidewalk la acera [athaira] see **pavement**

sight: the sights of ... los lugares de interés de ... [loogaress day eentairess]

sightseeing: we're going sightseeing vamos a hacer un recorrido turístico [bamoss a athair]

sightseeing tour el recorrido turístico

sign (notice) el letrero [letrairo] (roadsign) la señal de tráfico [sen-yal day]

signal: he didn't give a signal no hizo ninguna señal [no eetho]

signature la firma [feerma]

signpost el letrero [letrairo]

silence el silencio [seelenth-yo]

silk la seda [sayda]

silly tonto

silver la plata

silver foil el papel de aluminio [aloomeen-yo]

similar parecido [paretheedo]

simple (easy) sencillo [senthee-yo]

since: since yesterday desde ayer [desday a-yair]

since I got here desde que llegamos aquí [kay yegamoss akee]

sing cantar

singer el/la cantante [kantantay]

single: a single to ... un billete para ... [bee-yaytay]

I'm single soy soltero [soltairo]

single bed la cama individual [eendeebeedwal]

single room la habitación individual [abeetath-yon]

sink (in kitchen) el fregadero [fregadairo]

sister la hermana [airmana]

sister-in-law la cuñada [koon-yada]

sit: can I sit here? ¿puedo sentarme aquí? [pwaydo sentarmay akee]

sit down sentarse [sentarsay]

sit down! ¡siéntese! [s-yentaysay]

is anyone sitting here? ¿está ocupado este asiento? [estay as-yento]

size el tamaño [taman-yo]
(of clothes) la talla [ta-ya]

ski el esquí [eskee]
(verb) esquiar [esk-yar]

a pair of skis un par de esquís [day]

ski boots las botas de esquiar

skiing el esquí [eskee]

we're going skiing vamos a esquiar [bamoss – esk-yar]

ski instructor (man/woman) el monitor/la monitora de esquí

ski-lift el telesquí [teleskee]

skin la piel [p-yel]

skin-diving el buceo [boothay-o]

skinny flaco

ski-pants los pantalones de esquí [pantaloness day eskee]

ski-pass el abono

ski pole el bastón de esquí [day]

skirt la falda

ski run la pista de esquí [eskee]

ski slope la pista de esquí

ski wax la cera de esquís [thaira]

sky el cielo [th-yaylo]

sleep (verb) dormir

did you sleep well? ¿ha dormido bien? [a – b-yen]

I need a good sleep necesito

dormir bien [netheseeto]

sleeper (on train) el coche-cama [kochay-kama]

sleeping bag el saco de dormir [day]

sleeping car el coche-cama [kochay-kama]

sleeping pill la pastilla para dormir [pastee-ya]

sleepy: I'm feeling sleepy tengo sueño [swayn-yo]

sleeve la manga

slide (photographic) la diapositiva [d-yaposeeteeba]

slip (under dress) la combinación [kombeenath-yon]

slippery resbaladizo [resbaladeetho]

slow lento

slow down! ¡más despacio! [despath-yo]

slowly despacio

could you say it slowly? ¿podría decirlo despacio? [detheerlo]

very slowly muy despacio [mwee]

small pequeño [peken-yo]

smell: it smells! (smells bad) ¡apesta!

smile (verb) sonreír [sonray-eer]

smoke el humo [oomo]

do you mind if I smoke? ¿le importa si fumo? [lay – foomo]

I don't smoke no fumo

do you smoke? ¿fuma?

snack: I'd just like a snack

quisiera una tapa solamente
[kees-yaira – solamentay]

sneeze el estornudo

snorkel el tubo de buceo
[toobo day boothay-o]

snow la nieve [n-yaybay]

it's snowing está nevando

so: it's so good es tan bueno
[bwayno]

not so fast no tan de prisa
[preesa]

so am I yo también [tamb-yen]

so do I yo también

so-so más o menos
[maynoss]

soaking solution (for contact
lenses) el líquido preservador
[leekeedo]

soap el jabón [Habon]

soap powder el jabón en
polvo [em polbo]

sober sobrio [sobr-yo]

sock el calcetín [kaltheteen]

socket (electrical) el enchufe
[enchoofay]

soda (water) la soda

sofa el sofá

soft (material etc) suave
[swabay]

soft-boiled egg el huevo
pasado por agua [waybo –
agwa]

soft drink el refresco

soft lenses las lentes blandas
[lentess]

sole (of shoe, of foot) la suela
[swayla]

could you put new soles on

these? ¿podría cambiarles
las suelas? [kamb-yarless]

some: can I have some water?
¿me da un poco de agua?
[may – day]

can I have some rolls? ¿me
da unos bollos? [bo-yoss]

can I have some? ¿me da un
poco?

somebody, someone alguien
[alg-yen]

something algo

something to drink algo de
beber [bebair]

sometimes a veces [baythess]

somewhere en alguna parte
[partay]

son el hijo [eeHo]

song la canción [kanth-yon]

son-in-law el yerno [yairno]

soon pronto

I'll be back soon volveré
pronto [bolbairay]

as soon as possible lo antes
posible [antess poseeblay]

sore: it's sore me duele [may
dwaylay]

sore throat el dolor de
garganta

sorry: (I'm) sorry perdone
[pairdonay]

sorry? (didn't understand)
¿cómo?

sort: what sort of ...? ¿qué
clase de ...? [kay klassay day]

soup la sopa

sour (taste) ácido [atheedo]

south el sur [soor]

in the south en el sur

South Africa Sudáfrica
South African (adj) sudafricano
  I'm South African (man/woman) soy sudafricano/sudafricana
southeast el sudeste [sood-estay]
southwest el sudoeste [soodo-estay]
souvenir el recuerdo [rekwairdo]
Spain España [espan-ya]
Spaniard (man/woman) el español [espan-yol]/la española
Spanish español
  the Spanish los españoles [espan-yoless]
spanner la llave inglesa [yabay eenglaysa]
spare part el repuesto [repwesto]
spare tyre la rueda de repuesto [rwayda day]
spark plug la bujía [booHee-a]
speak: do you speak English? ¿habla inglés? [abla]
  I don't speak ... no hablo ... [ablo]

dialogue

can I speak to Pablo? ¿puedo hablar con Pablo? [pwaydo]
who's calling ¿quién llama? [k-yen yama]
it's Patricia soy Patricia
I'm sorry, he's not in, can I take a message? lo siento, no está, ¿quiere dejar algún recado? [s-yento – k-yairay dayHar]
no thanks, I'll call back later no gracias, llamaré más tarde [yamaray mass tarday]
please tell him I called por favor, dígale que he llamado [deegalay kay ay yamado]

speciality la especialidad [espeth-yaleeda]
spectacles las gafas
speed la velocidad [belotheeda]
speed limit el límite de velocidad [leemeetay day]
speedometer el velocímetro [belotheeemetro]
spell: how do you spell it? ¿cómo se escribe? [say eskreebay]
  see alphabet
spend gastar
spider la araña [aran-ya]
spin-dryer la secadora
splinter la astilla [astee-ya]
spoke (in wheel) el radio [rad-yo]
spoon la cuchara
sport el deporte [dayportay]
sprain: I've sprained my ... me he torcido el ... [may ay tortheedo]
spring (season) la primavera [preemabaira]

(of car, seat) el muelle [mway-yay]

square (in town) la plaza [platha]

stairs las escaleras [eskalairass]

stale (bread, taste) pasado

stall: the engine keeps stalling el motor se para a cada rato [say]

stamp el sello [say-yo]

dialogue

a stamp for England, please un sello para Inglaterra, por favor
what are you sending? ¿qué es lo que envía? [kay – embee-a]
this postcard esta postal

Stamps can be bought from tobacconist's (estanco), the Post Office (Correos) and sometimes from shops and stalls selling postcards and souvenirs.

standby el vuelo standby [bwaylo]

star la estrella [estray-ya]
(in film) el/la protagonista

start el principio [preentheep-yo]
(verb) comenzar [komenthar]
when does it start? ¿cuándo empieza? [kwando emp-yaytha]
the car won't start el coche no arranca [kochay]

starter (of car) el motor de arranque [arrankay]
(food) la entrada

starving: I'm starving me muero de hambre [may mwairo day ambray]

state (in country) el estado
the States (USA) los Estados Unidos [ooneedoss]

station la estación del ferrocarril [estath-yon]

statue la estatua [estatwa]

stay: where are you staying? ¿dónde se hospedan? [donday say ospaydan]
I'm staying at ... me hospedo en ... [may ospaydo]
I'd like to stay another two nights me gustaría quedarme otras dos noches [may – kedarmay – nochess]

steak el filete [feelaytay]

steal robar
my bag has been stolen me han robado el bolso [may an]

steep (hill) empinado

steering la dirección [deerekth-yon]

step: on the steps en las escaleras [eskalairass]

stereo el estéreo [estairay-o]

sterling las libras esterlinas [estairleenass]

steward (on plane) el auxiliar de vuelo [owkseel-yar day bwelo]

stewardess la azafata [athafata]

sticking plaster la tirita

still: I'm still waiting todavía estoy esperando [todabee-a]
is he still there? ¿está todavía ahí? [a-ee]
keep still! ¡quédese quieto! [kaydaysay k-yeto]
sting: I've been stung algo me ha picado [may a]
stockings las medias [maydyass]
stomach el estómago
stomach ache el dolor de estómago [day]
stone (rock) la piedra [p-yedra]
stop (verb) parar
please, stop here (to taxi driver etc) pare aquí, por favor [paray akee]
do you stop near ...? ¿para cerca de ...? [thairka day]
stop doing that! ¡deje hacer eso! [dayнay day athair ayso]
stopover la escala, la parada
storm la tormenta
straight: it's straight ahead todo derecho [dairecho]
a straight whisky un whisky solo
straightaway en seguida [segeeda]
strange (odd) extraño [estran-yo]
stranger (man/woman) el forastero [forastairo]/la forastera
I'm a stranger here no soy de aquí [day akee]
strap la correa [korray-a]

strawberry la fresa [fraysa]
stream el arroyo [arro-yo]
street la calle [ka-yay]
on the street en la calle
streetmap el mapa de la ciudad [thyooda]
string la cuerda [kwairda]
strong fuerte [fwairtay]
stuck atascado
the key's stuck la llave se ha atascado [yabay say a]
student el/la estudiante [estood-yantay]
stupid estúpido [estoopeedo]
subway (US) el metro
suburb el suburbio [sooboorb-yo]
suddenly de repente [repentay]
suede el ante [antay]
sugar el azúcar [athookar]
suit el traje [traнay]
it doesn't suit me (jacket etc) no me sienta bien [no may s-yenta b-yen]
it suits you te sienta muy bien [tay – mwee]
suitcase la maleta [malayta]
summer el verano [bairano]
in the summer en el verano
sun el sol
in the sun en el sol
out of the sun en la sombra
sunbathe tomar el sol
sunblock (cream) la crema protectora [krayma]
sunburn la quemadura de sol [kemadoora]
sunburnt quemado [kemado]

Sunday domingo
sunglasses las gafas de sol
sun lounger la tumbona
sunny: it's sunny hace sol
[athay]
sun roof (in car) el techo
corredizo [korraydeetho]
sunset la puesta de sol
[pwesta day]
sunshade la sombrilla
[sombree-ya]
sunshine la luz del sol [looth]
sunstroke la insolación
[eensolath-yon]
suntan el bronceado
[bronthay-ado]
suntan lotion la loción
bronceadora [loth-yon
bronthay-adora]
suntanned bronceado
suntan oil el aceite
bronceador [athay-eetay]
super fabuloso
supermarket el
supermercado
[soopairmairkado]
supper la cena [thayna]
supplement (extra charge) el
suplemento
sure: are you sure? ¿está
seguro?
sure! ¡por supuesto¡
[soopwesto]
surname el apellido [apay-
yeedo]
swearword la palabrota
sweater el suéter [swetair]
sweatshirt la sudadera
[soodadaira]

Sweden Suecia [swayth-ya]
Swedish (adj) sueco [swayko]
sweet (dessert) el postre
[postray]
(adj: taste) dulce [doolthay]
(sherry) oloroso
sweets los caramelos
[karamayloss]
swelling la hinchazón
[eenchathon]
swim (verb) nadar
I'm going for a swim voy a
nadar [boy]
let's go for a swim vamos a
nadar [bamoss]
swimming costume el
bañador [ban-yador]
swimming pool la piscina
[peestheena]
swimming trunks el traje de
baño [traHay day banyo]
switch el interruptor
[eentairrooptor]
switch off apagar
switch on encender
[enthendair]
swollen inflamado

T

table la mesa [maysa]
 a table for two una mesa
 para dos
tablecloth el mantel
table tennis el ping-pong
table wine el vino de mesa
[beeno day maysa]
tailback (of traffic) la caravana

129

de coches [karabana day kochess]

tailor el sastre [sastray]

take (lead) coger [koнair]

(accept) aceptar [atheptar]

can you take me to the airport? ¿me lleva al aeropuerto? [may yayba al a-airopwairto]

do you take credit cards? ¿acepta tarjetas de crédito? [athepta tarнaytass day kraydeeto]

fine, I'll take it está bien, lo compro [b-yen]

can I take this? (leaflet etc) ¿puedo llevarme esto? [pwaydo yebarmay]

how long does it take? ¿cuánto se tarda? [kwanto say]

it takes three hours se tarda tres horas [orass]

is this seat taken? ¿está ocupado este asiento? [estay as-yento]

a hamburger to take away una hamburguesa para llevar [yebar]

can you take a little off here? (to hairdresser) ¿puede quitarme un poco de aquí? [pwayday keetarmay – day akee]

talcum powder el talco

talk (verb) hablar [ablar]

tall alto

tampons los tampones [tamponess]

tan el bronceado [bronthay-ado]

to get a tan broncearse [bronthay-arsay]

tank (of car) el depósito [deposeeto]

tap el grifo

tape (for cassette) la cinta [theenta]

(sticky) la cinta adhesiva [adeseeba]

tape measure la cinta métrica

tape recorder el casete [kaset]

taste el sabor

can I taste it? ¿puedo probarlo? [pwaydo]

taxi el taxi

will you get me a taxi? ¿podría conseguirme un taxi? [konsegeermay]

where can I find a taxi? ¿dónde puedo coger un taxi? [donday pwaydo koнair]

dialogue

> **to the airport/to Hotel Sol please** al aeropuerto/al hotel Sol, por favor [a-airopwairto/otel]
>
> **how much will it be?** ¿cuánto costará? [kwanto]
>
> **1,000 pesetas** mil pesetas [pesaytass]
>
> **that's fine, right here, thanks** está bien, aquí mismo, gracias [b-yen akee meesmo]

taxi-driver el/la taxista

taxi rank la parada de taxis [day]

tea (drink) el té [tay]
tea for one/two please un té/dos tés, por favor

teabags las bolsas de té

teach: could you teach me? ¿podría enseñarme? [ensen-yarmay]

teacher (primary: man/woman) el maestro [ma-estro]/la maestra (secondary: man/woman) el profesor/la profesora

team el equipo [ekeepo]

teaspoon la cuchara de té [day tay]

tea towel el paño de cocina [pan-yo day kotheena]

teenager el/la adolescente [adolesthentay]

telegram el telegrama

telephone el teléfono [telayfono]
see phone

television la televisión [telebees-yon]

tell: could you tell him ...? ¿podría decirle ...? [detheerlay]

temperature (weather) la temperatura [temperatoora] (fever) la fiebre [f-yebray]

tennis el tenis

tennis ball la pelota de tenis [day]

tennis court la pista de tenis

tennis racket la raqueta de tenis [rakayta]

tent la tienda de campaña

[t-yenda day kampan-ya]

term (at university, school) el trimestre [treemestray]

terminus (rail) la estación terminal [estath-yon tairmeenal]

terrible terrible [terreeblay]

terrific fabuloso [fabooloso]

than* que [kay]
smaller than más pequeño que [pekayn-yo]

thanks, thank you gracias [grath-yass]
thank you very much muchas gracias [moochass]
thanks for the lift gracias por traerme [tra-airmay]
no thanks no gracias

dialogue

thanks gracias
that's OK, don't mention it
no hay de qué [ī day kay]

that: that man ese hombre [aysay ombray]
that woman esa mujer [mooHair]
that one ése
I hope that ... espero que ... [espairo kay]
that's nice (clothes, souvenir etc) es bonito
is that ...? ¿es ése ...? [aysay]
that's it (that's right) eso es

the* el, la; (pl) los, las

theatre el teatro [tay-atro]

their* su; (pl) sus [sooss]

theirs* su, sus; (pl) suyos [sooyoss], suyas; de ellos [day ay-yoss], de ellas

them* (things) los, las
(people) les
for them para ellos [ay-yoss]/ellas
with them con ellos/ellas
I gave it to them se lo di a ellos/ellas [say]
who? – them ¿quién? – ellos/ellas [k-yen]

then entonces [entonthess]

there allí [a-yee]
over there allí
up there allí arriba
is/are there ...? ¿hay ...? [ī]
there is/are ... hay ...
there you are (giving something) aquí tiene [akee t-yaynay]

thermometer el termómetro [tairmometro]

thermos flask el termo [tairmo]

these: these men estos hombres
these women estas mujeres
can I have these? ¿me puedo llevar éstos? [may pwaydo yebar]

they* (male) ellos [ay-yoss]
(female) ellas [ay-yass]

thick grueso [grwayso]
(stupid) estúpido [estoopeedo]

thief (man/woman) el ladrón/la ladrona

thigh el muslo [mooslo]

thin delgado

thing la cosa
my things mis cosas [meess]

think pensar
I think so creo que sí [kray-o kay]
I don't think so no lo creo
I'll think about it lo pensaré [pensaray]

third party insurance el seguro contra terceros [tairthaiross]

thirsty: I'm thirsty tengo sed [seth]

this: this man este hombre [estay]
this woman esta mujer
this one éste/ésta
this is my wife ésta es mi mujer
is this ...? ¿es éste/ésta ...?

those: those men aquellos hombres [akay-yoss]
those women aquellas mujeres [akay-yass]
which ones? – those ¿cuáles? – aquéllos/aquéllas [kwaless]

thread el hilo [eelo]

throat la garganta

throat pastilles las pastillas para la garganta [pastee-yass]

through a través de [day]
does it go through ...? (train, bus) ¿pasa por...?

throw (verb) tirar

throw away (verb) tirar

thumb el dedo pulgar [daydo]

thunderstorm la tormenta

Thursday jueves [Hwaybess]

ticket el billete [bee-yaytay]

dialogue

a return to Salamanca un billete de ida y vuelta a Salamanca [day **ee**da ee bw**e**lta]
coming back when? ¿cuándo piensa volver? [kwando p-y**e**nsa bolb**air**]
today/next Tuesday hoy/el martes que viene [oy/el m**a**rtess kay b-y**ay**nay]
that will be 2,000 pesetas son dos mil pesetas [pes**ay**tass]

ticket office (bus, rail) la taquilla [tak**ee**-ya]
tide la marea [mar**a**y-a]
tie (necktie) la corbata
tight (clothes etc) ajustado [aHoost**a**do]
  it's too tight es demasiado estrecho [daymas-y**a**do]
tights los panties
till la caja [k**a**Ha]
time* el tiempo [t-y**e**mpo]
  what's the time? ¿qué hora es? [kay **o**ra]
  this time esta vez [beth]
  last time la última vez [**oo**lteema]
  next time la próxima vez
  four times cuatro veces [b**e**thess]
timetable el horario [or**a**r-yo]
tin (can) la lata
tinfoil el papel de aluminio [aloom**ee**n-yo]

tin opener el abrelatas
tiny diminuto
tip (to waiter etc) la propina

 In Spain it is customary to leave a tip in restaurants, even though a service charge is included in the bill. Some people also leave tips in bars particularly when they have table service. Taxi drivers are not usually tipped, but often people let them keep the change. Hotel and station porters are tipped. In all but the most rock-bottom establishments, it is customary to leave a small tip: the amount is up to you, though ten per cent of the bill is quite sufficient.

tired cansado
  I'm tired estoy cansado/cansada
tissues los Kleenex®
to: to Barcelona/London a Barcelona/Londres
  to Spain/England a España/Inglaterra
  to the post office a la oficina de Correos
toast (bread) la tostada
today hoy [oy]
toe el dedo del pie [d**a**ydo del p-yay]
together junto [H**oo**nto]
  we're together (in shop etc) venimos juntos [ben**ee**moss]
  can we pay together? ¿podemos pagar todo junto, por favor? [pod**ay**moss]

toilet los servicios [sairbeeth-yoss]

where is the toilet? ¿dónde están los servicios? [donday]

I have to go to the toilet tengo que ir al servicio [kay]

Public toilets are rare in Spain. You should take advantage of toilets in bars and restaurants, museums and other tourist places you visit. They're usually marked **damas** and **caballeros**, though you may see the more confusing **señoras** (women) and **señores** (men).

toilet paper el papel higiénico [eeH-yayneeko]

tomato el tomate [tomatay]

tomato juice el zumo de tomate [thoomo]

tomato ketchup el ketchup

tomorrow mañana [man-yana]

tomorrow morning mañana por la mañana

the day after tomorrow pasado mañana

toner (for skin) el tonificador facial [fath-yal]

tongue la lengua [lengwa]

tonic (water) la tónica

tonight esta noche [nochay]

tonsillitis las anginas [anHeenass]

too (excessively) demasiado [demass-yado]
(also) también [tamb-yen]

too hot demasiado caliente [kal-yentay]

too much demasiado

me too yo también

tooth el diente [d-yentay]

toothache el dolor de muelas [day mwaylass]

toothbrush el cepillo de dientes [thepee-yo day d-yentess]

toothpaste la pasta de dientes

top: on top of ... encima de ... [entheema day]

at the top en lo alto

top floor el último piso [oolteemo]

topless topless

torch la linterna [leentairna]

total el total

tour el viaje [b-yaHay]

is there a tour of ...? ¿hay una gira por ...? [ī oona Heera]

tour guide el/la guía turístico [gee-a]

tourist el/la turista

tourist information office la oficina de información turística [ofeetheena day eenformath-yon]

tour operator la agencia de viajes [aHenth-ya day b-yaHess]

towards hacia [ath-ya]

towel la toalla [to-a-ya]

town la ciudad [th-yooda]

in town en el centro [thentro]

just out of town en las afueras de la ciudad [afwairass]

134

town centre el centro de la
ciudad
town hall el ayuntamiento
[a-yoontam-**y**ento]
toy el juguete [Hoog**ay**tay]
track (US) el andén
 see **platform**
tracksuit el chándal
traditional tradicional
[tradeeth-**yo**nal]
traffic el tráfico
traffic jam el
 embotellamiento de tráfico
[embotaym-**y**ento day]
traffic lights los semáforos
trailer (for carrying tent etc) el
 remolque [rem**o**lkay]
 (US: caravan) la caravana
 [kara**ba**na]
trailer park el camping
train el tren
 by train en tren

dialogue

is this the train for ...? ¿es
éste el tren para ....?
[**e**stay]
sure exacto
**no, you want that platform
there** no, tiene que ir a
aquel andén de allí
[t-**yay**nay kay eer a ak**ay**l – day
a-y**ee**]

trainers (shoes) las zapatillas
de deporte [thapat**ee**-yass day
dep**o**rtay]
train station la estación de

trenes [estath-y**on** day tr**ay**ness]
tram el tranvía [trambee-a]
translate traducir [tradoot**heer**]
 could you translate that?
 ¿podría traducir eso? [**ay**so]
translation la traducción
[tradookth-y**on**]
translator (man/woman) el
 traduct**o**r/la traduct**o**ra
trashcan el cubo de la basura
[k**oo**bo day la bas**oo**ra]
travel (verb) viajar [b-ya**Har**]
 we're travelling around
 estamos viajando [b-ya**Han**do]
travel agent's la agencia de
 viajes [a**Hen**th-ya day b-ya**Hess**]
traveller's cheque el cheque
 de viaje [ch**ay**kay day b-ya**Hay**]
tray la bandeja [band**ay**Ha]
tree el árbol
tremendous tremendo
trendy moderno [mod**air**no]
trim: just a trim please (to
 hairdresser) córtemelo sólo
 un p**o**co, por fav**o**r
[k**o**rtaymelo]
trip (excursion) la excursión
[eskoors-y**on**]
 I'd like to go on a trip to ...
 me gustaría hacer una
 excursión a ... [may – ath**air**]
trolley el carrito
trouble problemas
[probl**ay**mass]
 I'm having trouble with ...
 tengo problemas con ...
 sorry to trouble you perdone
 que le moleste [pairdonay kay
 lay mol**e**stay]

trousers los pantalones
[pantalo**ness**]

true verdadero [bairdad**ai**ro]
 that's not true no es verdad
 [**bair**da]

trunk (US) el maletero
 [male**tai**ro]

trunks (swimming) el bañador
 [ban-**yad**or]

try (verb) intentar
 can I have a try? ¿puedo
 probarlo? [**pway**do]

try on: can I try it on? ¿puedo
 probármelo?

T-shirt la camiseta
 [kamees**ay**ta]

Tuesday martes [**mar**tess]

tuna el atún [a**toon**]

tunnel el túnel [**too**nel]

turn: turn left/right gire a la
 izquierda/derecha [**Hee**ray]

turn off: where do I turn off?
 ¿dónde me desvío? [**don**day
 may des**bee**-o]

 can you turn the heating off?
 ¿puede apagar la
 calefacción? [**pway**day –
 kalefakth-**yon**]

**turn on: can you turn the
 heating on?** ¿puede
 encender la calefacción?
 [enthen**dair**]

turning (in road) el desvío
 [des**bee**-o]

TV la tele [**tay**lay]

tweezers las pinzas [**peen**thass]

twice dos veces [**bay**thess]
 twice as much el doble
 [**do**blay]

twin beds las camas gemelas
 [Haymay**lass**]

twin room la habitación
 doble [abeetath-yon **do**blay]

twist: I've twisted my ankle
 me he torcido el tobillo
 [may ay tor**thee**do el to**bee**-yo]

type el tipo
 a different type of ... un tipo
 diferente de ... [deefairay**ntay**
 day]

typical típico

tyre la rueda [**rway**da]

U

ugly (person, building) feo [**fay**-o]

UK el Reino Unido [**ray-ee**no
 oo**needo**]

ulcer la úlcera [**ool**thaira]

umbrella el paraguas
 [para**gwass**]

uncle el tío

unconscious inconsciente
 [eenkonsth-**yentay**]

under (in position) debajo de
 [de**ba**Ho day]
 (less than) menos de
 [**may**noss]

underdone (meat) poco hecha
 [**ay**cha]

underground (railway) el metro

underpants los calzoncillos
 [kalthonthee-**yoss**]

understand: I understand lo
 entiendo [ent-**yendo**]
 I don't understand no
 entiendo

do you understand?
¿entiende usted? [ent-yenday
oostay]

unemployed desempleado
[desemplay-ado]

United States los Estados
Unidos [ooneedoss]

university la universidad
[ooneebairseeda]

unleaded petrol la gasolina
sin plomo [gasoleena seen]

unlimited mileage sin límite
de kilometraje [seen
leemeetay day keelometraHay]

unlock abrir [abreer]

unpack deshacer las maletas
[desahair lass malaytass]

until hasta que [asta kay]

unusual poco común
[komoon]

up arriba

up there allí arriba [a-yee]

he's not up yet (not out of bed)
todavía no se ha levantado
[todabee-a no say a laybantado]

what's up? (what's wrong?)
¿qué pasa? [kay]

upmarket (restaurant, hotel, goods
etc) de lujo [day looHo]

upset stomach el malestar de
estómago

upside down al revés [rebayss]

upstairs arriba

urgent urgente [oorHentay]

us*: with us con nosotros

for us para nosotros

USA EE. UU., Estados
Unidos [ooneedoss]

use (verb) usar [oosar]

may I use ...? ¿podría
usar ...?

useful útil [ooteel]

usual habitual [abeetwal]

the usual (drink etc) lo de
siempre [day s-yempray]

V

**vacancy: do you have any
vacancies?** (hotel) ¿tiene
habitaciones libres? [t-yaynay
abeetath-yoness leebress]
see **room**

vacation las vacaciones
[bakath-yoness]
see **holiday**

vaccination la vacuna
[bakoona]

vacuum cleaner la aspiradora

valid (ticket etc) válido
[baleedo]

how long is it valid for?
¿hasta cuándo tiene
validez? [asta kwando t-yaynay
baleedeth]

valley el valle [ba-yay]

valuable (adjective) valioso
[bal-yoso]

**can I leave my valuables
here?** ¿puedo dejar aquí mis
objetos de valor? [pwaydo
dayHar akee meess obHaytoss day
balor]

value el valor

van la furgoneta [foorgonayta]

vanilla vainilla [ba-eenee-ya]

a vanilla ice cream un

helado de vainilla [elado]
vary: it varies depende
[daypenday]
vase el florero [florairo]
veal la ternera [tairnaira]
vegetables las verduras
[bairdoorass]
vegetarian (man/woman) el
vegetariano [beHetar-yano]/la
vegetariana
vending machine la máquina
[makeena]
very muy [mwee]
  very little for me un poquito
  para mí [pokeeto]
  I like it very much me gusta
  mucho [may goosta moocho]
vest (under shirt) la camiseta
[kameesayta]
via por
video el video [beeday-o]
view la vista [beesta]
villa el chalet [chalay]
village el pueblo [pwayblo]
vinegar el vinagre
[beenagray]
vineyard el viñedo [been-
yaydo]
visa la visa
visit (verb) visitar [beeseetar]
  I'd like to visit Valencia ...
  me gustaría ir a Valencia
  [may]
vital: it's vital that ... es de
vital importancia que ...
[day beetal eemportanth-ya kay]
vodka el vodka [bodka]
voice la voz [both]
voltage el voltaje [boltaHay]

The supply is 220V,
though anything requiring
240V will work. Most
plugs are two round pins: a travel
plug is useful.

vomit vomitar [bomeetar]

W

waist la cintura [theentoora]
waistcoat el chaleco
[chalayko]
wait esperar [espairar]
  wait for me espéreme
  [espairaymay]
  don't wait for me no me
  espere [may]
  **can I wait until my
  wife/partner gets here?**
  ¿puedo esperar hasta que
  llegue mi
  mujer/compañero? [pwaydo
  – asta kay yaygay]
  can you do it while I wait?
  ¿puede hacerlo mientras
  espero? [pwayday athairlo m-
  yentrass]
  could you wait here for me?
  ¿puede esperarme aquí?
  [espairarmay akee]
waiter el camarero [kamarairo]
  waiter! ¡camarero!
waitress la camarera
[kamaraira]
  waitress! ¡señorita! [sen-
  yoreeta]
wake: can you wake me up at

5.30? ¿podría despertarme a las cinco y media? [despertarmay]

wake-up call la llamada para despertar [yamada]

Wales Gales [galess]

walk: is it a long walk? ¿se tarda mucho en llegar andando? [say – moocho en yegar]

it's only a short walk está cerca [thairka]

I'll walk iré andando [eeray]

I'm going for a walk voy a dar una vuelta [boy – bwelta]

Walkman® el walkman [wolman]

wall: (inside) la pared [paray] (outside) la tapia

wallet la billetera [bee-yetaira]

wander: I like just wandering around me gusta caminar por ahí [may goosta – a-ee]

want: I want a ... quiero un/una ... [k-yairo]

I don't want ... no quiero ...

I want to go home quiero irme a casa [eermay]

I don't want to no quiero

he wants to ... quiere ... [k-yairay]

what do you want? ¿qué quiere? [kay]

ward (in hospital) la habitación [abeetath-yon]

warm caliente [kal-yentay]

I'm so warm tengo mucho calor [moocho]

was*: it was ... era ... [aira];

estaba ...

wash (verb) lavar [labar]

can you wash these? ¿puede lavarlos? [pwayday labarloss]

washer (for bolt etc) la arandela [arandayla]

washhand basin el lavabo [lababo]

washing (clothes) la ropa sucia [sooth-ya]

washing machine la lavadora [labadora]

washing powder el detergente [detairнentay]

washing-up liquid el (detergente) lavavajillas [daytairнentay lababaнee-yass]

wasp la avispa [abeespa]

watch (wristwatch) el reloj [rayloн]

will you watch my things for me? ¿puede cuidarme mis cosas? [pwayday kweedarmay meess]

watch out! ¡cuidado! [kweedado]

watch strap la correa [korray-a]

water el agua [agwa]

may I have some water? ¿me da un poco de agua? [may – day]

waterproof (adjective) impermeable [eempairmay-ablay]

waterskiing el esquí acuático [eskee akwateeko]

wave (in sea) la ola

way: it's this way es por aquí
[akee]
it's that way es por allí
[a-yee]
is it a long way to ...? ¿queda
lejos...? [kayda layHoss]
no way! ¡de ninguna
manera! [day – manaira]

dialogue

could you tell me the way
to ...? podría indicarme
el camino a ...?
[eendeekarmay]
go straight on until you
reach the traffic lights siga
recto hasta llegar al
semáforo [asta yegar]
turn left gire a la
izquierda [Heeray]
take the first on the right
tome la primera a la
derecha [tomay]
see where

we* nosotros, nosotras
weak (person, drink) débil
[daybeel]
weather el tiempo [t-yempo]

dialogue

what's the weather going
to be like? ¿qué tiempo
va a hacer? [kay – ba a
athair]
it's going to be fine va a
hacer bueno [bwayno]

it's going to rain va a
llover [yobair]
it'll brighten up later
despejará más tarde
[despayHara – tarday]

wedding la boda
wedding ring el anillo de
casado [anee-yo]
Wednesday miércoles
[m-yairkoless]
week la semana
a week (from) today dentro
de una semana [day]
a week (from) tomorrow
dentro de una semana a
partir de mañana [man-yana]
weekend el fin de semana
[feen]
at the weekend el fin de
semana
weight el peso [payso]
weird extraño [extran-yo]
weirdo: he's a weirdo es un
tipo raro
welcome: welcome to ...
bienvenido(s) a ...
[b-yenbeneeedo(ss)]
you're welcome (don't mention
it) de nada [day]
well: I don't feel well no me
siento bien [may s-yento b-yen]
she's not well no se siente
bien [say]
you speak English very well
habla inglés muy bien [abla
– mwee]
well done! ¡bravo! [brabo]
this one as well éste también

140

[**estay** tamb-yen]
well well! (surprise) ¡vaya,
vaya! [**ba**-ya]

dialogue

how are you? ¿cómo está?
very well, thanks muy
bien, gracias [mwee b-yen]
– and you? – ¿y usted? [ee
oo**stay**]

well-done (meat) muy hecho
[mwee **ay**cho]
Welsh galés [ga**lay**ss]
I'm Welsh (man/woman) soy
galés/ga**le**sa
were*: we were estábamos;
éramos [**ai**ramoss]
you were estabais [estaba-
eess]; erais [**ai**ra-eess]
they were estaban; eran
[**ai**ran]
west el oeste [o-**estay**]
in the west en el oeste
West Indian (adj) antillano
[antee-**ya**no]
wet mojado [mo**Ha**do]
what? ¿qué? [kay]
what's that? ¿qué es eso?
[**ay**so]
what should I do? ¿qué
hago? [**a**-go]
what a view! ¡qué vista!
[**bee**sta]
what number bus is it? ¿qué
autobús es ese? [**ay**say]
wheel la rueda [r**way**da]
wheelchair la silla de ruedas

[**see**-ya day r**way**dass]
when? ¿cuándo [**kwan**do]
when we get back cuando
volvamos [bol**ba**moss]
when's the train/ferry?
¿cuándo es el tren/ferry?
where? ¿dónde? [**don**day]
I don't know where it is no sé
dónde está [say]

dialogue

where is the cathedral?
¿dónde está la catedral?
it's over there está por ahí
[a-**ee**]
could you show me where
it is on the map? ¿puede
enseñarme en el mapa
dónde está? [p**way**day
ensen-**yar**may]
it's just here está justo ahí
[**Hoo**sto a-**ee**]
see way

which: which bus? ¿qué
autobús? [kay]

dialogue

which one? ¿cuál? [kwal]
that one ese [**ay**say]
this one? éste [**es**tay]
no, that one no, aquél
[a**kel**]

while: while I'm here mientras
esté aquí [m-**yen**trass es**tay**
a**kee**]

whisky el whisky
white blanco
white wine el vino blanco
[beeno]
who? ¿quién? [k-yen]
who is it? ¿quién es?
the man who ... el hombre
que... [kay]
whole: the whole week toda la
semana
the whole lot todo
whose: whose is this? ¿de
quién es esto? [day k-yen]
why? ¿por qué? [kay]
why not? ¿por qué no?
wide ancho
wife: my wife mi mujer [mee
mooHair]
will*: will you do it for me?
¿puede hacer esto por mí?
[pwayday athair]
wind el viento [b-yento]
window (of house) la ventana
[bentana]
(of ticket office, vehicle) la
ventanilla [bentanee-ya]
near the window cerca de la
ventana [thairka day]
in the window (of shop) en el
escaparate [escaparatay]
window seat el asiento junto
a la ventana [as-yento Hoonto a
la bentana]
windscreen el parabrisas
windscreen wiper el
limpiaparabrisas [leemp-ya-
parabreesass]
windsurfing el windsurf
windy: it's so windy hace

mucho viento [athay moocho
b-yento]
wine el vino [beeno]
can we have some more
wine? ¿podría traernos más
vino? [tra-airnoss]

Vino (wine) either tinto
(red) or blanco (white) or
rosado/clarete (rosé), is
the invariable accompaniment to
every meal and is, as a rule,
extremely inexpensive. The most
common bottle variety is
Valdepeñas, a good standard wine
from the central plains of La
Mancha; Rioja, from the area round
Logroño, is better but a lot more
expensive. Both are found all over
the country. There are also scores of
local wines – some of the best in
Catalunya (Bach, Sangre de Toro
and the champagne-like Cava) and
Galicia (Ribeiro, Fefiñanes and
Albariño) – but you'll rarely be
given any choice unless you're at a
good restaurant. Otherwise, it's
whatever comes out of the barrel,
or the house-bottled special (ask
for caserio or de la casa). This
can be great, it can be lousy, but
at least it will be distinctively
local.

wine list la lista de vinos
[leesta day beenoss]
winter el invierno [eemb-
yairno]
in the winter en el

Wh

142

invierno

winter holiday las vacaciones de invierno [bakath-yonayss day]

wire el alambre [alambray] (electric) el cable eléctrico [kablay]

wish: best wishes saludos [saloodoss]

with con

I'm staying with ... estoy en casa de ... [day]

without sin [seen]

witness el/la testigo [testeego]

will you be a witness for me? ¿acepta ser mi testigo? [athepta sair]

woman la mujer [mooHair]

wonderful estupendo [estoopendo]

won't*: it won't start no arranca

wood (material) la madera [madaira]

woods (forest) el bosque [boskay]

wool la lana

word la palabra

work el trabajo [trabaHo]

it's not working no funciona [foonth-yona]

I work in ... trabajo en ...

world el mundo [moondo]

worry: I'm worried estoy preocupado/preocupada [pray-okoopado]

worse: it's worse es peor [pay-or]

worst el peor

worth: is it worth a visit? ¿vale la pena visitarlo? [balay la payna beeseetarlo]

would: would you give this to ...? ¿le puede dar esto a ...? [lay pwayday]

wrap: could you wrap it up? ¿me lo envuelve? [may lo embwelbay]

wrapping paper el papel de envolver [day embolbair]

wrist la muñeca [moon-yayka]

write escribir [eskreebeer]

could you write it down? ¿puede escribírmelo? [pwayday]

how do you write it? ¿cómo se escribe? [say eskreebay]

writing paper el papel de escribir

wrong: it's the wrong key no es ésa la llave [aysa la yabay]

this is the wrong train éste no es el tren [estay]

the bill's wrong la cuenta está equivocada [kwenta – ekeebokada]

sorry, wrong number perdone, me he equivocado de número [pairdonay, may ay – day noomairo]

there's something wrong with ... le pasa algo a ... [lay]

what's wrong? ¿qué pasa? [kay]

X

X-ray la radiografía [radyografee-a]

Y

yacht el yate [yatay]
yard* (courtyard) el patio
year el año [an-yo]
yellow amarillo [amaree-yo]
yes sí
yesterday ayer [a-yair]
  yesterday morning ayer por la mañana [man-yana]
  the day before yesterday anteayer [antay-ayair]
yet

dialogue

is it here yet? ¿está aquí ya? [akee]
no, not yet no, todavía no [todabee-a]
you'll have to wait a little longer yet todavía tendrá que esperar un poquito más [kay espairar oon pokeeto]

yobbo el gamberro [gambairro]
yoghurt el yogur [yogoor]

you* (fam, sing) tú [too]
  (pol, sing) usted [oostay]
  (fam, pl) vosotros [bosotross]
  (pol, pl) ustedes [oostaydess]
this is for you esto es para tí/usted
with you contigo/con usted

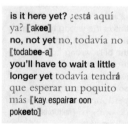

In Spanish, when you address people you don't know (especially older people) or those with whom you have a formal relationship, you should use '**usted**' which takes the third person singular of the verb. The plural form of usted is **ustedes** and it is used with the third person plural of the verb. If you talk to relatives, friends or younger people you should use '**tú**' or the plural '**vosotros**' when addressing more than one person.

young joven [Hoben]
your* (fam, sing) tu; (pl) tus [tooss]
  (fam, pl) vuestro [bwestro], vuestra; (pl) vuestros, vuestras
  (polite, sing) su; (pl) sus [sooss]
yours* (fam, sing) tuyo [too-yo], tuya
  (fam pl) vuestro [bwestro], vuestra
  (polite, sing) suyo [soo-yo], suya; de usted [day oostay]
youth hostel el albergue juvenil [albairgay Hoobayneel]

Z

zero cero [**tha**iro]
zip la cremallera [krema-**ya**ira]
 could you put a new zip in?
 ¿podría cambiar la
 cremallera? [kamb-**yar**]
zoo el zoo(lógico)
 [tho(lo**Hee**ko)]

Spanish

→

English

A

a to; at; per; from
abajo [abaHo] downstairs
abierto [ab-yairto] open
abierto de ... a ... open from
  ... to
abierto las 24 horas del día
  open 24 hours
abogado m/f lawyer
abonos mpl season tickets
aborrezco [aborethko] I hate
ábrase aquí open here
ábrase en caso de
  emergencia open in case of
  emergency
abrebotellas m [abray-botay-
  yass] bottle-opener
abrelatas m tin opener
abrigo m coat
abrigo de pieles [p-yayless] fur
  coat
abril m April
abrir to open
abróchense los cinturones
  fasten your seatbelts
abstenerse de fumar no
  smoking
abuela f [abwayla]
  grandmother
abuelo m grandfather
abuelos mpl grandparents
aburrido boring; bored
aburrirse [aboorreersay] to be
  bored; to get bored
acabar to finish
  acabo de ... I have just ...
acantilado m cliff

acceso a ... access to ...
acceso a los andenes to the
  trains
acceso playa to the beach
acceso prohibido no
  admittance
accidente m [aktheedentay]
  accident
  tener un accidente to have
  an accident
accidente de coche [kochay]
  car accident
accidente de montaña
  [montan-ya] mountaineering
  accident
accidente de tráfico road
  accident
accidente en cadena [kadayna]
  pile-up
acelerador m [athelairador]
  accelerator, gas pedal
acelerar [athelairar] to
  accelerate
acento m [athento] accent
aceptar [atheptar] to accept
acera f [athaira] pavement,
  sidewalk
acerca de [athairka day] about,
  concerning
acero m [athairo] steel
acetona f [athaytona] nail
  polish remover
ácido (m) [atheedo] sour; acid
acompañar [akompan-yar] to
  accompany
  le acompaño en el
  sentimiento condolences
acondicionador de pelo m
  [akondeeth-yonador day paylo]

hair conditioner

aconsejar [akonsay-Har] to advise

acordarse [akordarsay] to remember

acostar: irse a acostar [eersay] to go to bed

acostarse [akostarsay] to lie down; to go to bed
  al acostarse when you go to bed

actriz f [aktreeth] actress

acuerdo m [akwairdo] agreement
  estoy de acuerdo I agree
  de acuerdo OK

adaptador m adaptor

adelantado: por adelantado [adelantado] in advance

adelantar to overtake

adelante [adelantay] come in

además de [ademass day] besides, as well as

adentro inside

adiós [ad-yoss] goodbye

admitir to admit, to confess

adolescente m/f [adolesthentay] teenager

aduana f [ad-wana] customs

aduanero m [adwanairo] customs officer

aerobús m [a-airobooss] local train

aerodeslizador m [a-airo-desleethador] hovercraft

aerolínea f [a-airoleenay-a] airline

aeropuerto m [a-airopwairto] airport

afeitarse [afay-eetarsay] to shave

aficionado a [afeeth-yonado] keen on

afortunadamente [-mentay] fortunately

afueras fpl [afwairass] suburbs

agarrar un colocón to get sozzled

agárrese aquí hold on here

agencia f [a-Henth-ya] agency

agencia de viajes [b-yaHess] travel agency

agenda f [a-Henda] diary

agítese antes de usar(se) shake before use

agosto m August

agradable [agradablay] pleasant

agradar to please

agradecer [agradethair] to thank

agradecido [agradetheedo] grateful

agradezco [agradethko] I thank

agresivo aggressive

agricultor m farmer

agua f [agwa] water

agua de colonia [kolon-ya] eau de toilette

aguantar: no aguanto ... [agwanto] I can't stand ...

aguja f [agooHa] needle

agujero m [agooHairo] hole

ahora [a-ora] now

aire m [a-eeray] air

aire acondicionado [akondeeth-yonado] air-conditioning

ajedrez m [a-Hedreth] chess

ajustado [a-Hoostado] tight

ala f wing
alambre m [alambray] wire
alarma f alarm
  dar la señal de alarma [sen-yal] to raise the alarm
albergue m [albairgay] country hotel; hostel
albergue juvenil [Hoobeneel] youth hostel
albornoz m [albornoth] bathrobe
alcohómetro m Breathalyzer®
alegre [alegray] happy
alegro: ¡me alegro de verte! [bairtay] nice to see you!
alemán [alay-man] German
Alemania f [aleman-ya] Germany
alérgico a [alair-Heeko] allergic to
aletas fpl [alay-tass] flippers
alfarería f [alfarairee-a] pottery
alfiler m [alfeelair] pin
alfombra f rug, carpet
algo something
algo más something else
algodón m cotton; cotton wool, (US) absorbent cotton
alguien [alg-yen] somebody; anybody
algún some; any
alguno some; any
alianza f [al-yantha] wedding ring
alicates mpl pliers
alimentación f [aleementath-yon] groceries, foodstuffs
allá: más allá [a-ya] further

allí [a-yee] there
almacén m [almathen] department store; warehouse
almohada f [almo-ada] pillow
almuerzo m [almwairtho] lunch
alojamiento m [aloHam-yento] accommodation
alojamiento y desayuno [desa-yoono] bed and breakfast
alpinismo m mountaineering
alquilar [alkeelar] to rent; to hire
alquiler m [alkeelair] rental
alquiler de barcos boat hire
alquiler de bicicletas [beetheeklaytass] bike hire
alquiler de coches [kochess] car rental
alquiler de esquís [eskeess] (water-)ski hire
alquiler de sombrillas [sombree-yass] sunshade hire
alquiler de tablas surfboard hire
alquiler de tumbonas deckchair hire
alquileres rentals
alrededor (de) [alray-day-dor] around
alta costura f haute couture, high fashion
alto high; tall
¡alto! stop!
  en lo alto at the top
altura f altitude; height
altura máxima maximum headroom
aluminio m aluminium

amable [amablay] kind

amamantar to breastfeed

amanecer m [amanethair] sunrise, daybreak

amargo bitter

amarillo [amaree-yo] yellow

ambos both

ambulancia f [amboolanth-ya] ambulance

ambulatorio national health clinic

América del Norte f [nortay] North America

América del Sur [soor] South America

americano American

amiga f friend

amigo m friend

aminorar la marcha to slow down

amor m love

  hacer el amor to make love

amortiguador m [amorteegwador] shock-absorber

amperio m [ampair-yo] amp

ampliación f [amplee-ath-yon] enlargement

amplio loose-fitting

ampolla f [ampo-ya] blister

analgésico m [anal-Hayseeko] painkiller

análisis clínicos mpl clinical tests

anaranjado [anaran-Hado] orange

ancho wide

ancho m width, breadth

anchura f width, breadth

¡anda ya! get away!, come off it!

andaluz [andalooth] Andalusian

andar to walk

andén m platform, (US) track

  a los andenes to the trains

anduve [andoobay] I walked

anémico anaemic

anestesia f [anestays-ya] anaesthetic

anfiteatro m [anfeetay-atro] amphitheatre

angina (de pecho) f [an-Heena] angina

anginas fpl tonsillitis

anillo m [anee-yo] ring

anoche last night

anochecer m [anochethair] nightfall, dusk

ante m suede

anteayer [antay-a-yair] the day before yesterday

antepasado m ancestor

antes de before

  antes de que before

antes de ayer [a-yair] the day before yesterday

antes de entrar dejen salir let passengers off first

anticonceptivo m [anteekonthepteebo] contraceptive

anticongelante m [anteekon-Helantay] antifreeze

anticuado [anteek-wado] out of date

anticuario m antiques dealer

antigüedad: una tienda de

antigüedades [t-yenda day anteegway-dadess] an antique shop
antiguo [anteegwo] ancient
antihistamínico m [antee-eestameeneeko] antihistamine
anulado cancelled
anular to cancel
añadir [an-yadeer] to add
año m [an-yo] year
Año Nuevo m [nwaybo] New Year
  día de Año Nuevo m [dee-a] New Year's Day
  ¡feliz Año Nuevo! [feleeth] Happy New Year!
apagar to switch off
apagar los faros to switch off one's lights
apagar luces de cruce headlights off
apagón m power cut
apague el motor switch off your engine
apague las luces switch off your lights
aparato m device
aparatos electrodomésticos electrical appliances
aparcamiento m [aparkam-yento] car park, (US) parking lot
aparcamiento privado private parking
aparcamiento reservado this parking place reserved
aparcamiento subterráneo underground parking
aparcamiento vigilado supervised parking
aparcar to park
aparecer [aparethair] to appear
aparezco [aparethko] I appear
apartamento m apartment
apasionante [apass-yonantay] thrilling
apearse de [apay-arsay] to get off
apellido m [apay-yeedo] surname
apenado distressed, sorry
apenas [apaynass] scarcely
  apenas ... (cuando) [k-wando] hardly ... when
apetecer: me apetece [may apetaythay] I feel like
apetito m appetite
apodo m nickname
apoplejía f [apoplay-Hee-a] stroke
aprender [aprendair] to learn
aprensivo fearful, apprehensive
apresurarse [-arsay] to rush
aproveche: ¡que aproveche! [aprobay-chay] enjoy your meal!
aproximadamente [-mentay] about
aquel [akel] that
aquél that (one)
aquella [akay-ya] that
aquélla that (one)
aquellas [akay-yass] those
aquéllas those (ones)
aquellos [akay-yoss] those
aquéllos those (ones)
aquí [akee] here

aquí tiene [t-yaynay] here you are

árabe [arabay] Arabic

aragonés Aragonese

araña f [aran-ya] spider

arañazo m [aran-yatho] scratch

árbol m tree

arcén m [arthen] lay-by

ardor de estómago m heartburn

área de servicios m service area, motorway services

arena f [arayna] sand

Argelia f [arHaylee-a] Algeria

armario m cupboard

armería f [armairee-a] gunsmith's

arqueología f [arkay-oloHee-a] archaeology

arrancar to start up

arreglar to mend; to sort out, to arrange

arrepentido sorry

arriba up; upstairs; on top

arroyo m stream

arte m [artay] art

artesanía f crafts

artículos de artesanía mpl arts and crafts

artículos de baño [ban-yo] swimwear

artículos de boda wedding presents

artículos de deporte sports goods

artículos de limpieza household cleaning products

artículos de ocasión bargains; second hand goods

artículos de piel leather goods

artículos de playa beachwear

artículos de regalo gifts

artículos de viaje travel goods

artículos para el bebé babywear

artículos para el colegio schoolwear

artista m/f artist

artritis f [-treeteess] arthritis

asador m restaurant specializing in roast meats and/or fish

ascensor m [asthensor] lift, elevator

asegurar to insure

aseos mpl [asay-oss] toilets, rest room

así like this; like that

así que so (that)

asiático Asian

asiento m [ass-yento] seat

asma m asthma

aspiradora f hoover®

asqueroso [askairoso] disgusting

astigmático long-sighted

asturiano [astoor-yano] Asturian

asustado afraid

asustar to frighten

atacar to attack

atajo m [ataHo] shortcut

ataque m [atakay] attack

ataque al corazón [korathon] heart attack

atascado stuck

atasco (de tráfico) m traffic jam

atención [atenth-yon] please note

¡atención! take care!, caution!

atención al tren beware of trains

ateo [atay-o] atheist

aterrizaje m [atairreethaHay] landing

aterrizaje forzoso [forthoso] emergency landing

aterrizar [atairreethar] to land

atestado m report

atletismo m athletics

atracar to assault, to hold up

atracciones turísticas fpl [atrakth-yoness] tourist attractions

atraco a mano armada m hold-up

atractivo attractive

atrás at the back; behind

¡atrás! get back!

la parte de atrás [partay] the back

está más atrás it's further back

años atrás years ago

atravesar to go through

atravieso [atrab-yayso] I go through

atreverse [atrebairsay] to dare

atropellar [atropay-yar] to knock over

atroz [atroth] dreadful

audífono m [owdeefono] hearing aid

aun even

aún [a-oon] still; yet

aunque [a-oonkay] although

autobús m [owtobooss] bus

autobús sólamente buses only

autocar m coach, bus

auto-estopista m/f [-estopeesta] hitch-hiker

automotor m local short-distance train

automóvil m car

automovilista m/f car driver

autopista f motorway, (US) highway

autopista (de peaje) [pay-aHay] (toll) motorway/highway

auto-servicio m [owto-sairbeeth-yo] self-service

autorizada para mayores de 18 años for adults only

autorizada para mayores de 14 años y menores acompañados authorized for those over 14 and young people accompanied by an adult

autorizada para todos los públicos suitable for all

autostop m hitchhiking

hacer autostop to hitchhike

autovía f [-bee-a] dual carriageway, (US) divided highway

AVE m high-speed train on the Madrid-Seville line

avenida f avenue

avergonzado [abairgonthado] embarrassed

avería f [abairee-a] breakdown
averiado out of order
averiarse [abairee-arsay] to
 break down
avión m [ab-yon] aeroplane
 por avión by air
avisar to inform
aviso m information
aviso a los señores pasajeros
 passenger information
avispa f wasp
ayer [a-yair] yesterday
ayer por la mañana [man-yana]
 yesterday morning
ayer por la tarde [tarday]
 yesterday afternoon
ayuda f [a-yooda] help
ayudar to help
ayuntamiento m [ayoontam-
 yento] town hall
azafata f [athafata] air hostess
azul (m) [athool] blue
azul claro light blue
azul marino navy blue

B

baca f roof rack
bahía f [ba-ee-a] bay
bailar [ba-eelar] to dance
 ir a bailar to go dancing
baile m [ba-eelay] dance;
 dancing
bajar [baHar] to go down
 bajar de to get off
bajarse [baHarsay] to get off
bajo [baHo] low; short;
 under(neath)

balcón m balcony
Baleares [balay-aress]
 Balearics
balón m ball
balón volea [bolay-a]
 volleyball
baloncesto m [balonthesto]
 basketball
balonmano m handball
banco m bank; bench
bandeja f [bandayHa] tray
bandera f [bandaira] flag
bañador m [ban-yador]
 swimming costume
bañarse [ban-yarsay] to go
 swimming; to have a bath
bañera f [ban-yaira] bathtub
baño m [ban-yo] bathroom;
 bath
baraja f [baraHa] pack of cards
barato cheap, inexpensive
barba f beard
barbacoa f [barbako-a]
 barbecue
barbería f [barbairee-a] barber's
barbero m barber
barbilla f [barbee-ya] chin
barca de remos f rowing boat
barcas para alquilar boats to
 rent
barco m boat
barco de vela sailing boat
barra de labios f [lab-yoss]
 lipstick
barrio m [barr-yo] district, area
bastante [bastantay] enough
bastante más quite a lot
 more
bastante menos [maynoss]

quite a lot less

basura f litter

bata f dressing gown

bate m [batay] bat

batería f [batairee-a] battery

batería de cocina [kotheena] pots and pans

batín m dressing gown

bautismo m [bowteesmo] christening

bebé m baby

beber [bebair] to drink

bello [bay-yo] beautiful

benvengut [benvengoot] welcome (in Catalan)

besar to kiss

beso m kiss

betún m [betoon] shoe polish

biblioteca f [beebl-yotayka] library; bookcase

bici: ir a dar una vuelta en bici [bwelta en beethee] to go for a cycle

bicicleta f [beetheeklayta] bicycle

bien [b-yen] well

¡bien! good!

bien ... bien either ... or ...

o bien ... o bien either ... or ...

bienes mpl [b-yayness] possessions

¡bienvenido! welcome!

bifurcación f [beefoorkath-yon] fork

bigote m [beegotay] moustache

billete m [bee-yaytay] ticket

billete de andén platform

ticket

billete de banco banknote, (US) bill

billete de ida single ticket, one-way ticket

billete de ida y vuelta [bwelta] return ticket, round trip ticket

blanco (m) white

blusa f blouse

boca f mouth

bocina f [botheena] horn

boda f wedding

bodega f [bodayga] wine cellar; wine bar

boite f [bwat] night club

bolígrafo m biro®

bolsa f bag; stock exchange

bolsa de plástico plastic bag

bolsa de viaje [b-yaHay] travel bag

bolsillo m [bolsee-yo] pocket

bolso m handbag, (US) purse

bomba f bomb

bomberos mpl [bombaiross] fire brigade

bombilla f [bombee-ya] light bulb

bombona de gas f camping gas cylinder

bonito (m) nice; tuna fish

bonobús book of 10 reduced-price bus tickets

bordado embroidered

borracho drunk

bosque m [boskay] forest

bota f boot

botas de agua [agwa] wellingtons

botas de esquiar [eskee-**ar**] ski boots
botella f [bo**tay**-ya] bottle
botiquín m [boteek**een**] first aid kit
botón m button
botón desatascador coin return button
boxeo m [boks**ay**-o] boxing
boya f buoy
bragas fpl panties
brazo m [**bra**tho] arm
bricolaje m [breekola**Hay**] DIY
brillar [bree-**yar**] to shine
brisa f breeze
británico British
brocha de afeitar f [afay-ee**tar**] shaving brush
broche m [**bro**chay] brooch
bronce m [**bron**thay] bronze
bronceado m [bronthay-**a**do] suntan
bronceador m [bronthay-a**dor**] suntan oil/lotion
bronquitis f [bronk**ee**teess] bronchitis
brújula f [**broo**Hoola] compass
Bruselas Brussels
bucear [boothay-**ar**] to (skin-)dive
buceo m [booth**ay**-o] skin-diving
¡buenas! [bway**nass**] hello!
bueno [**bway**no] good; good-natured
buenas noches goodnight
buenas tardes good evening
buenos días [**dee**-ass] good morning

bufanda f scarf
bujía f [booH**ee**-a] spark plug
bulto m piece of luggage
burro m donkey
buscar to look for
busqué [boos**kay**] I looked for
butacas stalls
buzón [booth**on**] letter box, mail box

C

c/ (calle) street
c/c (cuenta corriente) current account
caballeros mpl [kaba-**yai**ross] gents, men's rest room
caballo m [kaba-yo] horse
cabello m [kab**ay**-yo] hair
cabeza f [kab**e**tha] head
cabida ... personas capacity ... people
cabina telefónica f telephone booth, phone box
cable alargador m [**kab**lay] extension lead
cabra f goat
cabrón m bastard
cacahuetes [kakaw**ay**tess] peanuts
cachondeo m [kachond**ay**-o] laugh
  lo digo de cachondeo I'm only joking
cada every
cadena f [kad**ay**na] chain
cadera f [kad**air**a] hip
caduca ... expires ...

caer [ka-**air**] to fall
caerse [ka-**air**say] to fall
cafetera f [kafetaira] coffee pot
cafetería f cafe, bar-type restaurant
caída f [ka-**eeda**] fall
cago: ¡me cago en diez! [d-yayth] for heaven's sake!
caja de cambios f [kaHa] gearbox
caja f [kaHa] cash desk; cashier
caja de ahorros [a-**o**rross] savings bank
cajera f [kaHaira], **cajero m** cashier
cajero automático [owtom**a**teeko] cash dispenser, (US) automatic teller
calambre m [kal**a**mbray] cramp
calcetines mpl [kalthet**ee**ness] socks
calcetines de algodón cotton socks
calcetines de lana woollen socks
calculadora f calculator
calefacción f [kalefakth-yon] heating
calefacción central [thentral] central heating
calendario m [-dar-yo] calendar
calidad f quality
caliente [kal-yentay] hot
calle f [ka-yay] street
calle comercial [komairth-yal] shopping street
calle de dirección única [deerekth-yon] one-way street

calle peatonal [pay-atonal] pedestrianized street
calle principal [preentheepal] main street
callejón sin salida m cul-de-sac, dead end
callo m [ka-yo] corn (on foot)
calmante m tranquillizer
calor m heat
hace calor it's warm/hot
calvo bald
calzada deteriorada poor road surface
calzada irregular uneven surface
calzados shoe shop
calzoncillos mpl [kalthonth**ee**yoss] underpants
cama f bed
cama de campaña [kampan-ya] campbed
cama de matrimonio double bed
cama individual single bed
cámara f camera; inner tube
cámara fotográfica camera
camarera f [kamaraira] waitress; chambermaid
camarero m waiter
camarote m [kamarotay] cabin
cambiar [kamb-yar] to change
cambiarse (de ropa) [kamb-yarsay] to get changed
cambio m change; exchange; exchange rate
cambio de divisas currency exchange
cambio de moneda currency exchange

cambio de sentido junction, take filter lane to exit and cross flow of traffic
caminar to walk
camino m path
camino cerrado (al tráfico) road closed to (traffic)
camino privado private road
camión m lorry, truck
camioneta f van
camisa f shirt
camiseta f T-shirt; vest
camisón m nightdress
campana f bell
camping m camping; campsite; caravan site, (US) trailer park
campo m countryside; pitch; court; field
campo de deportes sports field
campo de futból football ground
campo de golf golf course
Campsa State-owned oil company
canadiense [kanad-yensay] Canadian
Canal de la Mancha m English Channel
Canarias fpl [kanar-yass] Canaries
cancelado [kanthelado] cancelled
cancelar [kanthelar] to cancel
cancha f court; pitch
canción f [kanth-yon] song
canguro m/f [kangooro] baby-sitter

canoso greying; grey
cansado tired
cantar to sing
cantina f buffet
canto m singing
caña f [kan-ya] small glass of beer
caña de pescar fishing rod
capaz: ser capaz (de) [sair kapath] to be able (to)
capazo m [kapatho] carry-cot
capilla f [kapee-ya] chapel
capitán m captain
capó(t) m bonnet, (US) hood
cara f face
caramelos mpl [karamayloss] sweets, candies
caravana f caravan
carburador m carburettor
cárcel f [karthel] prison
cardenal m bruise
carne f [karnay] flesh
carné de conducir m [karnay day kondootheer] driving licence
carnet de identidad m identity card
carnicería f [karneethairee-a] butcher's
caro expensive
carpintería f [karpeentairee-a] joiner's, carpenter's
carrera f [karraira] race
carrete m [karraytay] film (for camera)
carretera f [karretaira] road
carretera comarcal district highway
carretera cortada road

blocked, road closed

carretera de circunvalación
by-pass

carretera de doble calzada
two-lane road

carretera nacional national
highway

carretera principal main
highway

carril m lane

carrito m trolley, cart

carrito portaequipajes [porta-
aykeepaHess] baggage trolley

carta f letter; menu

cartel m poster

cartelera de espectáculos f
[kartelaira] entertainments
guide

cartera f [kartaira] briefcase;
wallet

carterista m pickpocket

cartero m postman, mailman

cartón m cardboard; carton

casa f house
  en casa at home
  en casa de Juan at Juan's

casa de huéspedes
[wespedess] guesthouse

casa de socorro emergency
first-aid centre

casado married

casarse [kasarsay] to get
married

cascada f waterfall

casi almost

casino m leisure club; casino

caso m case
  en caso de que in case
  caso urgente [oorHentay]

emergency

casete f, cassette f [kaset]
cassette

casete m, cassette m cassette
player

caspa f dandruff

castaño (m) [kastan-yo] sweet
chestnut; brown

castañuelas fpl [kastan-waylass]
castanets

castellano [kastay-yano]
Castilian; another word for
the Spanish language

Castilla [kastee-ya] Castile

castillo m castle

casualidad: por casualidad
[kaswaleeda] by chance

Cataluña [kataloon-ya]
Catalonia

catarro: tengo catarro I've got
a cold

católico (m) Catholic

catorce [katorthay] fourteen

caucho m [kowcho] rubber

causa f [kowsa] cause
  a causa de because of

cayó [ka-yo] he fell

caza f [katha] hunting

cazadora f [kathadora] bomber
jacket, blouson

cazar [kathar] to hunt

cazo m [katho] saucepan

ceda el paso give way, yield

ceder el paso [thedair] to give
way

ceja f [thayHa] eyebrow

celoso [theloso] jealous

cementerio m [thementair-yo]
cemetery

cena f [thayna] dinner

cenar to have dinner

cenicero m [thayneethairo] ashtray

central telefónica f [thentral] telephone exchange

centro comercial m [thentro komairthee-al] shopping centre

centro urbano/ciudad m [th-yooda] city/town centre

ceñido [then-yeedo] tight-fitting

cepillo m [thepee-yo] brush

cepillo de dientes [d-yentess] toothbrush

cepillo del pelo hairbrush

cera f [thaira] wax

cerámica f [thairameeka] ceramics

cerca de [thairka] near

cercanías m [thairkanee-ass] local short-distance train

cerilla f [thairee-ya] match

cero [thairo] zero

cerrado [thairrado] closed

cerrado por defunción closed due to bereavement

cerrado por descanso del personal closed for staff holidays

cerrado por obras/reforma/vacaciones closed for alteration/renovation/holidays

cerradura f [thairradoora] lock

cerramos los ... we close on ...

cerrar [thairrar] to close

cerrar con llave [yabay] to lock

cerrojo m [thairroHo] bolt

certificado m [thairteefeekado] certificate; registered letter

cervecería f [thairbethair-ee-a] bar specializing in beer

cerveza f [thairbaytha] beer

césped m [thesped] lawn

cesta f [thesta] basket

cesto de la compra m shopping basket

CH (casa de huespedes) f [wespedess] boarding house, low-price hostel

chaleco m waistcoat

chalecos salvavidas life-jackets

chalet m [chalay] villa

champú m shampoo

chandal m tracksuit

chaparrón m shower; downpour

chaqueta f [chakayta] cardigan; jacket

chaquetón m [chaketon] jacket; three-quarter length jacket

charcutería f delicatessen

charlar to chat

cheque m [chaykay] cheque, (US) check

cheque de viaje m [day b-yaHay] travellers' cheque

chica f girl

chicle m [cheeklay] chewing gum

chico m boy

chillar [chee-yar] to shout

chino Chinese

chiringuito m [cheereengeeto] open-air bar

chiste m [cheestay] joke

chocar con to run into

chocolate con leche m [chokolatay kon lechay] milk chocolate

chocolate de hacer [athair] plain chocolate

chubasco m sudden short shower

chubasquero m [choobaskairo] cagoule

chupa-chups® m lollipop

Cía. (compañía) company

cicatriz f [theekatreeth] scar

ciclismo m [theekleesmo] cycling

ciclista m/f [theekleesta] cyclist

ciego [th-yaygo] blind

cielo m [th-yaylo] sky

cien [th-yen] hundred

ciencia f [th-yenth-ya] science

ciento ... [th-yento] a hundred and ...

cierren las puertas close the doors

cierro [th-yairro] I close

cigarrillo m [theegarree-yo] cigarette

cinco [theenko] five

cincuenta [theen-kwenta] fifty

cine m [theenay] cinema

cinta f [theenta] tape; ribbon

cintura f [theentoora] waist

cinturón m [theentooron] belt

cinturón de seguridad seat belt

circo m [theerko] circus

circulación f [theerkoolath-yon] traffic; circulation

circulación en ambas direcciones two-way traffic

circule despacio drive slowly

circule por la derecha keep to your right

circunvalación f [theerkoonbalath-yon] ring road

cistitis f [theesteeteess] cystitis

cita f [theeta] appointment

ciudad f [thee-oo-da] town, city

claro clear

¡claro! of course!

clase f [klasay] class

clavo m nail

claxon m [klakson] horn

clima m climate

climatizado [-thado] air-conditioned

clínica f hospital; clinic

cobrador m conductor

cobre m [kobray] copper

cocer [kothair] to cook; to boil

coche m [kochay] car
  en coche by car

coche-cama m sleeper, sleeping car

cochecito m [kochetheeto] pram

coche comedor dining car

coche de línea [leenay-a] long-distance bus

coche de niño [neen-yo] pram; pushchair, baby buggy

coche-restaurante m [-restowrantay] restaurant car

cocina f [kotheena] kitchen; cooker

cocinar [kotheenar] to cook

cocinera f [kotheenaira], cocinero m cook

código de la circulación m [theerkoolath-yon] highway code

código postal postcode, zip code

codo m elbow

coger [koнair] to catch; to take

cojo (m) [koнo] I catch; I take; person with a limp

cola f tail; queue
  hacer cola to queue

colchas fpl bedspreads

colchón m mattress

colchoneta inflable f [eenflablay] air mattress

colección f [kolekth-yon] collection

colegio m [kolayн-yo] school

colgante m [kolgantay] pendant

colina f hill

collar m [ko-yar] necklace

colocar to place, to put

color m colour

columna vertebral f spine

combinación f [kombeenath-yon] petticoat

combustible m [komboosteeblay] fuel

comedor m dining room

comenzar [komenthar] to begin

comer [komair] to eat

comerciante m [komairth-yantay] shopkeeper; dealer

comida f lunch; food; meal

comidas para llevar take-away meals

comienzo [kom-yentho] I begin

comisaría f police station

comisaría de policía [polee-thee-a] police station

como as; like

¿cómo? pardon?; how?
  ¿cómo dice? [deethay] pardon?
  ¿cómo está? how are you?
  ¿cómo le va? [lay] how are things?

como quieras [k-yairass] it's up to you

compañera f [kompan-yaira] girlfriend

compañero m mate; boyfriend

compañía f [kompan-yee-a] company

compañía aérea [a-airay-a] airline

comparar to compare

compartir to share

completamente [-mentay] completely

completo full, no vacancies

complicado complicated

compra: hacer la compra [athair] to do the shopping

compramos a ... buying rate

comprar to buy

comprender [komprendair] to understand

no comprendo I don't understand

compras: ir de compras to go shopping

compresa m [kompraysa] sanitary towel, sanitary napkin

comprimido efervescente m soluble tablet

comprimidos tablets

computadora f computer

comunicando engaged; busy

con with

concha f shell

concierne [konth-yairnay] it concerns

concierto m [konth-yairto] concert

condición: a condición de que [kondeeth-yon] on condition that

condón m condom

conducir [kondootheer] to drive

conductor m, **conductora** f driver

conduzca con cuidado drive with care

conduzco [kondoothko] I drive

conejo m [konay-нo] rabbit

confección f [konfekth-yon] clothing industry

confección de caballero [kaba-yairo] menswear

confección de señoras ladies' fashions

confecciones fpl ready-to-wear clothes

conferencia internacional f [konfairenth-ya eentairnath-yonal] international call

conferencia interurbana long-distance call

confesar to admit, to confess

confirmar to confirm

confitería f [konfeetairee-a] sweetshop, candy store

conforme [konformay] as

estar conforme to agree

conformidad f agreement

congelado [konнaylado] frozen

congelador m [konнaylador] freezer

congelados mpl [konнayladoss] frozen foods

conjunto m [konнoonto] group; band

conmigo with me

conmoción cerebral f [konmoth-yon thairebral] concussion

conocer [konothair] to know

conozco [konothko] I know

conque [konkay] so, so then

conserje m [konsairнay] janitor, porter

conservas fpl jams, preserves

consérvese en sitio fresco store in a cool place

consigna f [konseeg-na] left luggage (office), baggage check

consigna automática left luggage lockers

consigo with himself; with herself; with yourself; with themselves; with yourselves

consulado m consulate

consulta médica surgery, doctor's office

consúmase antes de ... best before ...

contable m/f [kontablay] accountant

contacto: ponerse en contacto con to contact

contado: pagar al contado to pay cash

contagioso [kontaH-yoso] contagious

contaminado polluted

contar to count; to tell

contener [kontenair] to contain

contenido m contents

contento happy

contestar to reply, to answer

contigo with you

continuación: a continuación [konteen-wath-yon] then, next

continuar [konteen-war] to continue

contorno de cadera m hip measurement

contorno de cintura [theentoora] waist measurement

contorno de pecho bust/chest measurement

contra against

contradecir [kontradetheer] to contradict

contraindicaciones fpl contra-indications

contraventanas fpl shutters

control de pasaportes m passport control

convalecencia f [konbalethenth-ya] convalescence

¡coño! [kon-yo] fuck!

copa f glass

coquetear [koketay-ar] to flirt

corazón m [korathon] heart

corbata f tie, necktie

cordero m [kordairo] lamb

cordones mpl [kordoness] (shoe)laces

correa del ventilador f [korray-a] fan belt

correo m [korray-o] mail

correo aéreo [a-airay-o] airmail

correo urgente [oorHentay] express

correos m post office

Correos y Telégrafos Post Office

correr [korrair] to run

corrida de toros f bullfight

corriente peligrosa dangerous current

corrimiento de tierras danger: landslides

cortadura f cut

cortar to cut

cortarse [kortarsay] to cut oneself

cortauñas m [korta-oon-yass] nail clippers

corte de pelo m [kortay] haircut

corte y confección [konfekth-yon] dressmaking

cortina f curtain

corto short

cosa f thing

coser [kosair] to sew

costa f coast

costar to cost
costilla f [kostee-ya] rib
costumbre f [kostoombray] custom
cráneo m [kranay-o] skull
crédito m credit; unit(s)
creer [kray-air] to believe
crema f [krayma] cream
crema base [basay] foundation cream
crema de belleza [bay-yaytha] cold cream
crema hidratante [eedratantay] moisturizer
crema limpiadora [leemp-yadora] cleansing cream
cremallera f [krema-yaira] zip, zipper
creyó [kray-yo] he believed
crisis nerviosa f [nairb-yosa] nervous breakdown
cristal m [kreestal] crystal; glass
cristalería f glassware
crítica f criticism
criticar to criticize
cruce m [kroothay] junction, intersection; crossing; crossroads
cruce de ganado danger: cattle crossing
cruce de ciclistas danger: cyclists crossing
crucero m [kroothairo] cruise
Cruz Roja f [krooth roHa] Red Cross
cruzar [kroothar] to cross
CTNE f Spanish national telephone company

cuaderno m [kwadairno] notebook
cuadrado [kwadrado] square
cuadro m [kwadro] painting
de cuadros checked
cual [kwal] which; who
¿cuándo? [kwando] when?
¿cuánto? [kwanto] how much?
en cuanto... as soon as...
¡cuánto lo siento! [s-yento] I'm so sorry!
¿cuántos? how many?
cuarenta [kwarenta] forty
cuartel de la guardia civil m civil guard barracks
cuartilla f [kwartee-ya] writing paper
cuarto (m) [kwarto] quarter; fourth; room
cuarto de hora [ora] quarter of an hour
cuarto de baño [ban-yo] bathroom
cuarto de estar sitting room
cuarto piso fourth floor, (US) fifth floor
cuatro [kwatro] four
cuatrocientos [kwatro-th-yentoss] four hundred
cubierta f [koob-yairta] deck
cubierto (m) covered; overcast; meal
cubiertos mpl cutlery
cubo m bucket; cube
cubo de la basura dustbin, trashcan
cucaracha f cockroach
cuchara f spoon

cucharilla f [koocharee-ya] teaspoon

cuchilla de afeitar f [koochee-ya day afay-eetar] razor blade

cuchillería f [koochee-yairee-a] cutlery

cuchillo m [koochee-yo] knife

cuelgue, espere y retire la tarjeta hang up, wait and remove card

cuello m [kway-yo] neck; collar

cuenco m [kwenko] bowl

cuenta f [kwenta] bill; account

cuentas corrientes current accounts

cuento m [kwento] tale

cuerda f [kwairda] rope; string

cuero m [kwairo] leather

cuerpo m [kwairpo] body

cuesta (f) [kwesta] it costs; slope

cueva f [kweba] cave

cuidado (m) [kweedado] take care; look out; care

cuidado con ... caution ...

cuidado con el perro beware of the dog

cuidado con el escalón mind the step

cuidar to look after; to nurse

culebra f snake

culpa f fault, blame; guilt

es culpa mía it's my fault

culturismo m body building

cumplas: ¡que cumplas muchos más! many happy returns!

cumpleaños m [koomplay-an-yoss] birthday

cuna f cot, (US) crib

cuneta f [koonayta] gutter

cuñada f [koon-yada] sister-in-law

cuñado m brother-in-law

cura m priest

curado cured; smoked

curar to cure; to dress

curarse [koorarsay] to heal up

curva f bend; curve

curva peligrosa dangerous bend

cuyo [koo-yo] whose; of which

D

D. (Don) Mr

damas fpl ladies' toilet, ladies' restroom

danés Danish

danza f [dantha] dancing; dance

daños mpl [dan-yoss] damage

dar to give

dar el visto bueno a [bwayno] to approve

dcha. (derecha) right

de of; from

de 2 metros de alto two metres high

debajo de [debaнo] under

deber (m) [debair] to have to; to owe; duty

deberes mpl [debairess] homework

débil weak

decepción f [dethepth-yon] disappointment

decepcionado [dethepth-yonado] disappointed

decidir [detheedeer] to decide

décimo [detheemo] tenth

decir [detheer] to say; to tell

declaración f [deklarath-yon] declaration; statement

declarar to declare, to state

dedo m [daydo] finger

dedo del pie [p-yay] toe

defectuoso [defekt-woso] faulty

degustación f [degoostath-yon] café specializing in coffee

dejar [dayнar] to leave; to let

  dejar de beber to stop drinking

delante de [delantay] in front of

delantera f [delantaira] front (part)

delantero front

  la parte delantera [partay] the front (part)

delgado thin

delicioso [deleeth-yoso] delicious

demás: los demás the others

demasiado [demass-yado] too

demasiados too many

demora f delay

dentadura postiza f [posteetha] dentures

dentista m/f dentist

dentro (de) inside

  dentro de dos semanas in two weeks' time

depende [dependay] it

depends

dependiente m/f [dependyentay] shop assistant

deporte m [deportay] sport

deportes de invierno mpl [eemb-yairno] winter sports

deportivo [deporteebo] sports

deportivos mpl trainers

depósito m tank; deposit

deprimido depressed

derecha f right

  a la derecha (de) on the right (of)

derecho: todo derecho straight ahead

derribar to wreck, to demolish

desacuerdo m [desak-wairdo] disagreement

desafortunadamente [-amentay] unfortunately

desagradable [-dablay] unpleasant

desagradar to displease

desaparecer [desaparaythair] to disappear

desastre m [desastray] disaster

desayunar [desa-yoonar] to have breakfast

desayuno m [desa-yoono] breakfast

descansar to rest

descarado cheeky

descarrilar to be derailed

descolgar el aparato lift receiver

descubierto [deskoob-yairto] discovered

descubrir to discover

descuelgue el auricular lift the receiver

descuentos [deskwentoss] discounts

descuidado [deskweedado] careless

desde (que) [desday] since

desde luego [lwaygo] of course

desear [desay-ar] to want; to wish

¿qué desea? [kay desay-a] what can I do for you?

desembarcadero m [desembarkadairo] quay

desfile de modelos m [desfeelay] fashion show

desgracia: por desgracia [desgrath-ya] unfortunately

deshacer las maletas [dessathair] to unpack

desinfectante m [-tantay] disinfectant

desmaquillarse [desmakeeyarsay] to remove one's makeup

desmayarse [desmayarsay] to faint

desnudo naked

desobediente [desobayd-yentay] disobedient

desodorante m [-rantay] deodorant

desordenado untidy

desorientarse [desor-yentarsay] to lose one's way

despachador automático m ticket machine

despacho de billetes m [bee-yaytess] ticket office

despacio [despath-yo] slowly

despedirse [despedeersay] to say goodbye

despegar to take off

despegue m [despay-gay] take-off

despejado [despayнado] clear

despertador m [despairtador] alarm clock

despertar to wake

despertarse [-tarsay] to wake up

despierto [desp-yairto] awake

desprendimiento de terreno danger: landslides

despreocupado [despray-okoopado] thoughtless

después [despwess] afterwards

después de after

destinatario m addressee

destino m destination

destornillador m [destorneeyador] screwdriver

destruir [destr-weer] to destroy

desvestirse [desbesteersay] to undress

desviación f [desb-yath-yon] diversion

desvío m [desbee-o] detour, diversion

desvío provisional temporary diversion

detener [detenair] to arrest; to stop

detergente en polvo m [detairнentay] washing powder

detergente lavavajillas

[lababaнee-yass] washing-up
liquid

detestar to detest

detrás (de) behind

devolver [debolbair] to give
back; to vomit

di I gave; tell me

día m [dee-a] day

día festivo public holiday

diamante m [d-yamantay]
diamond

diapositiva f [d-yaposeeteeba]
slide

diario (m) [d-yar-yo] diary;
daily newspaper

diarrea f [d-yarray-a] diarrhoea

días azules [athooless] cheap
travel days

días festivos public holidays

días laborables weekdays

dibujar [deebooнar] to draw

dibujos animados mpl
[deebooнoss] cartoons

diccionario m [deekth-yonar-yo]
dictionary

dice [deethay] he/she says;
you say

dicho said

¿qué ha dicho? what did
you say?; what did he/she
say?

diciembre m [deeth-yembray]
December

diecinueve [d-yetheenwaybay]
nineteen

dieciocho [d-yethee-ocho]
eighteen

dieciséis [d-yetheesay-eess]
sixteen

diecisiete [d-yethees-yaytay]
seventeen

diente m [d-yentay] tooth

dieron [d-yairon] they gave;
you gave

dieta f [d-yayta] diet

diez [d-yeth] ten

difícil [deefeetheel] difficult

diga tell me

dígame [deegamay] hello, yes

digo I say

dije [deeнay] I said

dijeron [deeнairon] they said;
you said

dijiste [deeнeestay] you said

dijo [deeнo] he/she said; you
say

diminuto tiny

Dinamarca f Denmark

dinero m [deenairo] money

dinero suelto [swelto] small
change

Dios m [dee-oss] God

¡Dios mío! [mee-o] my God!

dirección f [deerekth-yon]
direction; address; steering;
management

dirección única one-way
traffic

dirección prohibida no entry

director m, directora f
manager; director;
headteacher

dirigir [deereeнeer] to direct; to
lead

disco m record

disco compacto compact
disc

disco obligatorio parking disk

must be displayed

disconformidad f disagreement

discoteca f disco, discotheque

disculparse [deeskoolparsay] to apologize

disculpe [deeskoolpay] excuse me

disculpen las molestias we apologize for any inconvenience

discurso m speech

discusión f [deeskoos-yon] discussion; argument

discutir to argue

diseñador de modas m [deesen-yador] fashion designer

distancia f [deestanth-ya] distance

distinto different

distraído [deestra-eedo] absent-minded

distribuidor m [deestreebweedor] distributor

distrito postal m postcode, zip code

disuélvase en agua dissolve in water

divertido entertaining; funny

divertirse [deebairteersay] to have a good time

divisas fpl foreign currency

divorciado [deeborth-yado] divorced

divorciarse [deeborth-yarsay] to divorce

divorcio m [deeborth-yo]

divorce

doble [doblay] double

doce [dothay] twelve

docena (de) f [dothayna] dozen

dólar m dollar

doler [dolair] to hurt

dolor m pain

dolor de cabeza [kabaytha] headache

dolor de garganta sore throat

dolor de muelas toothache

dolor de oídos [o-eedoss] earache

doloroso painful

domicilio m [domeetheel-yo] place of residence; commercial headquarters

domingo m Sunday

domingos y festivos Sundays and public holidays

¡dominguero! [domeengairo] learn to drive!

don Mr

donaciones donations

donde [donday] where

doña [don-ya] Miss; Mrs

dorado gold, golden

dormido asleep

dormir to sleep

dormitorio m [dormeetor-yo] bedroom; dormitory

dos two

doscientos [doss-thyentoss] two hundred

doy I give

droga f drug

droguería f [drogairee-a] drugstore; household cleaning materials

ducha f shower
ducharse [doocharsay] to have a shower
dudar to doubt; to hesitate
duele [dwaylay] it hurts
dulce [doolthay] sweet; gentle
dunas fpl sand dunes
durante [doorantay] during
duro (m) hard; tough guy; five peseta coin

E

e and
ebanistería f [ebaneestairee-a] cabinetmaker's
echar to throw
echo de menos a mi ... [dee maynoss] I miss my ...
echar al buzón [boothon] to post, to mail
echar el cerrojo [thairroHo] to bolt
echar al correo [korray-o] to post, to mail
echarse la siesta [echarsay] to have a nap
edad f age
edificio m [edeefeeth-yo] building
edredón m quilt, eiderdown; duvet
educado polite
EE.UU. (Estados Unidos) USA
efectivo: en efectivo in cash
eje m [ayHay] axle
eje del cigüeñal [theegwen-yal] crankshaft

ejemplo m [eHemplo] example
por ejemplo for example
el the
él he; him
elástico elastic
electricidad f [elektreetheeda] electricity
electricista m [elektreetheeesta] electrician
eléctrico electric
electrodomésticos mpl electrical appliances
elegir [elayHeer] to choose
ella [ay-ya] she; her
ellas they; them
ellos they; them
embajada f [embaHada] embassy
embarazada [embarathada] pregnant
embarque m [embarkay] embarcation
embotellado en ... bottled in ...
embotellamiento m [embotay-yam-yento] traffic jam
embrague m [embragay] clutch
embudo m funnel
emergencia f [emairHenth-ya] emergency
emergencias casualty; emergencies
emisión f [emeess-yon] programme; emission; distribution date; issue
emocionante [emoth-yonantay] exciting
empalme m [empalmay] junction

Em

empaquetado m [empaketado] packing

empaste m [empastay] filling

empeorar [empay-orar] to get worse

empezar [empethar] to begin

empinado steep

empleada f [employ-ada], empleado m shop assistant, employee

empujar [empooHar] to push

en in; at; on; by

enagua de medio cuerpo f [enagwa day mayd-yo kwairpo] underskirt

enamorados: día de los enamorados m St Valentine's Day

encantado delighted

¡encantado! pleased to meet you!

encantador lovely

encantar to please

encendedor m [enthendedor] lighter

encender [enthendair] to light; to switch on

encender luces de cruce switch headlights on

encendido m [enthendeedo] ignition

enchufe m [enchoofay] plug; socket

encienda las luces switch on your lights

encierro [enth-yairro] bull-running in Pamplona, the bulls loose in the streets

encima [entheema] above

encima de on (top of)

encontrar to find

encontrarse (con/a) [-trarsay] to meet

encuentro (m) [enkwentro] meeting, encounter; I find

enero m [enairo] January

enfadado angry

enfadarse [-darsay] to get angry

enfermedad f [enfairmeda] disease

enfermedad venérea [benairay-a] VD

enfermera f [enfairmaira] nurse

enfermero m male nurse

enfermo [enfairmo] ill

enfrente de [enfrentay] opposite

enhorabuena: ¡enhorabuena! [enorabwayna] congratulations!

dar la enhorabuena a to congratulate

enlace m [enlathay] connection; wedding

enlatados mpl canned food

enorme [enormay] enormous

enseñar [ensen-yar] to teach

entender [entendair] to understand

entero [entairo] whole

entiendo [ent-yendo] I understand

entierro m [ent-yairro] funeral

entonces [entonthess] then; therefore

entrada f entrance, way in; ticket

entrada por delante entry at the front
entrada libre admission free
entrada gratis admission free
entrar to go in
entre [**e**ntray] among; between
entre sin llamar enter without knocking
entreacto m [entray-**a**kto] intermission
entretanto meanwhile
enviar [emb-**ya**r] to send
envolver [embolb**ai**r] to wrap up; to involve
equipaje m [ekeepa**Ha**y] luggage, baggage
equipaje de mano hand baggage
equipajes mpl left-luggage office, (US) baggage check
equipo m [ek**ee**po] team
equitación f [ekeetath-**yo**n] horse riding
equivocado [ekeebok**a**do] wrong
equivocarse [ekeebok**a**rsay] to make a mistake
equivocarse de número to dial the wrong number
era [**ai**ra] I/he/she/it was; you were
erais [**ai**ra-eess] you were
éramos we were
eran they were; you were
eras you were
eres you are
erupción f [airoopth-**yo**n] rash; eruption

es he is; you are
ésa [**ay**sa] that one
esa that
ésas those ones
esas those
escala f intermediate stop; scale; ladder
escalera automática f escalator
escaleras fpl stairs
escalón lateral ramp; uneven road surface; no hard shoulder
escandaloso shocking
Escandinavia f Scandinavia
escarcha f frost
escayola f [eska-**yo**la] plaster cast
escocés [eskoth**ay**ss] Scottish
Escocia f [eskoth-**ya**] Scotland
escoger [esko**Ha**ir] to choose
esconder [eskond**ai**r] to hide
escribir to write
escrito written
escuchar to listen; to listen to
escuela f [esk**way**la] school
escuela de párvulos kindergarten
escurrir a mano to wring by hand
ése [**ay**say] that one
ese that
esencial [esenth-**ya**l] essential
esfuerzo m [esfw**ai**rtho] effort
esmalte de uñas m [esm**a**ltay day **oo**n-yass] nail polish
esmeralda f emerald
eso [**ay**so] that

eso es that's it, that's right

ésos those ones

esos those

espalda f back

espantoso dreadful; frightening

España f [espan-ya] Spain

español (m) [espan-yol] Spanish; Spaniard

española f Spaniard, Spanish woman/girl

especialista m/f specialist

especialmente [espeth-yalmentay] especially

espejo m [espayHo] mirror

esperar [espairar] to wait; to hope

espere [espairay] please wait

¡espéreme! [espairemay] wait for me!

espere tono más agudo wait for higher pitched tone

espeso [espayso] thick

esponja f [esponHa] sponge

esposa f wife

esposo m husband

espuma de afeitar f [afay-eetar] shaving foam

esquí m [eskee] ski; skiing

esquí acuático [akwateeko] waterski; waterskiing

esquiar [eskee-ar] to ski

esquina f [eskeena] corner

esta this

ésta this one

estación f [estath-yon] station; season

estación de autobuses [owtoboosess] bus station

estación de servicio [sairbeeth-yo] service station

estación de trenes train station

estación principal central station

estacionamiento vigilado supervised parking

estacionamiento limitado restricted parking

estacionarse [estath-yonarsay] to park

estadio de fútbol m [estad-yo] football stadium

Estados Unidos mpl United States

estampado (m) pattern; printed

estanco m tobacconist's

estanque m [estankay] pond

estaño m [estan-yo] tin; pewter

estar to be

estárter m [estartair] choke

estas these

éstas these ones

estatua f [estatwa] statue

este m [estay] east

este this

éste this one

esterilizado [estaireeleethado] sterilized

esto this

estómago m stomach

estornudar to sneeze

estos these

éstos these ones

estoy I am

estrecho narrow; tight

Estrecho de Gibraltar m [Heebraltar] Strait of Gibraltar

estrella f [estray-ya] star

estrellarse contra [estray-yarsay] to run into

estreno m [estrayno] new film release

estreñido [estren-yeedo] constipated

estreñimiento m [estren-yeem-yento] constipation

estropear [estropay-ar] to damage

estudiante m/f [estood-yantay] student

estudiar [estood-yar] to study

estupendo wonderful, great

estúpido stupid

etiqueta f [eteekayta] label

... de etiqueta formal ...

europeo [ay-ooropay-o] European

evidente [ebeedentay] obvious

exactamente [-mentay] exactly

¡exacto! exactly!

excelente [esthelentay] excellent

excepto ... except ...

excepto domingos y festivos except Sundays and holidays

excepto sábados except Saturdays

exceso de equipaje m [esthayso day ekeepaHay] excess baggage

exceso de velocidad [belotheeda] speeding

excursión f [eskoors-yon] trip

expedir [espedeer] to dispatch

explicación f [espleekath-yon] explanation

explicar explain

explorar to explore

exportación f [esportath-yon] export

exposición f [esposeeth-yon] exhibition

exprés m slow night train stopping at all stations

expreso m fast train; special delivery

exterior (m) [estairee-or] exterior, outer; foreign; overseas

extintor (de incendios) m [eenthend-yoss] fire extinguisher

extra 4-star, (US) premium

extranjera f [estranHaira] foreigner

extranjero (m) [estranHairo] foreign; abroad; overseas; foreigner

en el extranjero abroad

extraño [estran-yo] strange

F

fábrica f factory

fabricado por ... made by ...

fácil [fatheel] easy

factura f bill; invoice

facturación f [faktoorath-yon] check-in

facturar el equipaje [ekeepaHay] to check in

Fa

falda f skirt; hillside
falda pantalón culottes
falso false
falta f lack; mistake; defect; fault
 no hace falta que ... [athay] it's not necessary to ...
falta de visibilidad poor visibility
familia f [fameel-ya] family
famoso famous
farmacia f [farmath-ya] chemist's, pharmacy
farmacia de guardia [gward-ya] emergency chemist's/pharmacy, duty chemist
faro m light; headlight; lighthouse
faro antiniebla [anteen-yebla] fog lamp
favor: a favor de [fabor] in favour of
 por favor please; please do; excuse me
febrero m [febrairo] February
fecha f date
fecha de caducidad [kadootheeda] expiry date
fecha de caducación [kadookath-yon] expiry date
fecha de nacimiento [natheem-yento] date of birth
fecha límite de venta sell-by date
¡felices Pascuas y próspero Año Nuevo! [feleethess paskwass ee prospairo an-yo nwaybo] merry Christmas and a happy New Year!

felicidad f [feleetheeda] happiness
 ¡felicidades! [feleetheedadess] happy birthday!; congratulations!
felicitar [feleetheetar] to congratulate
feliz [feleeth] happy
¡feliz cumpleaños! [koomplay-an-yoss] happy birthday!
feo [fay-o] ugly
feria de ... ... fair
ferias fpl [fair-yass] fair
ferretería f [fairraytairee-a] hardware store
ferrobús m local short-distance train
ferrocarril m railway, railroad
festividad f celebration
festivos bank holidays, public holidays
fibras naturales [natooraless] natural fibres
fiebre f [f-yebray] fever
fiebre del heno [ayno] hay fever
fiesta f public holiday; party
fiesta de ... feast of ...
fiesta nacional [nath-yonal] bullfighting
fila f row
filtro m filter
fin m [feen] end; purpose
 a fin de que [day kay] so that
fin de semana weekend
fin de serie [sair-yay] discontinued articles
final m [feenal] end
final de autopista end of

motorway/highway

fingir [feenHeer] to pretend

fino fine; delicate

firma f signature; company

firmar to sign

firme deslizante slippery surface

firme en mal estado bad surface

flaco skinny

flequillo m [flekee-yo] fringe

flor f flower

floristería f florist

flotador m rubber ring

flotadores mpl [flotadoress] lifebelts

folleto m [fo-yayto] leaflet

fonda f (simple) restaurant; boarding house

fondo m bottom; background

en el fondo (de) at the bottom (of)

fontanero m [fontanairo] plumber

footing m jogging

forma f form

en forma fit

foto f photograph

hacer fotos to take photographs

fotografía f photograph; photography

fotografiar [fotograf-yar] to photograph

fotógrafo m photographer

fotómetro m light meter

francamente [-mentay] frankly

francés [franthayss] French

Francia f [franth-ya] France

franqueo m [frankay-o] postage

fregadero m sink

fregar: fregar los platos to do the washing up

freír [fray-eer] to fry

frenar [frenar] to brake

freno m [frayno] brake

freno de mano handbrake

frente f [frentay] forehead

fresco fresh

frigorífico m fridge

frío [free-o] cold

hace frío [athay] it's cold

frontera f [frontaira] border

frutería f fruit shop/store; greengrocer

fue [fway] he/she/it went; he/she/it was; you went; you were

fuego m [fwaygo] fire

¿tiene fuego? have you got a light?

fuegos artificiales [arteefeeth-yaless] fireworks

fuente f [fwentay] fountain; source; font

fuera [fwaira] outside; he/she/it was; he/she/it went; you were; you went

fuera de servicio out of order

fuera de apart from

fuera de horas punta off-peak hours

fuerais [fwaira-eess] you were; you went

fuéramos [fwairamoss] we were; we went

fueran [fwairan] they were;

they went; you were; you
went

fueras [fwairass] you were;
you went

fueron [fwairon] they were;
they went; you were; you
went

fuerte [fwairtay] strong; loud

fuerza f [fwairtha] force;
strength

fui [fwee] I was; I went

fuimos [fweemoss] we were;
we went

fuiste [fweestay] you were;
you went

fuisteis [fweestay-eess] you
were; you went

fumadores smoking

fumar to smoke

funcionar [foonkth-yonar] to
work

funcionario m [foonkth-yonar-yo]
civil servant

funeraria f undertaker's

furgón m van

furgoneta f van

furioso [foor-yoso] furious

furúnculo m abscess; boil

fusible m [fooseeblay] fuse

fútbol m football

futuro (m) [footooro] future

G

gabardina f raincoat

gafas fpl glasses, eyeglasses

gafas de sol sunglasses

gafas de bucear [boothay-ar]

goggles

galería f [galairee-a] gallery

galería de arte [day artay] art
gallery

galerías fpl store

Gales m [galess] Wales

galés Welsh

gallego [ga-yay-go] Galician

ganar to win; to earn

ganga f bargain

ganso m goose

garaje m [garaHay] garage

garantía f guarantee

garganta f throat

gas-oil m diesel

gasóleo m [gasolay-o] diesel

gasolina f petrol, fuel

gasolina normal two-star
petrol, (US) regular (gas)

gasolina super four-star
petrol, (US) premium (gas)

gasolinera f [gasoleenaira]
petrol/gas station, filling
station

gastar to spend

gato m cat; jack

gemelos mpl [Haymayloss]
twins; cufflinks

generalmente [Henairalmentay]
generally; usually

¡genial! [Hayn-yal] great!,
fantastic!

genio: tener mal genio
[Hayn-yo] to be bad-
tempered

gente f [Hentay] people

gerente m [Hairentay] manager

¡gilipollas! [Heeleepo-yass]
stupid idiot!

gimnasia f [Heemn**a**s-ya] gymnastics

gimnasio m gymnasium

ginecólogo m [Heenek**o**logo] gynaecologist

girar [H**ee**rar] to turn

giro [H**ee**ro] money order; turn

gitano m [Hee**ta**no] gypsy

glorieta f [glor-y**ay**ta] roundabout

gobierno m [gob-y**ai**rno] government

gol m goal

Golfo de Vizcaya m [beethk**a**-ya] Bay of Biscay

golpe m [g**o**lpay] blow

de golpe all of a sudden

golpear [golpay-**ar**] to hit

goma f rubber; glue

goma elástica rubber band

gordo fat

gorra f cap

gorro m bonnet, cap

gorro de baño [ban-yo] bathing cap

gorro de ducha shower cap

gota f drop

gotera f [got**ai**ra] leak

gracias [gr**a**th-yass] thank you

gracias, igualmente [eegwalm**e**ntay] thank you, the same to you

gracioso [grath-y**o**so] funny

grados mpl degrees

gramática f grammar

gramo m gramme

Gran Bretaña f [bretan-ya] Great Britain

grande [gr**a**nday] big, large

grandes rebajas [reba**Ha**ss] sales

grandes almacenes mpl [almath**ay**ness] large department store

granizo m [gran**ee**tho] hail

granja f [gr**a**nHa] farm

granjero m [gran**Ha**iro] farmer

grano m spot

grasa f fat

grasiento [grass-y**e**nto] greasy

graso greasy

gratificación f [grateefeekath-y**o**n] reward; tip

gratis free

grave [gr**a**bay] serious

gravilla f [grabee-ya] loose chippings

Grecia f [gr**e**th-ya] Greece

grifo m tap, (US) faucet

gripe f [gr**ee**pay] flu

gris grey

gritar to shout

grosero [gros**ai**ro] rude

grúa f [gr**oo**-a] tow truck, breakdown lorry; crane

grueso [grw**ay**so] thick

grupo m group

grupo sanguíneo [sang**ee**nay-o] blood group

guante m [gw**a**ntay] glove

guapo [gw**a**po] handsome

guardacostas m/f [gwardak**o**stass] coastguard

guardar [gward**a**r] to keep; to put away

guardarropa m [gwardarr**o**pa] cloakroom, (US) checkroom guardería (infantíl) f [gwardairee-a (infanteel)] crèche; nursery school

guárdese en sitio fresco keep in a cool place

guardia civil m/f [gward-ya theebeel] police; policeman/policewoman

guateque m [gwatay-kay] party

guerra f [gairra] war

guerra civil civil war

guía m/f [gee-a] guide

guía telefónica f phone book, telephone directory

guía turística tourist guide

guisar [geesar] to cook

guitarra f [geetarra] guitar

gustar to please
me gusta ... I like ...

gusto: mucho gusto pleased to meet you!
con mucho gusto certainly, with great pleasure
el gusto es mío how do you do, it is a pleasure

H

h is not pronounced in Spanish

ha he/she/it has; you have

habéis [abay-eess] you have

habilidoso skilful

habitación f [abeetath-yon] room

habitación doble [doblay] double room

habitación individual

[eendeebeedwal] single room

habitación con dos camas twin room

habitar to live

hablador talkative

hablar to speak

hable aquí speak here

habrá there will be; he/she/it will have; you will have

habrán they will have; you will have

habrás you will have

habré [abray] I will have

habréis [abray-eess] you will have

habremos we will have

habría [abree-a] I would have; he/she/it would have; you would have

habríais [abree-a-eess] you would have

habríamos [abree-amoss] we would have

habrían [abree-an] they would have; you would have

habrías [abree-ass] you would have

hace [athay]: hace ... días ... days ago
hace calor it is hot

hacer [athair] to make; to do

hacerse [athairsay] to become

hacia [ath-ya] towards

hago I do; I make

hambre: tengo hambre [ambray] I'm hungry

hamburguesería f
[amboorgaysairee-a] restaurant
selling hamburgers, hot
dogs

han [an] they have; you have

haré [aray] I will do

harto: estar harto (de) [arto] to
be fed up (with)

has [ass] you have

hasta [asta] even; until

  hasta que [kay] until

¡hasta la vista! see you!

¡hasta luego! [lwaygo]
cheerio!; see you later!

¡hasta mañana! [man-yana] see
you tomorrow!

¡hasta pronto! see you soon!

hay [ī] there is; there are

  hay ... we sell ...

haya [ī-a] I have; he/she/it
has; you have

haz [ath] do; make

he [ay] I have

hecho m [ay-cho] fact

hecho made; done

hecho a la medida made-to-
measure

helada f frost

heladería f [eladairee-a] ice-
cream parlour

helado f [elado] ice-cream

helar to freeze

hembra female

hemos we have

herida f [aireeda] wound

herido injured

hermana f [airmano] sister

hermano m brother

hermoso [airmoso] beautiful

herramientas fpl [airram-
yentass] tools

hervir [airbeer] to boil

hice [eethay] I made; I did

hidratante: crema hidratante f
[eedratantay] moisturizer

hidropedales mpl
[eedropedaless] pedalos

hielo m [yaylo] ice

hierba f [yairba] grass

hierro m [yairro] iron

hija f [eeHa] daughter

hijo m son

hilo m thread

hipermercado [eepairmairkado]
hypermarket

hipo m hiccups

hipódromo m horse-racing
track

historia f [eestor-ya] history;
story

hizo [eetho] he/she made;
he/she did; you made; you
did

hogar m home; household
goods

hoja f [oHa] leaf; sheet of
paper

hoja de afeitar [day afay-eetar]
razor blade

¡hola! hello!, hi!

hombre m [ombray] man

¡hombre! hey there!; you
bet; oh come on!

hombre de negocios [negoth-
yoss] businessman

hombro m shoulder

hondo deep

honrado honest

h is not pronounced in Spanish

hora f [ora] hour
¿qué hora es? what time is it?
hora local local time
horario m [orar-yo] timetable, (US) schedule
horario de autobuses [owtoboosess] bus timetable/schedule
horario de invierno [eemb-yairno] winter timetable/schedule
horario de recogidas [rekoHeedass] collection times
horario de trenes train timetable/schedule
horario de verano summer timetable/schedule
horas de consulta surgery hours, (US) office hours (of doctor)
horas de oficina [ofeetheena] opening hours
horas de visita visiting hours
horas punta rush hour
hormiga f ant
horno m oven
horquilla f [orkee-ya] hairpin
hospedarse [ospedarsay] to stay
hostal m [ostal] restaurant specializing in regional dishes; boarding house
hostal-residencia m [reseedenth-ya] long-stay boarding house

hostería f [ostairee-a] restaurant specializing in regional dishes
hotel-residencia m residential hotel
hoy [oy] today
HR (hostal-residencia) m boarding house where no meals are served, often lower-priced, residential hotel
hube [oobay] I had
hubieron [oob-yairon] they had; you had
hubimos [oobeemoss] we had
hubiste [oobeestay] you had
hubisteis [oobeestay-eess] you had
hubo [oobo] he/she/it had; you had; there was/were
huelga f [welga] strike
hueso m [wayso] bone
huésped m/f [wesped] guest
huevo m [waybo] egg
humedad m humidity, dampness
húmedo damp
humo m smoke
humor m humour
hundirse [oondeersay] to sink
hurto m theft

I

idéntico (a/que) identical (to)
idioma m [eed-yoma] language
idiota m/f [eed-yota] idiot
iglesia f [eeglays-ya] church

igual [eegwal] equal; like
  me da igual it's all the same to me
imbécil (m) [eembaytheel] nutter; stupid
impaciente [eempath-yentay] impatient
imperdible m [eempairdeeblay] safety pin
impermeable (m) [eempairmay-ablay] waterproof; raincoat
importación f [eemportath-yon] imported goods
importante [eemportantay] important
importar: no importa it doesn't matter
  ¿le importa si ...? do you mind if ...?
importe m [eemportay] amount
importe del billete [bee-yaytay] fare
importe total total due
imposible [eemposeeblay] impossible
impreso m [eemprayso] form
impuesto m [eempwesto] tax
incendiar [eenthend-yar] to set fire to
incendio m [eenthend-yo] fire (blaze)
incluido [eenkl-weedo] included
incluso even
increíble [eenkray-eeblay] incredible
indemnizar [eendemneethar] to

compensate
independiente [eendependyentay] independent
indicaciones fpl instructions for use
indicador m indicator
indicador de nivel gauge
indicar to indicate
indicativos provinciales area codes
indicativos de paises country codes
indignado indignant
indispuesto [eendeespwesto] unwell
infantil children's
infarto m heart attack
infectarse [eenfektarsay] to become infected
inflamado swollen
inflamarse [eenflamarsay] to swell
influenciar [eenflwenth-yar] to influence
información f [eenformath-yon] information
información de vuelos [bwayloss] flight information
información turística tourist information
información y turismo tourist information office
informar to inform
informarse (de/sobre) [-marsay (day/sobray)] to get information (on/about)
infracción f [eenfrakth-yon] offence

Inglaterra f [eenglat**ai**rra] England

inglés (m) [een-gl**ay**ss] English; Englishman

inglesa f Englishwoman

ingresos mpl deposits; income

iniciales fpl [eeneeth-y**a**less] initials

inmediatamente [eenmed-yatam**entay**] immediately

inocente [eenoth**entay**] innocent

insertar monedas insert coins

inserte moneda insert coin

insistir to insist

insolación f [eensolath-y**on**] sunstroke

instituto de belleza m [bay-y**ay**tha] beauty salon

instrucciones de lavado mpl washing instructions

inteligente [eenteleeH**entay**] intelligent

intentar to try

interés m [eentair**ay**ss] interest

interesante [eentairesantay] interesting

interior (m) [eentairee-**or**] interior, inner; domestic, home

intermedio (m) [eentairm**ay**d-yo] intermediate; intermission, interval

intermitente m [eentairmeet**entay**] indicator

interruptor m switch

interurbana long-distance

intoxicación alimenticia f [eentokseekath-y**on** aleement**ee**th-ya] food poisoning

introduzca moneda insert coin

introduzca el dinero exacto insert exact amount

introduzca la tarjeta y marque insert card and dial

inútil useless, pointless

invierno m [eemb-y**ai**rno] winter

invitada f, **invitado** m guest

invitar to invite

inyección f [eenyekth-y**on**] injection

ir to go

ir de paseo [pas**ay**-o] to go for a walk

Irlanda f [eerl**a**nda] Ireland

Irlanda del Norte [n**or**tay] Northern Ireland

irlandés (m) [eerland**ay**ss] Irish; Irishman

irlandesa f Irishwoman

irse [**ee**rsay] to go away

isla f island

Islas Canarias fpl [kan**a**r-yass] Canary Islands

itinerario m [eeteenair**a**r-yo] itinerary

IVA (impuesto sobre el valor añadido) [**ee**ba] VAT

izq. (izquierda) left

izquierda f [eethk-y**ai**rda] left

a la izquierda (de) on the left (of)

J

jabón m [Hab**on**] soap
jabón de afeitar [afay-ee**tar**]
  shaving soap
jamonería f [Hamonai**ree**-a]
  hams (shop)
jarabe m [Ha**ra**bay] syrup
jardín m [Har**deen**] garden
jardines públicos [Har**dee**ness]
  park, public gardens
jarra f [**Ha**rra] jug
jarrón m [Ha**rron**] vase
jefe m [**Ha**yfay] boss
jefe de tren guard
jersey m [Hair**say-ee**] jumper
jersey de cuello alto [**kway**-yo]
  polo neck jumper
¡Jesús! [Hay**sooss**] bless you!
¡joder! [Ho**dair**] hell!
joven (m/f) [**Ho**ben] young;
  young man; young woman
joyas fpl [**Ho**yass] jewellery
joyería f [Hoyai**ree**-a] jewellery;
  jeweller's
judío [Hoo**dee**-o] Jewish
juego (m) [**Hway**go] game; I
  play
jueves m [**way**bess] Thursday
jugar [Hoo**gar**] to play
juguete m [Hoo**gay**tay] toy
juguetería f [Hoogaytai**ree**-a] toy
  shop
juicio m [Hw**eeth**-yo]
  judgement; opinion;
  reason
julio m [**Hool**-yo] July
junio m [**Hoon**-yo] June

junto (a) [**Hoo**nto] next (to)
juntos together
justo [**Hoo**sto] just

K

kiosko de periódicos m
  [k-**yo**sko day pairee-o**dee**koss]
  newsagent's, newsstand
kiosko de prensa
  newsagent's, newsstand

L

la the; her; it
labio m [**lab**-yo] lip
laborables [labo**rab**less]
  weekdays, working days
laca f hair spray
lado m side
  al lado de beside, next to
ladrillo m [la**dree**-yo] brick
ladrón m thief
lagartija f [lagar**tee**Ha] lizard
lago m lake
lámpara f lamp
lana f wool
lana pura pure wool
lanas al peso wool sold by
  weight
lápiz m [**lapeeth**] pencil
lápiz de ojos [o**Hoss**] eyeliner
largo (m) length; long
  a lo largo de along
largura f length
las the; them; you
  las que ... the ones that ...

lástima: es una lástima it's a pity

lastimarse la espalda [lasteemarsay] to hurt one's back

lata f can; nuisance

latón m brass

lavabo m [lababo] washbasin

lavabos toilets, rest room

lavado m [labado] washing

lavadora f [labadora] washing machine

lavandería f [labandairee-a] laundry

lavandería automática [owtomateeka] launderette, laundromat

lavaplatos m [labaplatoss] dishwasher

lavar [labar] to wash

lavar a mano wash by hand

lavar en seco dry clean

lavar la ropa to do the washing

lavarse [labarsay] to wash

lavar separadamente wash separately

laxante m [laksantay] laxative

le [lay] him; her; you

lección f [lekth-yon] lesson

leche f [lechay] milk

leche limpiadora f [leemp-yadora] skin cleanser

lechería f [lechairee-a] dairy shop; dairy produce

leer [lay-air] to read

lejía f [leнee-a] bleach

lejos [layнoss] far away

lejos de far from

lencería f [lenthairee-a] drapery

lentillas fpl [lentee-yass] contact lenses

lentillas blandas soft lenses

lentillas duras hard lenses

lentillas porosas gas permeable lenses

lento slow

leotardos mpl [lay-otardoss] tights, pantyhose

les them; you

letra f letter; banker's draft

levantar [lebantar] to raise, to lift

levantarse [lebantarsay] to get up

ley f [lay-ee] law

libra f pound

libre [leebray] free; vacant

libre de impuestos duty-free

librería f [leebrairee-a] bookshop, bookstore

libreta de ahorros f [leebrayta day a-orross] savings account book

libreta de direcciones [deerekth-yoness] address book

libro m book

libro de frases phrase book

libros de bolsillo [bolsee-yo] paperbacks

líder m [leedair] leader

ligero [leeнairo] light

lima de uñas f [oon-yass] nailfile

límite f [leemeetay] limit

límite de altura maximum height

límite de peso [**pay**so] weight limit

límite de velocidad [day belothee**dad**] speed limit

limpiaparabrisas m [leemp-yapara**bree**sass] windscreen wiper

limpiar [leemp-**yar**] to clean

limpieza f [leemp-**yay**tha] cleanliness; cleaning

limpieza de coches car wash

limpieza en seco dry-cleaning

limpio [**leemp**-yo] clean

línea f [**lee**nay-a] line

linterna f [leen**tair**na] torch

lío m [**lee**-o] mess

liquidación f [leekeedath-**yon**] sale

liquidación total clearance sale

liso flat; plain; straight

lista f list

lista de correos [kor**ray**-oss] poste restante, (US) general delivery

lista de espera [esp**air**a] standby

listo clever; ready

litera f [lee**tair**a] couchette

litro m litre

llamada f [ya**ma**da] call

llamada a cobro revertido [rebair**tee**do] reverse charge call

llamar [ya**mar**] to call; to name

llamar por teléfono [te**lay**fono] to call, to phone

llamarse [yamar**say**] to be called

llame a la puerta please knock

llame al timbre please ring

llame antes de entrar knock before entering

llamo: me llamo ... [may **ya**mo] my name is ...

llave f [**ya**bay] key; spanner

llave inglesa [eeng**lay**sa] spanner

llegada f [yay**ga**da] arrival

llegadas internacionales international arrivals

llegadas nacionales domestic arrivals

llegar [ye**gar**] to arrive; to get to

llegué [ye**gay**] I arrived

llenar [ye**nar**] to fill

llenar el depósito to fill up

lleno [**yay**no] full

llevar [ye**bar**] to carry; to take; to bring; to give a lift to

llevar a juicio [Hwee**th**-yo] to prosecute

llevarse [yebar**say**] to take away

llorar [yo**rar**] to cry

llover [yo**bair**] to rain

lloviendo: está lloviendo [yob-**yen**do] it's raining

llovizna f [yo**beeth**na] drizzle

llueve [y-**way**-bay] it is raining

lluvia f [**yoob**-ya] rain

lo it; the

localidad f place

localidades tickets
loción antimosquitos f [loth-**yon** anteemoskeetoss] insect repellent
loción bronceadora [bronthay-a**do**ra] suntan lotion
loción para después del afeitado [desp**wess** del afay-ee**ta**do] after-shave
loco (**m**) mad; madman
locomotora f engine
locutorio telefónico m telephone booth
Londres [**lon**dress] London
longitud f [lonHee**too**] length
los the
  los que ... the ones that ...
loza f [**lo**tha] crockery
luces de posición fpl [**loo**thess day poseeth-**yon**] sidelights
luces traseras [tras**ai**rass] rear lights
luego [l**way**go] then
  luego que after
lugar m place
  en lugar de instead of
lugar de veraneo [bairan**ay**-o] summer resort
lugares de interés places of interest
lujo m [**loo**Ho] luxury
lujoso luxurious
luna f moon
lunes m [**loo**ness] Monday
luz f [**looth**] light
luz de carretera main beam
luz de cruce [kr**oo**thay] dipped headlights

M

machista m male chauvinist, sexist
madera f [mad**ai**ra] wood
madre f [**ma**dray] mother
madrileño [madree**layn**-yo] from Madrid, Madrid
madrugada f small hours
maduro ripe
maestra f [ma-**e**stra], **maestro m** primary school teacher
mal (**m**) badly; unwell, ill, sick; evil
¡maldita sea! [**say**-a] damn!
maleducado rude
malentendido m misunderstanding
maleta f suitcase
  hacer las maletas to pack
maletero m [male**tai**ro] boot, (US) trunk
mal genio m [**Hay**n-yo] bad temper
mal humor m bad mood; bad temper; anger
Mallorca [ma-**yor**ka] Majorca
malo bad
mamá f mum
manantial m [manant-**yal**] spring
mancha f stain
mandar to send; to order
mandíbula f jaw
manera: de esta manera [man**ai**ra] in this way
  de manera que so (that)
mano f hand

manoplas fpl mittens

manta f blanket

mantel m tablecloth

mantelerías fpl [mantelairee-ass] table linen

mantenga limpia España keep Spain tidy

mantenga limpia la ciudad keep our city tidy

manténgase en sitio fresco store in a cool place

manténgase alejado de los niños keep out of the reach of children

manual de conversación m [manwal day konbairsath-yon] phrasebook

mañana (f) [man-yana] morning; tomorrow

  por la mañana in the morning

  ¡hasta mañana! see you tomorrow!

mañana por la mañana tomorrow morning

mañana por la tarde [tarday] tomorrow afternoon; tomorrow evening

mapa m map

mapa de carreteras road map

mapa de recorrido network map

maquillaje m [makee-yaHay] make-up

maquillarse [makee-yarsay] to put one's makeup on

máquina de afeitar eléctrica f [makeena day afay-eetar] electric shaver

máquina de escribir typewriter

máquina de fotos camera

máquina tragaperras [makeena] slot machine

maquinaria f [makeenar-ya] machinery

maquinilla de afeitar f [makeenee-ya] razor

mar m sea

  la mar de ... lots of ...; very ...

maravilloso [marabee-yoso] marvellous

marca registrada f [reHeestrada] registered trade mark

marcar to dial

marcar el número dial the number

marcha f gear

marcha atrás reverse gear

marcharse [marcharsay] to go away

marea f [maray-a] tide

mareado [maray-ado] sick; merry, drunk

mares: a mares loads

marica m poofter

marido m husband

mariposa f butterfly; fairy, pansy

marisquería f [mareeskairee-a] shellfish restaurant

marque ... dial ...

marrón brown

marroquinería f [marrokeen-airee-a] fancy leather goods

Marruecos m [marrway-koss] Morocco

martes m [martess] Tuesday
martes de carnaval Shrove
Tuesday
martillo m [martee-yo] hammer
marzo m [martho] March
más more
 más de more than
 más pequeño smaller
 el más caro the most
 expensive
 ya no más no more
 más o menos [maynoss] more
 or less
matar to kill
matrícula f number plate;
 registration; registration
 fees
máximo personas maximum
 number of people
mayo m [ma-yo] May
mayor [mayor] adult; bigger;
 older; biggest; oldest
 la mayor parte (de) [partay]
 most (of)
 mayor de edad of age, adult
mayoría: la mayoría [mayoree-a]
 most
me me; myself
 me duele aquí [dwaylay] I
 have a pain here
mecánico m mechanic
mechas fpl highlights
media docena (de) f [dothayna]
 half a dozen
media hora f half an hour
media pensión f [pens-yon]
 half board, (US) European
 plan
mediano [mayd-yano] medium;

average
medianoche f [mayd-yanochay]
 midnight
medias fpl [mayd-yass]
 stockings
 ir/pagar a medias to go
 Dutch
medias panty tights,
 pantyhose
medicina f [medeetheena]
 medicine
médico m [maydeeko] doctor
médico general [Hay-nairal] GP
medida: a medida que as
medida del cuello f [kway-yo]
 collar size
medio m [mayd-yo] middle
 por medio de by (means of)
medio: de tamaño medio
 medium-sized
medio billete m [bee-yaytay]
 half(-price ticket)
medio litro half a litre
mediodía m [mayd-yodee-a]
 midday
medir to measure
medusa f jellyfish
mejor [mayHor] best; better
mejorar [mayHorar] to improve
mejoría f [mayHoree-a]
 recovery
mencionar [menth-yonar] to
 mention
menor [menor] smaller;
 younger; smallest; youngest
menor de edad minor
menos [maynoss] less; fewest;
 least
 a menos que unless

menudo tiny, minute
  a menudo often
menú turístico m set menu
mercadillo m [mairkadee-yo]
  street market
mercado m market
mercado cubierto [koob-yairto]
  indoor market
mercado de divisas exchange
  rates
mercería f [mairthairee-a]
  haberdashery
merendar to have an
  afternoon snack
merendero m [mairendairo]
  open-air café
merienda f [mair-yenda] tea,
  afternoon snack
mes m month
mesa f table
mesón m inn
meta [mayta] goal
metro m metre;
  underground, (US) subway
mezquita f [methkeeta] mosque
mí me
mi my
mía [mee-a] mine
microbús m minibus
miedo m [m-yaydo] fear
  tengo miedo (de/a) I'm
  afraid (of)
mientras [m-yentrass] while
mientras que whereas
mientras tanto meanwhile
miércoles m [m-yairkoless]
  Wednesday
miércoles de ceniza [theneetha]
  Ash Wednesday

¡mierda! [m-yairda] shit!
mil [meel] thousand
militar m serviceman
millón m [mee-yon] million
minifalda f mini-skirt
ministerio de ... ministry
  of ...
minúsculo tiny
minusválido (m) disabled;
  disabled person
minuto m minute
mío [mee-o] mine
miope [m-yopay] short-sighted
mirador m scenic view,
  vantage point
mirar to look (at)
mis my
misa f mass
mismo same
mitad f half
mitad de precio [prayth-yo]
  half price
mobilette f [mobeelettay]
  moped
mochila f rucksack
moda f fashion
  de moda fashionable
moda jóvenes [Hobayness]
  young fashions
moda juvenil [Hoobayneel]
  young fashions
modas caballeros [kaba-
  yaiross] men's fashions
modas niños/niñas [neen-yoss]
  children's fashions
modas pre-mamá maternity
  fashions
modas señora ladies'
  fashions

modelo m model; design; style

moderno [modairno] modern

modista f dressmaker; fashion designer

modisto m fashion designer

modo: de modo que so (that)

modo de empleo instructions for use

mojado [moHado] wet

moldeado con secador de mano [molday-ado] blow-dry

molestar to disturb; to bother

molesto annoying

monedas fpl coins

monedero m [monedairo] purse

montacargas m service lift, service elevator

montaña f [montan-ya] mountain

montañismo m [montan-yeesmo] climbing

montar to get in; to ride; to assemble

montar a caballo [kaba-yo] to go horse-riding

montar en bici [beethee] to cycle

moquetas fpl [mokaytass] carpets

morado purple

mordedura f bite

moreno [morayno] dark-haired

morir to die

moros mpl Moors

morriña: tengo morriña [morreen-ya] I'm homesick

mosca f fly

mostrador m counter

mostrador (de equipajes) [day ekeepaHess] check-in

mostrar to show

moto f motorbike

motora f motorboat

mover [mobair] to move

mozo m [motho] porter

muchacha f girl

muchacho m boy

muchas gracias [grath-yass] thank you very much

muchísimas gracias thank you very much indeed

muchísimo enormously, a great deal

mucho much; a lot; a lot of

mucho más a lot more

mucho menos [maynoss] a lot less

muchos/muchas a lot; a lot of; many

muebles mpl [mwaybless] furniture

muela f [mwayla] back tooth

muela del juicio [Hweeth-yo] wisdom tooth

muelle m [mway-yay] spring; quay

muerte f [mwairtay] death

muerto [mwairto] dead

mujer f [mooHair] woman; wife

muletas fpl crutches

multa f fine; parking ticket

multa por uso indebido penalty for misuse

mundo m world

muñeca f [moon-yeka] wrist; doll

muro m wall

músculo m muscle

museo m [moosay-o] museum

museo de arte [artay] art gallery

música f music

muslo m thigh

musulmán Muslim

muy [mwee] very

muy bien [b-yen] very well

N

N (carretera nacional) national highway

nacido [natheedo] born

nacimiento m [natheem-yento] birth

nacional [nath-yonal] domestic

nacionalidad f [nath-yonaleeda] nationality

nada nothing

de nada you're welcome, don't mention it

nada que declarar nothing to declare

nadar to swim

nadie [nad-yay] nobody

naranja f [naranHa] orange

nariz f [nareeth] nose

natación f [natath-yon] swimming

naturaleza f [natooralaytha] nature

naturalmente [-mentay] naturally; of course

náusea: siento náuseas [s-yento nowsay-ass] I feel sick

navaja f [nabaHa] penknife

Navidad f Christmas

¡feliz Navidad! [feleeth] merry Christmas!

neblina f mist

necesario [nethesar-yo] necessary

necesitar: necesito ... [netheseeto] I need ...

negar to deny

negativo (m) negative

negocio m [negoth-yo] business

negro (m) black; furious

nena f [nayna] baby girl; little girl

nene m [naynay] baby boy; little boy

nervioso [nairb-yoso] nervous

neumático m [nay-oomateeko] tyre

neumáticos - se reparan, se arreglan tyres repaired

neurótico [nay-ooroteeko] neurotic

nevar to snow

ni neither, nor

ni ... ni ... neither ... nor ...

niebla f [n-yebla] fog

nieta f [n-yayta] grand-daughter

nieto m grandson

nieva [n-yayba] it is snowing

nieve f [n-yaybay] snow

ningún [neengoon] nobody; none; not one; no ...

en ningún sitio [seet-yo] nowhere

ninguno nobody; none; not one; no ...

niña f [neen-ya] child

niñera f [neen-yaira] nanny

niño m [neen-yo] child

nivel del aceite m [athay-eetay] oil level

no no; not

no admite plancha do not iron

no aparcar no parking

no aparcar, llamamos grúa illegally parked vehicles will be towed away

no contiene alcohol does not contain alcohol

no entrada por detrás no entry at the rear

no exceda la dosis indicada do not exceed the stated dose

no fumadores no smoking

no funciona out of order

no hay de qué [no ī day kay] you are welcome

no hay localidades sold out

no molestar do not disturb

no para en ... does not stop in ...

no ... pero sí not ... but

no pisar el césped keep off the grass

no recomendada para menores de 18 años not recommended for those under 18 years of age

no se admiten caravanas no caravans allowed

no se admiten devoluciones no refunds given

no se admiten perros no dogs allowed

no tocar please do not touch

no utilizar lejía do not bleach

noche f [nochay] night

  esta noche tonight

  por la noche at night

nochebuena f [nochay-bwayna] Christmas Eve

nochevieja f [nochay-b-yayHa] New Year's Eve

nombre m [nombray] name

nombre de soltera [soltaira] maiden name

nombre de pila first name

nordeste m [nordestay] northeast

normal (m) [normal] normal; lower grade petrol, (US) regular

normalmente [-mentay] usually

noroeste m [noro-estay] northwest

norte m [nortay] north

  al norte de la ciudad north of the town

Noruega f [norwayga] Norway

nos us; ourselves

nosotras, nosotros we; us

noticias fpl [noteeth-yass] news

novecientos [nobay-th-yentoss] nine hundred

novela f novel

noveno [nobayno] ninth

noventa ninety

novia f [nob-ya] girlfriend; fiancée; bride

noviembre m [nob-yembray]

November

novillada f [nobee-**ya**da] bullfight featuring young bulls

novio m [**nob**-yo] boyfriend; fiancé; groom

nube f [**noo**bay] cloud

nublado cloudy

nuboso cloudy

nuera f [**nwai**ra] daughter-in-law

nuestra [**nwe**stra], **nuestras, nuestro, nuestros** our

Nueva York [**nway**ba] New York

nueve [**nway**bay] nine

nuevo new

número m [**noo**mairo] number

número de teléfono phone number

número (de calzado) [day **kal**thado] (shoe) size

nunca never

O

o or

o ... o ... either ... or ...

objeción f [ob-Heth-**yon**] objection

objetar [obH**ay**tar] to object

objetivo m [obH**ay**teebo] lens; objective

objetos de escritorio [obH**ay**toss day eskreet**or**-yo] office supplies

objetos perdidos lost property, lost and found

obra f work; play

obras fpl roadworks

obstruido [obstr-w**ee**do] blocked

obturador m shutter

ocasión f [okass-**yon**] occasion; opportunity; bargain

de ocasión second hand

occidental [oktheed**en**tal] Western

ochenta eighty

ocho eight

ocho días mpl [**dee**-ass] week

ochocientos [ochoth-**yen**toss] eight hundred

octavo eighth

octubre m [okt**oo**bray] October

oculista [okool**ee**sta] optician

ocupado engaged; occupied; busy

ocupantes del coche mpl [ok**oo**pantess del k**o**chay] passengers

odiar [od-**yar**] to hate

oeste m [o-**estay**] west

al oeste de la ciudad west of the town

ofender [ofend**air**] to offend

oferta (especial) f [of**air**ta (espeth-**yal**)] special offer

oficina f [ofeet**hee**na] office

oficina de reclamaciones [reklamath-**yon**ess] complaints department

oficina de registros [reH**ee**stross] registrar's office

oficina de turismo tourist information office

oficina de objetos perdidos

[obHaytoss] lost property office, lost and found

oficina de información y turismo [eenformath-yon] tourist information office

oficina de correos [korray-oss] post office

oficina de correos y telégrafos post office and telegrams

oficinista m/f [ofeetheeneesta] office worker

oficio m [ofeeth-yo] job

ofrecer [ofrethair] to offer

oído (m) [o-eedo] ear; hearing; heard

¡oiga! [oyga] listen here!; excuse me!

oigo I hear

oír [o-eer] to hear

ojo m [oHo] eye

ojo al tren beware of the train

ola f wave; fashion

ola de calor heatwave

oler [olair] to smell

olor m smell

olvidar to forget

omnibús m local short-distance train

once [onthay] eleven

operadora f operator

operarse [opairarsay] to have an operation; to come about

oportunidad f chance, opportunity

oportunidades bargains

óptica f optician's

óptico m optician

optimista optimistic

orden m order

ordenador m computer

oreja f [oray-Ha] ear

organizar [organeethar] to organize

orgulloso [orgoo-yoso] proud

orilla f [oree-ya] shore

oro m gold

orquesta f [orkesta] orchestra

os you; to you

oscuro dark

otoño m [oton-yo] autumn, (US) fall

otorrinolaringólogo ear, nose and throat specialist

otra vez [bayth] again

otro another (one); other

oveja f [obayHa] sheep

oye [o-yay] he/she hears; you hear; listen

P

p (paseo) street; parking

paciente [path-yentay] patient

pacotilla: de pacotilla [pakotee-ya] rubbishy; second-rate

padecer de [padethair] to suffer from

padecer del corazón [korathon] to have a heart condition

padre m [padray] father

padres mpl parents

pagadero payable

pagar to pay

página f [paHeena] page

páginas amarillas [amaree-yass]

yellow pages

pagos mpl deposits

pague el importe exacto (please tender) exact money

país m [pa-eess] country

País Vasco Basque Country

País de Gales: el País de Gales [galess] Wales

paisaje m [pa-eesaHay] scenery

pájaro m [paHaro] bird

pala f spade

palabra f word

palacio m [palath-yo] palace

palacio real [ray-al] royal palace

palacio de congresos conference hall

Palacio de Justicia [Hoosteeth-ya] Law Courts

Palacio de la Opera opera house

palanca de velocidades f [belotheedadess] gear lever

palco m box (at theatre)

palomitas de maíz fpl [ma-eeth] popcorn

palos de golf mpl golf clubs

pan m bread

panadería f [panadairee-a] baker's

pantalla f [panta-ya] screen

pantalón corto m shorts

pantalones mpl [pantaloness] trousers, (US) pants

pantalones cortos mpl shorts

pantalones vaqueros [bakaiross] jeans

panties mpl tights

pantorrilla f [pantorree-ya] calf

pañal m [pan-yal] nappy, (US) diaper

pañería f [pan-yairee-a] drapery

pañuelo m [panwaylo] handkerchief; scarf

pañuelo (de cabeza) [day kabaytha] (head)scarf

papá m dad

papel m [papel] paper; rôle

papel celo® [thaylo] sellotape®, Scotch tape®

papel de envolver [embolbair] wrapping paper

papel de escribir writing paper

papel de plata silver foil

papel higiénico [eeH-yayneeko] toilet paper

papelera f litter; litter bin

papelería f [papelairee-a] stationery, stationer's

papeles pintados mpl wallpaper

paquete m [pakaytay] packet

par m pair

para for; in order to

para automáticas for automatic washing machines

para que [kay] in order that

para uso del personal staff only

para uso externo not to be taken internally

parabrisas m windscreen

paracaidismo m [paraka-eedeesmo] parachuting

parachoques m [parachokess]

bumper, (US) fender

parada f stop

parada de autobuses bus stop

parada de taxis taxi rank

parador m hotel restaurant; luxury hotel

parador nacional [nath-yonal] state-owned hotel, often a historic building which has been restored

paraguas m [paragwass] umbrella

parar to stop

parecer [parethair] to seem; to resemble

parecido [paretheedo] similar

pared f [parayd] wall

pareja f [paray-Ha] pair; couple

parezco [parethko] I seem

pariente m/f [par-yentay] relative

parking m car park, (US) parking lot

paro: en paro unemployed

parque m [parkay] park

parque de atracciones [atraktth-yoness] amusement park

parque de bomberos [bombaiross] fire station

parque de recreo [rekray-o] amusement park

parque infantil children's park; playpen

parrilla f [parree-ya] grill

parte f [partay] part

  en todas partes everywhere

  en otra parte elsewhere

  en alguna parte somewhere

  ¿de parte de quién? [day k-yen] who's calling?

parte antigua [anteegwa] old town

parte meteorológico m [maytay-oroloHeeko] weather forecast

particular private

partida f game

partido m match

pasado last

  la semana pasada last week

  pasado mañana the day after tomorrow

  pasado de moda out of fashion

  poco pasado rare

pasador m hairslide

pasaje m [pasaHay] plane ticket

pasajero m [pasaHairo] passenger

pasajeros de tránsito transit passengers

pasaporte m [pasaportay] passport

pasaportes passport control

pasar to pass; to overtake; to happen

pasar la aduana [ad-wana] to go through customs

pasarlo bien [b-yen] to enjoy oneself

pasarlo bomba to have a great time

pasatiempo m [pasat-yempo] hobby

Pascua [pask-wa] Easter

pasear [pasay-ar] to go for a walk

pasen enter; cross, walk

paseo m [pasay-o] walk; drive; ride

paseo de ... ... avenue

pasillo m [pasee-yo] corridor

paso m passage; pass; step
  estar de paso to be passing through

paso a nivel level crossing, (US) grade crossing

paso de cebra [thaybra] zebra crossing

paso de contador unit

paso de peatones [pay-atoness] pedestrian crossing

paso subterráneo pedestrian underpass

pasta de dientes f [d-yentess] toothpaste

pastelería f [pastelairee-a] cake shop

pastilla f [pastee-ya] tablet

pastillas para la garganta throat pastilles

patatas fritas chips, French fries; crisps, potato chips

patinaje m [pateenaHay] skating

patinar to skid; to skate

patio de butacas m stalls

peaje m [pay-aHay] toll

peatón m [pay-aton] pedestrian

peatón, camine por la izquierda pedestrians keep to the left

peatón, circula por tu izquierda pedestrians keep to the left

peatonal pedestrian

peatones pedestrians

peatones, caminen por la izquierda pedestrians keep to the left

pecho m chest; breast

pedazo m [pedatho] piece

pediatra m/f [pedee-atra] pediatrician

pedir to order; to ask for

pedir disculpas to apologize

pedir hora [ora] to make an appointment

peinar [pay-eenar] to comb

peinarse [pay-eenarsay] to comb one's hair

peine m [pay-eenay] comb

pelea f [pelay-a] fight

peletería f [peletairee-a] furs, furrier

película f film, movie

película en color colour film

película en versión original [bairs-yon oreeHeenal] film in the original language

peligro m danger

peligro de incendio danger: fire hazard

peligro deslizamientos slippery road surface

peligroso dangerous
  es peligroso bañarse danger: no swimming
  es peligroso asomarse al exterior do not lean out

pelirrojo [peleerroHo] redheaded

pelo m [paylo] hair
  me está tomando el pelo you're pulling my leg

pelón bald

pelota f ball
peluca f wig
peluquería f [pelookair**ee**-a] hairdresser's
peluquería de caballeros [kaba-y**ai**ross] gent's hairdresser's
peluquería de señoras ladies' salon
peluquera f [pelook**ai**ra], **peluquero** m hairdresser
pena f [**pay**na] grief, sorrow
¡qué pena! [kay] what a pity!
pendiente de pago outstanding
pendientes mpl [pend-y**en**tess] earrings
pene m [**pay**nay] penis
penicilina f [peneetheel**ee**na] penicillin
pensar to think
pensión f [pens-y**on**] guesthouse, boarding house; pension
pensión completa [kompl**ay**ta] full board, (US) American plan
pensionista m [pens-yon**ee**sta] old-age pensioner
peor [pay-**or**] worse; worst
pequeño (m) [pek**ayn**-yo] small; child
percha f [**pair**cha] coathanger
perder [paird**air**] to lose; to miss
perderse [paird**air**say] to get lost
pérdida f loss
perdón sorry, excuse me; pardon, pardon me
perezoso [paireth**o**so] lazy
perfecto [pairf**e**kto] perfect
perfumería f [pairfoomair**ee**-a] perfumes (shop)
periódico m [pairee-**o**deeko] newspaper
periodista m [pair-yod**ee**sta] journalist
período m [pairee-odo] period
perla f [**pair**la] pearl
permanente f [pairman**en**tay] perm
permiso m [pairm**ee**so] licence
permitido allowed
permitir to allow
pero [**pai**ro] but
perra: no tengo una perra I'm broke
perro m [**pai**rro] dog
persona f [pairs**o**na] person
persuadir [pairswad**ee**r] to persuade
pesadilla f [pesad**ee**-ya] nightmare
pesado heavy
pésame: dar el pésame [**pay**samay] to offer one's condolences
pesar weight
 a pesar de que despite the fact that
 a pesar de in spite of
pesca f fishing
 ir de pesca to go fishing
pescadería f [peskadair**ee**-a] fishmonger's
pescar to fish; to catch out
peso m [**pay**so] weight

peso neto net weight
peso máximo maximum weight
pestañas fpl [pestan-yass] eyelashes
petición de mano f [peteeth-yon] engagement
pez m [peth] fish
picadura f bite
picante [peekantay] hot
picar to sting; to itch
picor m itch
pidió [peed-yo] he/she asked for; you asked for
pie m [p-yay] foot
 a pie on foot
piedra f [p-yedra] stone
piedra preciosa [preth-yosa] precious stone
piel f [p-yayl] skin
pienso [p-yenso] I think
pierna f [p-yairna] leg
pieza de repuesto f [p-yaytha day repwesto] spare part
piezas de recambio [rekamb-yo] spares
pijama m [peeHama] pyjamas
pila f battery; pile
píldora f pill
piloto m pilot
pilotos mpl rear lights
pincel m [peenthayl] paint brush
pinchazo m [peenchatho] puncture
pintar to paint
pintura f painting; paint
pinza de la ropa f clothes peg
pinzas fpl [peenthass] tweezers

piña f [peen-ya] pineapple
pipa f pipe
piragua f [peeragwa] canoe
piragüismo m [peeragweesmo] canoeing
Pirineos mpl [peereenay-oss] Pyrenees
piscina f [peestheena] swimming pool
piscina cubierta [koob-yairta] indoor swimming pool
piso m floor; flat, apartment
piso amueblado [amweblado] furnished apartment
piso bajo [baHo] ground floor, (US) first floor
piso sin amueblar [amweblar] unfurnished apartment
pista f track; clue
pista de baile [ba-eelay] dance floor
pista de patinaje [pateenaHay] skating rink
pista de tenis tennis court
pistas de esquí [eskee] ski runs
pistola f gun
plancha f iron
planchar to iron
plano (m) flat; map
planta f plant; floor
planta baja [baHa] ground floor, (US) first floor
planta primera [preemaira] first floor, (US) second floor
planta sótano lower floor; basement
planta superior [soopair-yor] upper floor

plástico (**m**) plastic
plata f silver
plateado [platay-**ado**] silver
platillo m [plat**ee**-yo] saucer
plato m plate; dish, course
playa f [pla-ya] beach
playeras fpl [pla-y**ai**rass]
  trainers
plaza f [pl**atha**] square; seat
  en plaza current prices
plaza de abastos marketplace
plaza de toros bullring
plazas libres [l**ee**bress] seats
  available
pluma f pen; feather
población f [poblath-y**on**]
  village; town; population
pobre [p**o**bray] poor .
poco little
poco profundo shallow
pocos few
  unos pocos a few
poder (**m**) [pod**air**] to be able
  to; power
podrido rotten
policía f [poleeth**ee**-a] police
policía m/f policeman;
  policewoman
policía municipal f
  [mooneetheep**al**] municipal
  police
polideportivo m sports centre
polígono industrial m
  industrial estate
política f politics
político political
póliza de seguros f insurance
  policy
polo m ice lolly

polvos mpl powder
pomada f ointment
pon put
poner [pon**air**] to put
ponerse en marcha [pon**air**say]
  to set off
ponerse en pie [p-yay] to
  stand up
poney m pony
pongo I put
poquito: un poquito [pok**ee**to] a
  little bit
por by; through; for
  por allí [a-y**ee**] over there
  por fin at last
  por lo que [kay] for which
  reason
  por lo menos [m**ay**noss] at
  least
  por qué [kay] why
  por semana per week
  por si in case
por ciento [th-y**en**to] per cent
por favor please
por favor, use un carrito
  please take a trolley
por favor, use una cesta
  please take a basket
porcelana f [porthel**ana**]
  porcelain
porque [p**o**rkay] because
portaequipajes m [porta-
  ekeepa**Hess**] luggage rack
portátil [portat**eel**] portable
portero m [port**ai**ro] porter;
  doorman; goalkeeper
portugués [portoog**ay**ss]
  Portuguese
posada f inn

posible [po**see**blay] possible

postal f postcard

precaución f [prekowth-**yon**] caution

precio m [**preth**-yo] price

precioso [preth-**yo**so] beautiful; precious

precio unidad unit price

precios fijos [fee**Hoss**] fixed prices

preferencia f [prefair**enth**-ya] right of way; preference

preferir [prefair**eer**] to prefer

prefijo m [prefee**Ho**] dialling code, area code

pregunta f question

preguntar to ask

prendas fpl clothing

prensa f press; newspapers

preocupado [pray-okoo**pa**do] worried

preocupes: ¡no te preocupes! [no tay pray-ok**oo**pess] don't worry

preparar to prepare

prepararse [prepar**ar**say] to get ready

presentar to introduce

preservativo m [presairbat**ee**bo] condom

presión f [press-**yon**] pressure

presión de los neumáticos [nay-oom**a**teekoss] tyre pressure

prestado: pedir prestado to borrow

prestar to lend

prima f cousin

primavera f [preemab**ai**ra] spring

primer [pree**mair**] first

primer piso m first floor, (US) second floor

primer plato m first course

primera (clase) f [**kla**say] first class

primero first

primeros auxilios [owk-**seel**-yoss] first-aid post

primo m cousin

princesa f [preen**thay**sa] princess

principal [preenthee**pal**] main

príncipe m [preen**thee**pay] prince

principiante m/f [preentheep-**yan**tay] beginner

principio m [preen**theep**-yo] beginning

principio de autopista start of motorway/highway

prioridad de paso priority

prioridad a la derecha give way/yield to vehicles coming from your right

prisa: darse prisa [**dar**say] to hurry

¡dese prisa! [**day**say] hurry up!

privado private

probablemente [probable**men**tay] probably

probador m fitting room

probar to try

probarse to try on

problema m problem

procesiones de Semana Santa fpl [prothess-**yo**ness] Holy

Week processions

producido en ... produce of ...

producto preparado con ingredientes naturales product prepared using natural ingredients

productos alimenticios [aleement**eeth**-yoss] foodstuffs

productos de belleza [bay-y**ay**tha] beauty products

profesor m, profesora f teacher; lecturer

profundidad f depth

profundo deep

programa infantil m children's programme

prohibida la entrada a menores de ... no admission for those under ... years of age

prohibida su reproducción copyright reserved

prohibida su venta not for sale

prohibida la entrada no entry, no admission

prohibido [pro-eeb**ee**do] prohibited, forbidden; no

prohibido acampar no camping

prohibido adelantar no overtaking, no passing

prohibido aparcar no parking

prohibido aparcar excepto carga y descarga no parking except for loading and unloading

prohibido asomarse do not lean out

prohibido asomarse a la ventana do not lean out of the window

prohibido asomarse a la ventanilla do not lean out of the window

prohibido bañarse no swimming

prohibido cambiar de sentido no U-turns

prohibido cantar no singing

prohibido el paso no entry; no trespassing

prohibido encender fuego no campfires

prohibido escupir no spitting

prohibido estacionar no parking

prohibido fijar carteles stick no bills

prohibido fumar no smoking

prohibido girar a la izquierda no left turn

prohibido hablar con el conductor do not speak to the driver

prohibido hacer auto-stop no hitch-hiking

prohibido hacer sonar el claxon/la bocina do not sound your horn

prohibido pescar no fishing

prohibido pisar el césped keep off the grass

prohibido pisar la hierba keep off the grass

prohibido tirar basura no litter

prohibido tirar escombros no dumping

prohibido tocar la bocina/el claxon do not sound your horn

prohibido tomar fotografías no photographs

prometer [prometair] to promise

prometida f fiancée

prometido (m) engaged; fiancé

pronóstico del tiempo m [t-yempo] weather forecast

pronto soon

¡hasta pronto! [asta] see you soon!

llegar pronto [yegar] to be early

pronunciar [pronoonth-yar] to pronounce

propiedad privada private property

propietario m [prop-yetar-yo] owner

propina f tip

propósito: a propósito deliberately

proteger [protay-Hair] to protect

provecho: ¡buen provecho! [bwen probay-cho] enjoy your meal!

provincia f [probeenth-ya] district

provocar to cause

próximo next

la semana próxima next week

prudente [proodentay] careful

prueba de alcoholemia f [pr-wayba day alko-olaym-ya] breath test

pts (pesetas) pesetas

pub bar in which no meals are served, often higher priced and disco music played

público (m) public; audience

pueblo m [pweblo] village; people

puede [pwayday] he/she can; you can

puede ser [sair] maybe

puedo [pwaydo] I can

puente m [pwentay] bridge

puente aéreo [a-airay-o] shuttle plane

puente de fuerte pendiente humpbacked bridge

puente de peaje [pay-aHay] toll bridge

puente romano Roman bridge

puerta f [pwairta] door; gate

por la otra puerta use other door

puerta de embarque [embarkay] gate

puerta nº. gate no.

puerto m harbour; pass; port

puerto deportivo marina

puerto de montaña [montan-ya] (mountain) pass

pues [pwayss] since; so

puesta de sol f [pwesta] sunset

puesto de periódicos [pairee-odeekoss] newspaper kiosk

puesto de socorro m first-aid post

puesto que [kay] since

pulga f flea

pulmones mpl lungs

pulmonía f [poolmonee-a] pneumonia

pulse botón para cruzar press button to cross

pulsera f [poolsaira] bracelet

pulso m pulse

puntual: llegar puntual [poont-wal] to arrive on time

punto de vista m point of view

punto: hacer punto [athair] to knit

¡puñeta! [poon-yayta] hell!

¡vete a hacer puñetas! [baytay a athair] bugger off!

pura lana virgen [beerHen] pure new wool

puro m cigar

puse [poosay] I put

Q

que [kay] who; that; which; than

que ... o que whether ... or

¿qué? what?

¿qué hay? [i] how's things?

¿qué tal?, mucho gusto how do you do?, nice to meet you

¡qué va! no way!

quedarse [kedarsay] to stay

quedarse con to keep

quedarse sin gasolina to run out of petrol/gas

quejarse [kayHarsay] to complain

quemadura f [kemadoora] burn

quemadura de sol sunburn

quemar [kemar] to burn

quemarse [kemarsay] to burn oneself

querer [kerair] to love; to want

querido [kaireedo] dear

¿quién? [k-yen] who?

quiero [k-yairo] I want; I love

no quiero I don't want to

quince [keenthay] fifteen

quince días [dee-ass] fortnight

quinientos [keen-yentoss] five hundred

quinto [keento] fifth

quiosco m [k-yosko] kiosk

quisiera [keess-yaira] I would like; he/she would like; you would like

quiso [keeso] he/she wanted; you wanted

quitaesmalte m [keeta-esmaltay] nail polish remover

quitar [keetar] to remove

quizá(s) [keetha(ss)] maybe

R

rabioso [rab-yoso] furious

R.A.C.E (Real Automóvil Club de España) Spanish Royal Automobile Club

ración f [rath-yon] portion
radiador m [rad-yador] radiator
radio m [rad-yo] spoke
radio f radio
radiografía f [rad-yografee-a] X-ray
rápidamente [-mentay] quickly
rápido fast
rápido m train stopping at many stations
raqueta de tenis f [rakayta] tennis racket
raro rare; strange
rata f rat
ratón m mouse
rayas: a rayas [ra-yass] striped
razón f [rathon] reason; rate
  razón aquí apply within
  tiene razón you're right
razonable [rathonablay] reasonable
rea sale
realmente [ray-almentay] really
rebajado [rebaHado] reduced
rebajas fpl [rebaHass] reductions, sale
rebajas de verano [bairano] summer sale
rebanada f slice
recado m message
recepción f [rethepth-yon] reception
recepcionista m/f [rethepth-yoneesta] receptionist
receta f [rethayta] recipe; prescription
  con receta médica only available on prescription
recetar [rethaytar] to prescribe

recibir [retheebeer] to receive
recibo m [retheebo] receipt
recién [reth-yen] recently
recién pintado wet paint
reclamación de equipajes f [reklamath-yon day ekeepaHess] baggage claim
reclamaciones fpl [reklamath-yoness] complaints
recoger [rekoHair] to collect; to pick up
recogida de equipajes f [rekoHeeda] baggage claim
recoja su ticket take your ticket
recomendar to recommend
reconocer [rekonothair] to recognize; to examine
recordar to remember
recorrido m journey
recto straight
recuerdo (m) [rekwairdo] souvenir; I remember
red f network; net
redondo round
reduzca la velocidad reduce speed now
reembolsar [ray-embolsar] to refund
reembolsos refunds
reestreno [ray-estrayno] re-release (of a classic movie)
regalo m present
regatear [regatay-ar] to haggle
régimen m [ray-Heemen] diet
registrar [reHeestrar] to search
regla f rule; period
registro de equipajes m [reHeestro day ekeepaHess]

check in

registros sanitarios government health certificate

regresar to return

reina f [ray-eena] queen

Reino Unido m United Kingdom

reír [ray-eer] to laugh

rejoneador m [reHonay-ador] bullfighter on horseback

relajarse [relaHarsay] to relax

rellenar [ray-yaynar] to fill in

reloj m [ray-loH] watch; clock

reloj de pulsera [poolsaira] (wrist)watch

relojería f [ray-loHairee-a] watches and clocks

remar to row

remite m [remeetay] sender's name and address

remitente m/f [remeetentay] sender

remo m [raymo] oar

remolque m [remolkay] trailer

remonte m [remontay] ski tow

Renacimiento m [renatheemyento] Renaissance

RENFE (Red Nacional de Ferrocarriles Españoles) Spanish Railways/Railroad

reparación f [reparath-yon] repair(s)

reparación de calzado shoe repairs

reparaciones faults service

reparar to repair

repente: de repente [repentay] suddenly

repetir to repeat

replicar to reply

reponerse [reponairsay] to recover

reposar to rest

representante m/f [repraysentantay] representative, agent

repuestos mpl [repwestoss] spare parts

repugnante [repoognantay] disgusting

resaca f hangover

resbaladizo [resbaladeetho] slippery

resbalar to slip

rescatar to rescue

reserva f [resairba] reservation

reserva de asientos seat reservation

reservado reserved

reservado el derecho de admisión the management reserve the right to refuse admission

reservado socios members only

reservar to reserve; to book

reservas fpl reservations

resfriado m [resfree-ado] cold

respirar to breathe

responder [respondair] to answer

responsable [responsablay] responsible

respuesta f [respwesta] answer

resto m rest

retales mpl [retaless] remnants

retrasado late

retrasado mental mentally handicapped
retraso m delay
retrete m [retray**tay**] toilets, (US) rest rooms
reumatismo m [ray-ooma**tee**smo] rheumatism
reunión f [ray-oon-y**o**n] meeting
revelado m film processing
revelar to develop; to reveal
revisar to check
revisor m ticket collector
revista m magazine
rey m [ray] king
Reyes: día de los Reyes m [**dee**-a day loss **ray**-ess] 6th of January, Epiphany
rico rich
ridículo ridiculous
rímel m mascara
rincón m corner
riñón m [reen-y**o**n] kidney
río m [**ree**-o] river
rizado [reet**ha**do] curly
robar to steal
robo m theft
roca f rock
rodilla f [ro**dee**-ya] knee
rojo [**ro**Ho] red
románico romanesque
rómpase en caso de emergencia break in case of emergency
romper to break
ropa f clothes
ropa confeccionada ready-to-wear clothes
ropa de caballeros [kaba-**yair**oss] men's clothes

ropa de cama bed linen
ropa de señoras ladies' clothes
ropa infantil children's clothes
ropa interior f [eentair-y**o**r] underwear
ropa sucia [**soo**th-ya] laundry
rosa (f) pink; rose
roto broken
rotulador m felt-tip pen
rubéola f [roo**bay**-ola] German measles
rubí m [roo**bee**] ruby
rubio [**roo**b-yo] blond
rueda f [rw**ay**da] wheel
rueda de repuesto f [rep**wes**to] spare wheel
ruedo m bullring
ruego [rw**ay**go] I request
ruido m [rw**ee**do] noise
ruidoso [rwee**do**so] noisy
ruinas fpl [rw**ee**nass] ruins
rulo m roller, curler
rulot(a) f caravan, (US) trailer
ruta f route

S

S.A. (Sociedad Anónima) PLC, Inc
sábado m Saturday
sábana f sheet
saber [sab**air**] to know
saber a to taste of
sabor m taste
sabroso tasty
sacacorchos m [saka**kor**choss]

corkscrew

sacar to take out; to get out

sacar un billete [bee-yaytay] to buy a ticket

saco de dormir m sleeping bag

sal (f) salt; leave

sala f room; hall

sala climatizada air conditioned

sala de baile [ba-eelay] dance hall

sala de cine [theenay] cinema, movie theater

sala de conciertos [konth-yairtoss] concert hall

sala de embarque [embarkay] departure lounge

sala de espera [espaira] waiting room

sala de exposiciones [esposeeth-yoness] exhibition hall

sala de tránsito transit lounge

sala X X-rated cinema

salado salty

saldar to sell at a reduced price

saldo m clearance; balance

saldos sales

sales de baño fpl [saless day ban-yo] bath salts

salgo I leave

salida f exit; departure

salida ciudad take this direction to leave the city

salida de ambulancias ambulance exit

salida de autopista end of motorway/highway; motorway exit

salida de camiones heavy goods vehicle exit, works exit

salida de emergencia [aymairHenth-ya] emergency exit

salida de fábrica factory exit

salida de incendios fire exit

salida de socorro f emergency exit

salidas fpl departures

salidas de noche night life

salidas internacionales international departures

salidas nacionales domestic departures

salir to go out; to leave

salón m lounge

salón de belleza [bay-yaytha] beauty salon

salón de demostraciones exhibition hall

salón de peluquería [pelookairee-a] hairdressing salon

saltar to jump

salud f [saloo] health

¡salud! cheers!

saludar to greet

saludos best wishes

salvo que [kay] except that

sandalias fpl [sandal-yass] sandals

San Fermín [fairmeen] July 7th, when the 'encierro' happens

sangrar to bleed

sangre f [sangray] blood
sano healthy
Santiago [sant-yago] July 25th, a national holiday
sarampión m [saramp-yon] measles
sartén f frying pan
sastre m [sastray] tailor
se [say] himself; herself; itself; yourself; themselves; yourselves; oneself
sé [say] I know
no sé I don't know
se aceptan tarjetas de crédito we accept credit cards
se alquila for hire, to rent
se alquila piso flat to let, apartment for rent
se alquilan habitaciones rooms to rent
se alquilan hidropedales pedalos for hire
se alquilan sombrillas parasols for hire
se alquilan tumbonas deckchairs for hire
se habla inglés English spoken
se hacen fotocopias photocopying service
se necesita ... ... needed
se precisa ... ... needed
se prohibe ... ... forbidden
se prohibe fumar no smoking
se prohibe hablar con el conductor do not speak to the driver
se prohibe la entrada no entry, no admittance

se prohibe tirar basura no litter
se ruega ... please ...
se ruega desalojen su habitación antes de las doce please vacate your room by 12 noon
se ruega no ... please do not ...
se ruega no aparcar no parking please
se ruega no molestar please do not disturb
se ruega pagar en caja please pay at the desk
se vende for sale
secador de pelo m [paylo] hair dryer
secadores mpl dryers
secar to dry
secarse el pelo [sekarsay] to dry one's hair, to have a blow-dry
sección f [sekth-yon] department
seco dry
secretaria f, secretario m secretary
secreto secret
sed: tengo sed [seth] I'm thirsty
seda f silk
seda natural pure silk
seguida: en seguida [segeeda] immediately, right away
seguir [segeer] to follow
según according to
segunda clase f [klasay] second class

segundo (**m**) second

de segunda mano second-hand

segundo piso m second floor, (US) third floor

segundo plato m main course

seguridad f [segooree**da**] safety; security

seguro (**m**) safe; sure; insurance

seguro de viaje m [b-ya**Hay**] travel insurance

seis [say-eess] six

seiscientos [say-eess-th-y**en**toss] six hundred

sello m [**say**-yo] stamp

semáforos mpl traffic lights

semana f week

Semana Santa Holy Week

semanarios mpl weeklies

sencillo [senth**ee**-yo] simple

sensible [sens**ee**blay] sensitive

sentar: sentar bien (**a**) [b-yen] to suit

sentarse [sent**ar**say] to sit down

sentido m direction; sense; meaning

sentir to feel

señal de tráfico f [sen-y**al** day tra**fee**ko] roadsign

señas fpl [**sen**-yass] address

señor [sen-y**or**] gentleman, man; sir

el señor Brown Mr Brown

señora f [sen-y**or**a] lady, woman; madam

la señora Brown Mrs Brown

señoras fpl ladies' toilet,

ladies' room; ladies' department

señores mpl [sen-y**or**ess] gents' toilet, men's room

señorita f [sen-yor**ee**ta] young lady, young woman; miss

la señorita Brown Miss Brown

separado separate; separated

por separado separately

septiembre m [sept-y**em**bray] September

séptimo seventh

sequía f [sek**ee**-a] drought

ser [sair] to be

a no ser que unless

serio [**sair**-yo] serious

servicio m [sairb**ee**th-yo] service; toilet

servicio a través de operadora operator-connected calls

servicio automático direct dialling

servicio de habitaciones room service

servicio de fotocopias photocopying service

servicio (no) incluido service charge (not) included

servicios mpl [sairb**ee**th-yoss] toilets, (US) rest rooms

servicios de rescate mountain rescue

servicios de socorro emergency services

servilleta f [sairbee-y**ay**ta] serviette

servir [sairb**eer**] to serve

sesenta [say**sen**ta] sixty

sesión continua continuous showing
sesión de noche late showing
sesión de tarde early showing
setecientos [saytay-th-yentoss] seven hundred
setenta [setenta] seventy
sexto [sesto] sixth
si [see] if
sí [see] yes; oneself; herself; itself; yourself; themselves; yourselves; each other
si no otherwise
SIDA m AIDS
sido been
siempre [s-yempray] always
siempre que [kay] whenever; so long as
siento [s-yento] I sit down; I feel; I regret
  lo siento I'm sorry
siete [s-yaytay] seven
siga adelante straight ahead
siglo m century
siglo de oro XVI–XVII century
significar to mean
siguiente [seeg-yentay] next
  el día siguiente [dee-a] the day after
silencio m [seelenth-yo] silence
silla f [see-ya] chair
silla de ruedas [rwaydass] wheelchair
sillita de ruedas [see-yeeta] pushchair, buggy
sillón m [see-yon] armchair
similar (a) similar (to)

simpático nice
sin [seen] without
sin duda undoubtedly
sin embargo however
sin plomo unleaded
sinagoga f synagogue
sincero [seenthairo] sincere
sino but
sino que [kay] but
siquiera [seek-yaira] even if
sírvase [seerbasay] please
sírvase coger una cesta please take a basket
sírvase frío serve cold
sírvase usted mismo help yourself
sitio m [seet-yo] place
  en ningún sitio [neen-goon] nowhere
smoking m dinner jacket
sobrar to be left over; to be too many
sobre (m) [sobray] envelope; on; above
sobrecarga [sobraykarga] excess weight; extra charge
sobrina f niece
sobrino m nephew
sobrio [sobr-yo] sober
sociedad f [soth-yayda] society; company
socio m [soth-yo] associate; member
socorrer [sokorair] to help
socorrista mf lifeguard
¡socorro! help!
sois [soyss] you are
sol m sun
  al sol in the sun

solamente [solamentay] only
soleado [solay-ado] sunny
solo alone
sólo only
  no sólo ... sino también [tamb-yen] not only ... but also
sólo carga y descarga loading and offloading only
sólo laborables weekdays only
sólo monedas de nueva emisión only new coins
sólo motos motorcycles only
solo para residentes (del hotel) hotel patrons only
soltero (m) [soltairo] single; bachelor
solterón m bachelor
solterona f spinster
solución ... gotas solution ... drops
sombra f shade; shadow
sombra de ojos [oHoss] eye shadow
sombrero m [sombrairo] hat
sombrilla f [sombree-ya] parasol
somnífero m [somneefairo] sleeping pill
somos we are
son they are; you are
sonreír [sonray-eer] to smile
sordo deaf
sorprendente [sorprendentay] surprising
sorpresa f surprise
sortija f [sorteeHa] ring
sótano m basement
soy [soy] I am

sport: de sport casual
Sr (Señor) Mr
Sra (Señora) Mrs
Sres (Señores) Messrs
Srta (Señorita) Miss
starter m choke
stop m stop sign
su [soo] his; her; its; their; your
suave [swabay] soft
subir to go up; to get on; to get in; to put up
subtitulada sub-titled
subtítulos mpl subtitles
suburbios mpl [sooboorb-yoss] suburbs
suceder [soothedair] to happen
sucio [sooth-yo] dirty
sucursal f branch
sudar to sweat
Suecia f [swayth-ya] Sweden
sueco [swayko] Swedish
suegra f [swaygra] mother-in-law
suegro m father-in-law
suela f [swayla] sole
suelo (m) floor; I am used to
suelto m [swelto] change
sueño m [swayn-yo] dream; I dream
  tener sueño to be sleepy
suerte f [swairtay] luck
  por suerte luckily, fortunately
  ¡buena suerte! [bwayna] good luck!
suéter m [swaytair] sweater
suficiente: es suficiente

[soofeeth-**yen**tay] that's enough
sugerencias de presentación
serving suggestions
Suiza f [**swee**tha] Switzerland
sujetador m [sooHay-**tador**] bra
sumar to add
supe [**soo**pay] I knew
súper soopair] four-star
petrol, (US) premium (gas);
supermarket
supermercado m
[soopairmair**ka**do] supermarket
supuesto: por supuesto
[soop**wes**to] of course
sur m south
al sur de south of
sureste m [soo**res**tay] southeast
suroeste m [sooro-**es**tay] southwest
surtido m assortment
sus [**soo**ss] his; her; its; their;
your
susto m shock
susurrar to whisper
sutil subtle
suyo [**soo**-yo] his; hers; its;
theirs; yours

T

T.V.E. (Television Española)
Spanish Television
Tabacalera SA Spanish
tobacco monopoly
tabaco m tobacco
tabla de surf f surfboard
tabla de windsurf sailboard

tablero de instrumentos m
dashboard
tablón de anuncios m notice
board, (US) bulletin board
tablón de información [tab**lon**
day eenformath-**yon**] indicator
board
tacón m heel
tacones altos [ta**ko**ness] high
heels
tacones planos flat heels
TAF m slow diesel train
Tajo m [**ta**Ho] Tagus
tal such
con tal (de) que provided
that
tal vez [**bayth**] maybe
talco m talcum powder
TALGO m fast diesel train,
luxury train (supplement
required)
talla f [**ta**-ya] size
tallas sueltas odd sizes
tallas grandes large sizes
taller (de reparaciones) m [ta-
yair (day reparath-**yo**ness)] garage
talón m heel
talón de equipajes [ekeepa**Hess**]
baggage slip
talonario de cheques m
[talonar-yo day **che**kess] cheque
book
tamaño m [ta**man**-yo] size
también [tamb-**yen**] also
yo también me too
tampoco neither, nor
yo tampoco me neither
tan: tan bonito so beautiful
tan pronto como as soon as

tancat closed (in Catalan)

tanto (m) so much; point

tanto ... como ... both ... and ...

tantos so many

tapa f lid

tapas fpl savoury snacks, tapas

tapón m plug

taquilla f [takee-ya] ticket office

tarde (f) [tarday] afternoon; evening; late

a las tres de la tarde at 3 p.m.

esta tarde this afternoon, this evening

por la tarde in the evening

llegar tarde [yegar] to be late

tarifa f charge, charges

tarifa especial estudiante [espeth-yal estood-yantay] student reduced rate

tarifa normal standard rate

tarifa reducida [redootheeda] reduced rate

tarifas de servicio fares

tarjeta f [tarHayta] card

tarjeta bancaria cheque card

tarjeta de crédito credit card

tarjeta de embarque [embarkay] boarding pass

tarjeta de transporte público [transportay] travel card

tarjeta postal postcard

tarjeta telefónica phonecard

tauromaquia f [towromak-ya] bullfighting

taxista m/f taxi driver

taza f [tatha] cup

te [tay] you; yourself

teatro m [tay-atro] theatre

techo m ceiling

teclado m keyboard

tejado m [teHado] roof

tejanos mpl [teHanoss] jeans

tejidos mpl [teHeedoss] materials, fabrics

tela f [tayla] material; dosh

tele f [taylay] TV

telecabina f cable car

teleférico m cable car

telefonear [telefonay-ar] to telephone

teléfono m telephone

teléfono interurbano long-distance phone

teléfonos para casos urgentes emergency telephone numbers

telesilla m [telesee-ya] chairlift

telesquí m [teleskee] ski lift

televisor m television (set)

temer [temair] to fear

temor m fear

tempestad f storm

temporada f season

temprano early

ten hold

tenedor m fork

tener [tenair] to have

tener derecho to have the right

tener prisa to be in a hurry

tener prioridad [pree-oreeda] to have right of way

tener que [kay] to have to

tengo que I have to, I must

¡tenga cuidado! [kweedado] be careful!

tenis m tennis

tensión f [tens-yon] blood pressure

teñirse el pelo [ten-yeersay el paylo] to dye one's hair, to have one's hair dyed

TER m fast luxury diesel trains, a supplement is required

tercer piso m [tairthair] third floor, (US) fourth floor

tercero [tairthairo] third

tercio m [tairth-yo] third

terciopelo m [tairth-yopaylo] velvet

terco stubborn

terminal f [tairmeenal] terminus; terminal

terminal nacional domestic terminal

terminar to finish

termo m vacuum flask

termómetro m thermometer

test del embarazo [embaratho] pregnancy test

testigo m witness

tetera f [tetaira] teapot

tfno (teléfono) telephone

ti [tee] you

tía f [tee-a] aunt; bird, woman

tibio [teeb-yo] lukewarm

tiburón m shark

tiempo m [t-yempo] time; weather

a tiempo on time

tiempo de recreo [rekray-o] leisure

tiempo libre [leebray] free time

tienda f [t-yenda] shop, store; tent

esta tienda se translada a ... business is transferred to ...

tienda de artículos de piel [p-yayl] leather goods shop

tienda de artículos de regalo gift shop

tienda de comestibles [komesteebless] grocer's

tienda de deportes [deportess] sports shop

tienda de discos record shop

tienda de electrodomésticos electrical goods shop

tienda de lanas woollen goods shop

tienda de muebles [mwaybless] furniture shop

tienda de regalos gift shop

tienda de ultramarinos grocer's

tienda de vinos y licores off-licence, (US) liquor store

tienda libre de impuestos [leebray day eempwestoss] duty-free shop

tiendas: ir de tiendas to go shopping

tiene que [t-yaynay kay] he must

¿tiene ...? have you got ...?

tierra f [t-yairra] earth

tijeras fpl [teeHairass] scissors

timbre m [teembray] bell

timbre de alarma alarm bell

tímido shy

tintorería f [teentorairee-a] dry-cleaner's

tío m [tee-o] uncle; bloke, guy

tipo de cambio m [kamb-yo] exchange rate

tirar to pull; to throw; to throw away

tirita f Elastoplast®, Bandaid®

toalla f [to-a-ya] towel

toalla de baño [ban-yo] bath towel

tobillo m [tobee-yo] ankle

tocadiscos m record player

tocar to touch; to play

todavía [todabee-a] still; yet
  todavía no not yet

todo all, every; everything
  todos los días every day

todo derecho straight on

todo seguido [segeedo] straight ahead

todos everyone

tomamos la tensión we take your blood pressure

tomar to take

tomar el sol to sunbathe

tomavistas m cine-camera

tome usted take

tómese antes de las comidas to be taken before meals

tómese después de las comidas to be taken after meals

tómese ... veces al día to be taken ... times per day

tonelada f tonne

tono m dialling tone; shade

tonto silly

torcer [torthair] to twist; to sprain

torcerse un tobillo [oon tobee-yo] to twist one's ankle

torero m [torairo] bullfighter

tormenta f storm

tormentoso stormy

tornillo m [tornee-yo] screw

toro m bull

toros mpl bullfighting

torpe [torpay] clumsy

torre f [torray] tower

tos f cough

toser [tosair] to cough

tosferina f [tosfaireena] whooping cough

total: en total altogether

totalmente [-mentay] absolutely

tóxico [tokseeko] poisonous

trabajador [trabaHador] industrious

trabajar [trabaHar] to work

trabajo m [trabaHo] work

traducir [tradootheer] to translate

traer [tra-air] to bring

tragar to swallow

traigo [tra-eego] I bring

traje [traHay] I brought

traje m suit; dress

traje de baño [ban-yo] swimming costume

traje de noche [nochay] evening dress

traje de señora lady's suit

traje típico traditional regional costume

tranquilizante [trankeeleethantay]

tranquillizer

tranquilizarse [trankeeleetharsay] to calm down

tranquilo [trankeelo] quiet

transbordo m transfer; change

hacer transbordo en ... change at ...

transferencia f [transfairenth-ya] transfer

tras after

trasero (m) [trasairo] bottom; back; rear

tratar to treat

través: a través de across, through

travieso [trab-yayso] mischievous

trece [traythay] thirteen

treinta [tray-eenta] thirty

tren m [tren] train

tren de carga goods train

trenes de cercanías [treness day thairkanee-ass] local trains, suburban trains

tren de lavado automático car wash

tren de pasajeros [pasaHaiross] passenger train

tren directo through train

tren tranvía [tranbee-a] stopping train

tres [tress] three

tres cuartos de hora mpl three quarters of an hour

trescientos [tress-th-yentoss] three hundred

tripulación f [treepoolath-yon] crew

triste [treestay] sad

tristeza f [treestaytha] sadness

tronco m body; buddy

tropezar [tropethar] to trip

trozo (de) m [trotho (day)] piece (of)

trueno m [trwayno] thunder

tu [too] your

tú [too] you

tú mismo yourself

tubería f [toobairee-a] pipe

tubo de escape m [eskapay] exhaust

tubo de respirar snorkel

tuerza [twairtha] turn

tumbona f deck chair

túnel m tunnel

Túnez m [tooneth] Tunisia

turista m/f tourist

turno m turn; round

es mi turno it's my turn/round

turrón m [toorron] nougat

tus [tooss] your

tuyo [tooyo] yours

U

u [oo] or

Ud (usted) [oostay] you (sing)

Uds (ustedes) [oostaydess] you (plural)

úlcera (de estómago) f [oolthaira] (stomach) ulcer

últimamente [oolteemamentay] recently, lately

último last; latest

últimos días [dee-ass] last days

ultramarinos m grocer's

un [oon] a

una [oona] a

unas some

uno one; someone

unos some; a few

uña f [oon-ya] fingernail

urbana local

urbanización f [oorbaneethath-yon] housing estate

urgencias [oorHenth-yass] casualty department, emergencies

usado used; secondhand

usar to use

uso use

el uso del tabaco es perjudicial para su salud smoking can damage your health

uso externo not to be taken internally

uso obligatorio cinturón de seguridad seatbelts must be worn

Usted [oostay] you

Ustedes [oostaydess] you

útil useful

utilice sólo moneda fraccionaria small change only

V

v is pronounced more like a **b** than an English **v**

va he/she/it goes; you go

vaca f cow

vacaciones fpl [bakath-yoness] holiday, vacation

vacío [bathee-o] empty

vacuna f vaccination

vacunarse [bakoonarsay] to be vaccinated

vado permanente no parking at any time

vagón m carriage

vagón restaurante [restowrantay] restaurant car

vagón de literas [leetairass] sleeping car

vainilla f [ba-eenee-ya] vanilla

vais [ba-eess] you go

vajilla f [baHee-ya] crockery

vale [balay] OK

valer [balair] to be worth

valiente [bal-yentay] brave

valla f [ba-ya] fence

valle m [ba-yay] valley

valores mpl [baloress] securities

válvula f valve

vamos we go

van they go; you go

vapor m steamer

vaqueros mpl [bakaiross] jeans; cowboys

varicela f [bareethay-la] chickenpox

varios [bar-yoss] several

varón m male

varonil manly

vas you go

vasco Basque

Vascongadas fpl the Basque country

vaso m glass

vaya [ba-ya] go; I/he/she go; you go

¡vaya por Dios! [dee-oss] oh Christ!

¡váyase! [ba-yasay] go away!

¡váyase a paseo! [pasay-o] get lost!

Vd (usted) [oostay] you (sing)

Vds (ustedes) you (plural)

ve [bay] go; he/she sees; you see

veces: a veces [baythess] sometimes

vecino m [betheeno] neighbour

vehículos pesados heavy vehicles

veinte [bay-eentay] twenty

vejiga f [beHeega] bladder

vela f [bayla] candle; sail

velero m [belairo] sailing boat

velocidad f [belotheeda] speed

velocidad controlada por radar radar speed checks

velocidad limitada speed limits apply

velocidades fpl [belotheedadess] gears

velocímetro m [belotheemetro] speedometer

ven [ben] come; they see; you see

vena f [bayna] vein

venda f bandage

vendar to dress (wound)

vendemos a ... selling rate

vender [bendair] to sell

veneno m [benayno] poison

vengo I come

venir to come

venta f sale

de venta aquí on sale here

venta de localidades tickets (on sale)

venta de sellos stamps sold here

ventana f window

ventanilla f [bentanee-ya] window; ticket office

ventas a crédito credit terms available

ventas a plazos hire purchase, (US) installment plan

ventas al contado cash sales

ventilador m fan

ver [bair] to see; to watch

veraneante m [bairanay-antay] holidaymaker, vacationer

veranear [bairanay-ar] to holiday

verano m [bairano] summer

verbena f [bairbayna] open-air dance

verdad f [bairda] truth

¿de verdad? is that so?

¿verdad? don't you?; do you?; isn't he?; is he? etc

verdadero m [bairdadairo] true

verde (m) [bairday] green

versión f [bairs-yon] version

en versión original in the original language

vestido m dress

vestir to dress

de vestir formal

v is pronounced more like a **b** than an English **v**

vestirse [best**ee**rsay] to get dressed

vestuarios mpl [bestwar-yoss] fitting rooms

vez f [bayth] time
 una vez once
 en vez de instead of

vi [bee] I saw

vía aérea: por vía aérea by air mail

vía oral orally

vía rectal per rectum

viajar [b-ya**H**ar] to travel

viaje m [b-ya**H**ay] journey
 ¡buen viaje! [bwen] have a good trip!

viaje de negocios [neg**o**th-yoss] business trip

viaje de novios [n**o**b-yoss] honeymoon

viaje organizado [organeeth**a**do] package tour

viajero m [b-ya**H**airo] passenger

vida f life

vidrio m [b**ee**dr-yo] glass

viejo [b-y**ay**Ho] old

viene: la semana que viene [b-y**ay**nay] next week

viento m [b-y**e**nto] wind

vientre m [b-y**e**ntray] stomach

viernes [b-y**ai**rness] Friday

Viernes Santo m Good Friday

vine [b**ee**nay] I came

vinos y licores wines and spirits

viñedo [been-y**ay**do] vineyard

violación f [b-yolath-y**o**n] rape

violar [b-yolar] to rape

violento [b-yol**e**nto] violent; embarrassing, awkward
 sentirse violento to feel awkward

visado m visa

visita f visit

visita con guía [g**ee**-a] guided tour

visitante m/f [beeseet**a**ntay] visitor

visitar to visit

visor m viewfinder

víspera f [b**ee**spaira] the day before

vista f view
 ¡hasta la vista! see you!

vista turística scenic view

visto seen

viuda f [b-y**oo**da] widow

viudo m widower

vivir to live

vivo alive; I live

VO (versión original) original language

volante m [bol**a**ntay] steering wheel

volar to fly

voltaje [bolta**H**ay] voltage

volver [bolb**ai**r] to come back

volver a hacer algo to do something again

volver a casa to go home

vomitar to vomit

vosotras, vosotros you

v.o. subtitulada version in the original language with

subtitles
voy I go
voz f [both] voice
vuelo m [bwaylo] flight
vuelo nacional [nath-yonal] domestic flight
vuelo regular scheduled flight
vuelta f [bwelta] change
 la vuelta al colegio [kolay-Hyo] back to school
vuelvo [bwelbo] I return
vuestra [bwestra], **vuestras, vuestro, vuestros** your; yours

cobbler; shoe repairer
zapatillas fpl [thapatee-yass] slippers
zapatos mpl [thapatoss] shoes
zona f [thona] area
zona de avalanchas frequent avalanches
zona monumental historic monuments
zona (reservada) para peatones pedestrian precinct
zona azul [athool] restricted parking area, permit holders only
zona de servicios [sairbeeth-yoss] service area
zurdo [thoordo] left-handed

W

wáter [batair] toilet, rest room

Y

y [ee] and
ya already
 ya está there you are
 ya ... ya sometimes ... sometimes
 ya que [kay] since
yerno m [yairno] son-in-law
yo I; me
 yo mismo myself

Z

zapatería f [thapatairee-a] shoe shop/store
zapatero m [thapatairo]

Zu

Menu Reader
Food

aceite [athay-eetay] oil

aceite de oliva [day oleeba] olive oil

aceitunas [athay-eetoonass] olives

aceitunas aliñadas [aleen-yadass] olives with salad dressing

aceitunas negras black olives

aceitunas rellenas [ray-yaynass] stuffed olives

aceitunas verdes [bairdess] green olives

acelgas [athelgass] chard, spinach beet

achicoria [acheekor-ya] chicory

aguacate [agwakatay] avocado

aguja de ternera [agooHa day tairnaira] veal for stewing

ahumados [a-oomadoss] smoked fish

ahumados variados [baree-adoss] smoked fish

ajillo [aHee-yo] garlic

ajo [aHo] garlic

alaju [ala-Hoo] nougat–type sweet made from walnuts or pine nuts, toasted breadcrumbs and honey

albahaca [alba-aka] basil

albaricoque [albareekokay] apricot

albóndigas meatballs

albóndigas de lomo [day] pork meatballs

alcachofas artichokes

alcachofas en vinagreta [beenagrayta] artichokes in vinaigrette dressing

alcachofas a la andaluza [andalootha] artichokes with ham and bacon

alcachofas a la romana artichokes in batter

alcaparras capers

aliñada [aleen-yada] with salad dressing

ali oli garlic mayonnaise

almejas [almay-Hass] clams

almejas a la buena mujer [bwayna mooHair] clams stewed with chillies, white wine, lemon and herbs

almejas a la marinera [mareenaira] clams stewed in white wine and parsley

almejas a la valenciana [balenth-yana] clams in a white wine sauce

almejas al natural [natooral] live clams

almejas en salsa verde [bairday] clams in parsley and white wine sauce

almejas naturales [natooraless] live clams

almendra almond

alubias [aloob-yass] beans

alubias blancas white kidney beans

alubias rojas [roHass] red kidney beans

ancas de rana frogs' legs

ancas de rana albuferena [alboofairayna] frogs' legs in a sauce made from chicken soup, mushrooms and paprika anchoas [ancho-ass] anchovies

anchoas a la barquera [barkaira] marinated anchovies with capers

anguila [angeela] eel

anguila ahumada [a-oomada] smoked eel

angulas baby eels

angulas al all-i-pebre [all-ee-pebray] baby eels with garlic and black pepper

añojo [an-yoHo] veal

apio [ap-yo] celery

arenques frescos [arenkess] fresh herrings

arroz [arroth] rice

arroz a la cubana boiled rice with fried eggs and either bananas or tomato sauce

arroz a la emperatriz [empairatreeth] rice with milk, apricots, truffles, raisins, Cointreau and gelatine

arroz a la turca [toorka] boiled rice with curry sauce, onions and tomatoes

arroz a la valenciana [balenth-yana] paella

arroz blanco boiled white rice

arroz con leche [lechay] rice pudding

asado roast

asados roast meats

asadurilla [asadooree-ya] lambs' liver stew

atún [atoon] tuna

atún al horno [orno] baked tuna

avellana [abay-yana] hazelnut

aves [abess] poultry

azafrán [athafran] saffron

azúcar [athookar] sugar

bacalao a la catalana [bakala-o] cod with ham, almond, garlic and parsley

bacalao al ajo arriero [aHo arr-yairo] cod with garlic, peppers and chillies

bacalao a la vizcaína [beethka-eena] cod served with ham, peppers and chillies

bacalao al pil pil [peel] cod cooked in olive oil

baveresa de coco [babairaysa day] cold coconut sweet

becadas snipe

becadas a la vizcaína [beethka-eena] snipe served with bacon, onion and sherry sauce

becadas asadas baked snipe

berenjena [bairenHayna] aubergine, eggplant

berenjenas a la mallorquina [ma-yorkeena] aubergines/eggplants with garlic mayonnaise

berza [bairtha] cabbage

besugo bream

besugo al horno [al orno] baked sea bream

besugo asado baked sea bream

besugo mechado sea bream stuffed with ham and bacon

bien hecho [b-yen echo] well done

bistec a la riojana [r-yoнana] steak with fried red peppers

bistec de ternera [tairn**ai**ra] veal steak

bizcocho [beethk**o**cho] sponge finger

bocadillo [bokadee-yo] sandwich, snack

bogavante [bogab**a**ntay] lobster

bollo [bo-yo] roll

bomba helada [el**a**da] baked alaska

bonito tuna

bonito al horno [**o**rno] baked tuna

boquerones en vinagre [bokair**o**ness en been**a**gray] anchovies in vinaigrette

boquerones fritos fried fresh anchovies

brandada de bacalao [bakal**a**-o] creamy cod purée

brazo de gitano [br**a**tho day нe**e**tano] swiss roll

brevas [br**e**bass] figs

broqueta de riñones [brok**e**ta day reen-y**o**ness] kidney kebabs

buey [boo-**ay**] beef

buñuelos [boon-yw**ay**loss] light fried pastry

buñuelos de bacalao [bakal**a**-o] fried pastry containing flaked, dried, salted cod

buñuelos de cuaresma rellenos [day kwar**e**sma ray-y**ay**noss] light fried pastries with chocolate and cream

butifarra Catalan sausage – contains bacon

butifarra con rovellons [robay-y**o**ns] Catalan sausage with mushrooms

butifarra con setas Catalan sausage with mushrooms

buvangos rellenos [boob**a**ngoss ray-y**ay**noss] stuffed courgettes/zucchini

cabello de ángel [kab**ay**-yo day] sweet pumpkin filling (used in cakes)

cabracho mullet

cabrito asado roast kid

cacahuetes [kakaw**ay**tess] peanuts

cachelada [kachel**a**da] pork stew with eggs, tomato, onion and boiled potatoes

cachelos [kach**ay**loss] boiled potatoes served with spicy sausage and bacon

calabacines [kalabath**ee**ness] courgettes, zucchini; marrow

calabaza [kalab**a**tha] pumpkin

calamares a la romana [kalam**a**ress] squid rings fried in batter

calamares en su tinta [t**ee**nta] squid cooked in their ink

calamares fritos fried squid

caldeirada [kalday-eer**a**da] fish soup

caldera de dátiles de mar [kald**ai**ra day d**a**teeless] seafood stew

caldereta de cordero a la pastora [kaldair**ay**ta day kord**ai**ro] lamb and vegetable stew

caldereta gallega [ga-**yay**ga] vegetable stew

caldo clear soup

caldo de gallina [ga-**yee**na] chicken soup

caldo de perdiz [pair**deeth**] partridge soup

caldo de pescado clear fish soup

caldo gallego [ga-**yay**go] clear soup with green vegetables, beans and pork

caldo guanche [**gwan**chay] soup made from potatoes, onions, tomatoes and courgettes/zucchini

callos a la madrileña [ka-yoss a la madreel**en**-ya] tripe cooked with chillies

camarones [kama**ron**ess] baby prawns

canela [ka**nay**la] cinnamon

canelones [kanel**on**ess] canneloni

cangrejo [kan**gray**-нo] crab

cangrejos de río river crabs

caracoles [kara**kol**ess] snails

caracoles a la madrileña [madreel**en**-ya] snails cooked with chillies

carbonada de buey [boo-**ay**] beef cooked in beer

cardo type of thistle, eaten as a vegetable

carne [**kar**nay] meat

carne de cerdo [**thair**do] pork

carne de membrillo [membr**ee**-yo] quince jelly (dessert)

carne de vaca [**bak**a] beef

carne picada minced meat

carnero [kar**nair**o] mutton

carnes [**kar**ness] meat; meat dishes

carro de queso [**kay**so] cheese board

carta menu

castaña [kas**tan**-ya] chestnut

caza [**kath**a] game

cazuela [kath**way**la] casserole

cazuela de chichas meat casserole

cazuela de hígado [**ee**gado] liver casserole

cebolla [the**bo**-ya] onion

cebolletas [thebo-**yet**ass] spring onions

cecina [the**thee**na] dry cured meat

centollo [then**to**-yo] spider crab

centollo relleno [ray-**yay**no] spider crab cooked in its shell

cerdo [**thair**do] pork, pig

cereza [thair**ay**tha] cherry

cesta de frutas [**thes**ta day **froot**ass] a selection of fresh fruit

champiñón a la crema [champeen-**yon** – kr**ay**ma] mushrooms in cream sauce

champiñón al ajillo [aн**ee**-yo] mushrooms fried with garlic

champiñón a la plancha grilled mushrooms

champiñones [champeen-**yon**ess] mushrooms

chanfaina [chanfa-**ee**na] rice

and black pudding stew

chanfaina castellana [kastay-**ya**na] rice and sheeps' liver stew

changurro spider crab cooked in its shell

chanquetes [chank**ay**tess] fish (like whitebait)

chateaubrian [chatobr**ee**-an] thick steak

chicharros horse mackerel

chipirones [cheepeer**o**ness] baby squid

chipirones en su tinta [**tee**nta] baby squid cooked in their ink

chipirones rellenos [ray-**yay**noss] stuffed baby squid

chirimoyas [cheereem**o**-yass] custard apples

chocos squid

chocos con habas [**a**bass] squid with broad beans

chorizo [chor**ee**tho] spicy red sausage

chuleta [chool**ay**ta] chop

chuleta de buey [day boo-**ay**] beef chop

chuleta de cerdo [th**ai**rdo] pork chop

chuleta de cerdo empanada breaded pork chop

chuleta de cordero [kord**ai**ro] lamb chop

chuleta de ternera [tairn**ai**ra] veal chop

chuleta de ternera empanada breaded veal chop

chuletas de gamo venison chops

chuletas de lomo ahumado [a-oom**a**do] smoked pork chops

chuletas de venado [ben**a**do] venison chops

chuletitas de cordero [day kord**ai**ro] small lamb chops

chuletón large chop

chuletón de ternera a la diable roja [d-y**a**blay ro**H**a] large, grilled, breaded veal chop

churros fried pastry strips

cigala [the**e**gala] crayfish

cigalas a la parrilla [parr**ee**-ya] grilled crayfish

cigalas cocidas [koth**ee**dass] boiled crayfish

ciruela [theerw**ay**la] plum, greengage

ciruelas pasas prunes

civet de liebre [the**e**bet day l-y**ay**bray] marinated hare

coca amb pinxes [k**o**ka am pe**e**nsess] sardine pie

cochinillo asado [kocheen**ee**-yo] roast sucking pig

cocido [koth**ee**do] stew made from meat, chickpeas and vegetables

cocido castellano/madrileño [kastay-y**a**no/madreel**e**n-yo] stew made from meat, chickpeas, vegetables etc

cocochas (de merluza) [mairl**oo**tha] hakes' gills

cóctel de bogavante [bogab**a**ntay] lobster cocktail

cóctel de gambas prawn

233

cocktail

cóctel de langostinos king prawn cocktail

cóctel de mariscos seafood cocktail

codillo de cerdo con chucrut [kodee-yo day thairdo kon chookroot] pigs' trotters with sauerkraut

codoñate [kodon-yatay] cake made with chestnuts, honey and quince

codoñate de nueces [nwaythess] cake made with walnuts

codornices [kodorneethess] quail

codornices con uvas [oobass] quail stewed with grapes

codornices estofadas braised quail

col cabbage

coles de Bruselas [koless day broosaylass] Brussels sprouts

coliflor cauliflower

coliflor con bechamel cauliflower cheese

comino cumin

conejo [konay-Ho] rabbit

conejo encebollado [entheboyado] rabbit served with onions

conejo estofado braised rabbit

congrio [kongr-yo] conger eel

consomé al jerez [konsomay al Haireth] consommé with sherry

consomé con yema [yayma] consommé with egg yolk

consomé de ave [abay] chicken consommé

consomé de pollo [po-yo] chicken consommé

contra de ternera con guisantes [tairnaira kon geesantess] veal stew with peas

contrafilete de ternera [kontrafeelaytay day] veal fillet

copa de helado [elado] assorted ice cream served in a stemmed glass

cordero [kordairo] lamb

cordero chilindrón lamb stew with onion, tomato, peppers and eggs

corvina [korbeena] Mediterranean fish, similar to sea bass

costillas de cerdo [kostee-yas day thairdo] pork ribs

costillas de cerdo con chucrut [chookroot] pork ribs with sauerkraut

crema catalana [krayma] crème caramel

cremada dessert made from egg, sugar and milk

crema de cangrejos [krayma day kangray-Hoss] cream of crab soup

crema de espárragos cream of asparagus soup

crema de espinacas cream of spinach soup

crema de legumbres/verduras [legoombrays/bairdoorass] cream of vegetable soup

crep(e) pancake

crep(e)s imperiales [eempair-**yaless**] crêpe suzette

criadillas [kree-a**dee**-yass] bulls' testicles; truffles (edible fungus); root vegetable

criadillas de ternera [tair**nair**a] calves' testicles

criadillas de tierra [t-**yair**ra] truffles (edible fungus)

criadillas en salsa verde [**bair**day] root vegetable in parsley sauce

crocante [krok**an**tay] ice cream with chopped nuts

croquetas [krok**ay**tass] croquettes

crudo raw

cuajada [kwa**Ha**da] junket, curds

dátiles [**dat**eeless] dates

dátiles de mar shellfish

delicias de queso [de**lee**th-yass day **kay**so] cheese croquettes

dulce de membrillo [**dool**thay day membr**ee**-yo] quince jelly

embutidos cured pork sausages

embutidos de la tierra [t-**yair**ra] local sausages

empanada gallega [ga-**yay**ga] pie with chicken, chorizo sausage, peppers, ham, onions and tuna

empanada santiaguesa [sant-yag**ays**a] fish pie

empanado in breadcrumbs

empanadillas [empana**dee**-yass]

small pies

empanadillas de chorizo [chor**eet**ho] small pies filled with spicy sausage

endivias [end**eeb**-yass] endive

ensaimada mallorquina [ensa-eem**a**da ma-york**een**a] large, spiral-shaped bun

ensalada salad

ensalada de frutas fruit salad

ensalada ilustrada mixed salad

ensalada mixta [**mees**ta] mixed salad

ensalada simple [**seem**play] green salad

ensaladilla [ensala**dee**-ya] Spanish salad

ensaladilla rusa [**roo**sa] Russian salad

entrantes [entr**an**tess] entrées, starters

entrecot a la parrilla [entre**kot** – parr**ee**-ya] grilled entrecôte steak

entrecot a la pimienta [peem-**yen**ta] entrecôte in black pepper sauce

entremés [entre**mayss**] hors d'oeuvre, starter

entremeses [entre**may**sess] hors d'oeuvres

entremeses de la casa hors d'oeuvres – house speciality

entremeses variados [bar-**yad**oss] assorted hors d'oeuvres

escabeche de ... [eska**be**chay] marinated ...

escalibada flaked cod and vegetable salad (Catalan dish)
escalope a la milanesa [eskalopay] breaded veal escalope with cheese
escalope a la parrilla [parree-ya] grilled veal
escalope a la plancha grilled veal
escalope Cordon Bleu veal escalope with ham and cheese
escalope de cerdo [thairdo] pork escalope
escalope de lomo de cerdo escalope of fillet of pork
escalope de ternera [tairnaira] veal escalope
escalopines al vino de Marsala [eskalopeeness – beeno] veal escalopes cooked in wine
escalopines de ternera [tairnaira] veal escalopes
escarola endive
espadín a la toledana kebab
espaguetis italiana [espagayteess eetal-yana] spaghetti
espárragos asparagus
espárragos calientes [kal-yentess] grilled asparagus with béchamel sauce
espárragos dos salsas asparagus with mayonnaise and vinagrette dressing
espárragos en vinagreta [beenagrayta] asparagus in vinaigrette dressing

espárragos trigueros [treegayross] green asparagus
especia [espayth-ya] spice
especialidad speciality
espina fishbone
espinacas spinach
espinazo de cerdo con patatas [espeenatho day thairdo] pork ribs with potatoes
espuma de jamón [day Hamon] boiled ham mousse
estofado stew; stewed
estofado de liebre [l-yaybray] hare stew
estofado de liebre con níscalos hare stew with wild mushrooms
estofados stews
estragón tarragon
fabada (asturiana) [astoor-yana] bean stew with red sausage, black pudding and pork
fabricación: de fabricación casera homemade
faisán [fa-eesan] pheasant
faisán trufado [troofado] pheasant with truffles
farinato fried sausage
fiambres [f-yambress] cold meats, cold cuts
fideos [feeday-oss] thin pasta; noodles; vermicelli
filete [feelaytay] steak; fillet
filete a la parrilla [parree-ya] grilled beef steak
filete a la plancha grilled beef steak
filete de cerdo [thairdo] pork steak

filete de ternera [tairn**ai**ra] veal steak

flan crème caramel

flan con nata crème caramel with whipped cream

flan de café [day kaf**ay**] coffee-flavoured crème caramel

flan de caramelo [karam**ay**lo] crème caramel

flan (quemado) al ron [kem**a**do] crème caramel with rum

frambuesa [frambw**ay**sa] raspberry

fresa [fr**ay**sa] strawberry

fresas con nata strawberries and cream

fritanga al modo de Alicante [day aleek**a**ntay] dish of fried peppers, tuna and garlic

frito fried

fritos de la casa fried hors d'oeuvres – house speciality

fritos variados [bar-y**a**doss] fried hors d'oeuvres

fruta fruit

frutas en almíbar fruit in syrup

fruta variada [bar-y**a**da] assorted fresh fruit

gachas manchegas type of sweet or savoury porridge

galleta [ga-y**ay**ta] biscuit

gallina a la cairatraca [ga-y**ee**na a la ka-eeratr**a**ka] stewed chicken

gallina en pepitoria [pepeet**or**-ya] stewed chicken with peppers, onions and tomato

gamba prawn

gambas a la americana prawns with brandy and garlic

gambas al ajillo [aн**ee**-yo] prawns with garlic

gambas a la plancha grilled prawns

gambas cocidas [koth**ee**dass] boiled prawns

gambas en gabardina prawns in batter

gambas rebozadas [reboth**a**dass] prawns in batter

garbanzos [garb**a**nthoss] chickpeas

garbanzos a la catalana chickpeas with sausage, boiled eggs and pine nuts

gazpacho andaluz [gathp**a**cho andal**ooth**] cold soup made from tomatoes, onions, garlic, peppers and cucumber

gazpacho manchego rabbit stew with tomato and garlic, sometimes also with partridge meat

gelatina [Helat**ee**na] jelly

gratén de ... ... au gratin

grelo turnip

guisado de cordero [gees**a**do day kord**ai**ro] stewed lamb

guisado de costillas de ternera [kostee-y**a**ss day tairn**ai**ra] rib of veal stew

guisado de ternera stewed veal

guisantes [gees**a**ntess] peas

habas [**a**bass] broad beans

habas fritas fried young broad beans

habichuelas [abeechwaylass] haricot beans; white kidney beans

hamburguesa [amboorgaysa] hamburger

harina [areena] flour

helado [elado] ice cream

helado de caramelo [karamaylo] caramel ice cream

helado de mantecado dairy ice cream

helado de nata dairy ice cream

helado de vainilla [ba-eenee-ya] vanilla ice cream

hierbas [yairbass] herbs

hígado [eegado] liver

hígado de ternera estofado [tairnaira] braised calves' liver

hígado encebollado [enthebo-yado] liver in an onion sauce

hígado estofado braised liver

higos [eegoss] figs

higos secos dried figs

hornazo [ornatho] Easter cake

horno: al horno baked

huevo [waybo] egg

huevo duro [dooro] hard-boiled egg

huevo hilado [eelado] shredded boiled eggs used as a garnish

huevo pasado por agua [ag-wa] boiled egg

huevos a la española [espan-yola] fried eggs

huevos a la flamenca baked eggs with sausage, tomato, peas, asparagus and peppers

huevos cocidos [kotheedoss] hard-boiled eggs

huevos con picadillo [peekadee-yo] eggs with minced sausage meat

huevos duros con mayonesa [ma-yonaysa] egg mayonnaise

huevos escalfados poached eggs

huevos fritos fried eggs

huevos fritos con chorizo [choreetho] fried eggs with Spanish sausage

huevos pasados por agua [ag-wa] boiled eggs

huevos rellenos [ray-yaynoss] stuffed eggs

huevos revueltos [rebweltoss] scrambled eggs

incluye pan, postre y vino includes bread, dessert and wine

IVA no incluido VAT not included

jamón [Hamon] ham

jamón con huevo hilado [waybo eelado] ham with shredded egg garnish

jamón de Jabugo [day Haboogo] jamón ibérico from Jabugo, Huelva

jamón ibérico [eebaireeko] Spanish ham

jamón serrano [sairrano] cured ham, similar to Parma ham

jamón York boiled ham

jarrete de ternera [Harray tay day tairnaira] veal hock

jeta [Heta] pigs' cheeks

jeta rebozada [rebothada] pigs' cheek in batter

judías [Hoodee-ass] beans

judías verdes [bairdess] green beans

judías verdes a la española [espan-yola] French bean stew

judías verdes al natural [natooral] plain green beans

judías verdes con jamón [Hamon] French beans with ham

judiones [Hood-yoness] broad beans

lacón con grelos bacon with turnip tops

langosta lobster

langosta a la americana lobster with brandy and garlic

langosta a la catalana lobster with mushrooms and ham in a white sauce

langosta con mahonesa [ma-onaysa] lobster with mayonnaise

langosta fría con mayonesa cold lobster with mayonnaise

langosta gratinada lobster au gratin

langostinos a la plancha grilled king prawns

langostinos dos salsas king prawns cooked in two sauces

laurel [lowrel] bay leaves

lebrato hare

leche frita [lechay freeta] slices of thick custard fried in breadcrumbs

leche merengada cold milk with meringues and cinnamon

lechuga [lechooga] lettuce

lengua [lengwa] tongue

lengua de buey [boo-ay] ox tongue

lenguado a la parrilla [lengwado a la parree-ya] grilled sole

lenguado a la plancha grilled sole

lenguado a la romana sole in batter

lenguado al chacolí con hongos [ongoss] sole with mushrooms and white wine

lenguado frito fried sole

lenguado grillado [gree-yado] grilled sole

lenguado menie/meuniere [men-yair] sole meunière – sole coated in flour, fried and served with butter, lemon juice and parsley

lenguado rebozado [rebothado] sole in batter

lentejas [lentay-Hass] lentils

lentejas aliñadas [aleen-yadass] lentils in vinaigrette dressing

lentejas onubenses [onoobensess] lentils with spicy sausage, onion and garlic

liba rebozada [rebothada] sea bass fried in batter

liebre estofada [l-yaybray] stewed hare

lima [leema] lime

limón lemon

lombarda red cabbage

lomo curado [koorado] cured pork sausage

lomo de liebre [l-yaybray] loin of hare

lonchas de jamón [Hamon] slices of cured ham

longaniza [longaneetha] cooked Spanish sausage

lubina a la cantábrica sea bass with garlic, lemon juice and white wine

lubina a la marinera [mareenaira] sea bass in a parsley sauce

macarrones [makarroness] macaroni

macarrones gratinados macaroni cheese

macedonia de fruta [mathedon-ya] fruit salad

maduro [madooro] ripe

magdalena [magdalayna] muffin

magras con tomate [tomatay] slices of cured ham with tomato

mahonesa [ma-onaysa] mayonnaise

maíz [ma-eeth] sweetcorn

mandarinas tangerines

manises [maneesess] peanuts

manitas de cordero [kordairo]

leg of lamb

manos de cerdo [thairdo] pigs' trotters

mantecadas small sponge cakes

mantecado vanilla ice cream

mantequilla [mantekee-ya] butter

manzana [manthana] apple

manzanas a la malvasía [malbassee-a] apples in syrup

manzanas asadas baked apples

mariscada cold mixed shellfish

mariscos seafood

mariscos del día fresh shellfish

mariscos del tiempo [t-yempo] seasonal shellfish

marmitako tuna and vegetable stew

mayonesa [ma-yonaysa] mayonnaise

mazapán [mathapan] marzipan

medallones de anguila [meda-yoness day angeela] eel steaks

medallones de merluza [mairlootha] hake steaks

mejillones [may-нее-yoness] mussels

mejillones a la marinera [mareenaira] mussels in wine sauce with garlic and parsley

mejillones con salsa mussels with tomato and herb sauce

melocotón peach

melocotones en almíbar

[melokotoness] peaches in syrup

melón melon

melón al calisay [kaleesi] melon with a spirit or liqueur poured over it

melón con jamón [Hamon] melon with cured ham

membrillo [membree-yo] quince

menestra de legumbres [legoombress] vegetable stew made from pulses

menestra de verduras [bairdoorass] vegetable stew

menú [menoo] set menu

menú de la casa fixed price menu

menú del día today's set menu

merluza a la castellana [mairlootha – kastay-yana] hake with clams, prawns, linseeds, eggs and chilli

merluza a la cazuela [kathwayla] hake casserole

merluza al ajo arriero [aHo arr-yairo] hake with garlic and chillies

merluza a la riojana [r-yoHana] hake with chillies

merluza a la romana hake steaks in batter

merluza a la vasca [baska] hake in a garlic sauce

merluza caldo corto hake with vegetable sauce

merluza en salsa verde [bairday] hake in parsley and white wine sauce

merluza fría [free-a] cold hake

merluza frita fried hake

merluza koskera [koskaira] hake in a garlic sauce

merluza (lomos de) con angulas y almejas [ee almay-Hass] hake fillet with baby eels and clams

mermelada [mairmelada] jam; marmalade

mero [mairo] grouper (fish)

mero a la levantina [lebanteena] grouper with lemon juice and rosemary

mero en salsa verde [bairday] grouper with garlic, parsley and white wine sauce

miel [m-yel] honey

mojete [moHay-tay] 'dipping' sauce for bread, usually made from vegetables

mojojones [moHoHoness] mussels

mollejas con setas [mo-yay-Hass] lambs' gizzards with mushrooms

mollejas de ternera [tairnaira] calves' sweetbreads

mora blackberry

morcilla [morthee-ya] black pudding, blood sausage

morcilla de ternera [tairnaira] black pudding made from calves' blood

morros de cerdo [thairdo] pigs' cheeks

morros de vaca [day baka] cows' cheeks

morros de vaca pastora cows'

cheeks with vegetables

mortadela salami-type sausage

morteruelo [mortair-**way**lo] breaded minced liver

mostaza [most**ath**a] mustard

mousse de limón lemon mousse

mújol guisado [moo**Hol** gees**a**do] red mullet

nabo turnip

naranja [naran**Ha**] orange

nata cream

nata batida whipped cream

natillas [nat**ee**-yass] cold custard with cinnamon

natillas de chocolate [choko**latay**] cold custard with chocolate

níscalos wild mushrooms

nísperos [**nee**spaiross] medlars – fruit similar to crab apple

nueces [nw**ay**thess] walnuts

nuez [nw**ayth**] nut

ñoquis [n-**yo**keess] potato gnocchi

oca en adobo marinaded goose

orejas de cerdo [or**ay**-Has day th**air**do] pigs' ears

orejas y pie de cerdo [ee p-**yay**] pigs' ears and trotters

ostra oyster

otros mariscos según precios en plaza other shellfish, depending on current prices

pa amb tomaquet bread spread with olive oil and

tomato sauce

paella [pa-**ay**-ya] fried rice with seafood and chicken

paella castellana [kastay-**ya**na] meat paella

paella de marisco shellfish paella

paella de pollo [po-yo] chicken paella

paella especial [espeth-**yal**] paella house speciality

paella mixta [**mee**sta] shellfish and chicken paella

paella valenciana [balenth-**ya**na] paella with assorted shellfish and chicken

paleta de cordero lechal [kord**air**o] shoulder of lamb

paloma pigeon

pan bread

panaché de verduras [panach**ay** day baird**oo**rass] vegetable stew

pan blanco white bread

panceta [panth**ay**ta] bacon

pan de higos [**ee**goss] dried fig cake with cinnamon

pan integral wholemeal bread

parrilla: a la parrilla grilled

parrillada de caza [parree-**ya**da day **ka**tha] mixed grilled game

parrillada de mariscos mixed grilled shellfish

pasas raisins

pasta biscuit; pastry; pasta

pastel cake; pie

pastel de hígado de cerdo [**ee**gado day th**air**do] pigs' liver pie pastel de higos [**ee**goss] fig cake

pastel de ternera [tairn**ai**ra] veal pie

pastel de verduras con salsa de champiñones silvestres [baird**oo**rass –champeen-**yo**ness seelb**e**stress] vegetable pie with wild mushroom sauce

pasteles [past**ay**less] cakes

patas de cordero [kord**ai**ro] stewed leg of lamb

patata potato

patatas a la pescadora potatoes with fish

patatas asadas roast potatoes

patatas bravas [br**a**bass] potatoes in cayenne sauce

patatas con nabos potatoes with turnips

patatas estofadas boiled potatoes

patatas fritas chips, French fries; crisps, potato chips

patitos rellenos [ray-y**ay**noss] stuffed duckling

pato duck

pato a la naranja [naran-Ha] duck à l'orange

pavipollo [pabeep**o**-yo] large chicken

pavo [p**a**bo] turkey

pavo a la Asturiana [astoor-y**a**na] turkey with red wine and paprika

pavo relleno a la catalana turkey stuffed with sausage, pork and plums

pavo trufado turkey stuffed

with truffles

pecho de ternera [tairn**ai**ra] breast of veal

pechuga de pollo [p**o**-yo] breast of chicken

peixo-palo a la marinera [p**e**sho – mareen**ai**ra] stock-fish with potatoes and tomato

pepinillos [pepeen**ee**-yoss] gherkins

pepinillos en vinagreta [beenagr**ay**ta] gherkins in vinaigrette dressing

pepino cucumber

pera pear

percebes [pairth**ay**bess] barnacles (shellfish)

perdices [paird**ee**thess] partridges

perdices a la campesina partridges with vegetables

perdices a la manchega partridges cooked in red wine, garlic, herbs and pepper

perdiz encebollada [pairde**e**th enthebo-y**a**da] partridge with onion sauce

perejil [pairay-H**ee**l] parsley

pescaditos fritos fried sprats

pescado fish

pestiños [pest**ee**n-yoss] sugared pastries flavoured with aniseed

pestiños con miel [m-yel] fried sugared pastries flavoured with aniseed and honey

pez [payth] fish

pez espada ahumado

[a-oo**ma**do] smoked swordfish

picadillo [peeka**dee**-yo] salad of diced vegetables; stew of pork, bacon, garlic and eggs

picadillo de ternera [tair**nai**ra] minced veal

pichones estofados [peecho**ness**] stewed pigeon

pimentón paprika

pimienta (negra) [peem-**yen**ta] black pepper

pimienta blanca white pepper

pimienta de cayena [ka-**yay**na] cayenne pepper

pimiento pepper

pimientos a la riojana [r-yo**Ha**na] baked red peppers fried in oil and garlic

pimientos fritos fried peppers

pimientos morrones [mor**ro**ness] strong peppers

pimientos rellenos [ray-**yay**noss] stuffed peppers

pimientos verdes [**bair**dess] green peppers

pinchitos snacks/appetizers served in bars; kebabs

pinchos snacks served in bars

pinchos morunos kebabs

pintada guinea fowl

piña [**peen**-ya] pineapple

piña al gratén pineapple au gratin

piña fresca fresh pineapple

piñones [peen-**yo**ness] pine nuts

piparrada vasca [**bas**ca] pepper and tomato stew with ham and eggs

piriñaca [peereen-**ya**ka] tuna and vegetable salad

pisto fried peppers, onions, tomatoes and courgettes/zucchini

pisto manchego marrow, onion and tomato stew

plancha: a la plancha grilled

plátano banana

plátanos flameados [flamay-**a**doss] flambéed bananas

platos combinados meat and vegetables, hamburgers and eggs etc, mixture of various foods served as one dish; set menu

pochas con almejas [almay-**Hass**] white beans with clams

poco hecho [**ech**o] rare

pollo [**po**-yo] chicken

pollo al ajillo [a**Hee**-yo] fried chicken with garlic

pollo a la parrilla [par**ree**-ya] grilled chicken

pollo a la riojana [r-yo**Ha**na] chicken with peppers and chillies

pollo asado roast chicken

pollo braseado [brasay-**a**do] braised chicken

pollo en cacerola [kathai**ro**la] chicken casserole

pollo en chanfaina [chanfa-**ee**na] chicken with fried peppers, onions, tomatoes and courgettes/zucchini

pollo en pepitoria [pepee**tor**-ya] chicken in wine with saffron, garlic and almonds

pollo reina clamart [**ray-ee**na] roast chicken with vegetables

pollos tomateros con zanahorias [tomat**ai**ros kon thana-**or**-yass] baby chickens with carrots

polvorones [polbor**o**ness] sugar-based dessert (eaten at Christmas)

pomelo grapefruit

postre [**po**stray] dessert

postre sorpresa al DYC [sorpr**ay**sa al deek] whisky-flavoured dessert

potaje castellano [pota**H**ay kast**ay**-yano] thick broth

potaje de garbanzos [garb**a**nthoss] chickpea stew

potaje de habichuelas [habeechw**ay**lass] white bean stew

potaje de lentejas [lent**ay**-Hass] lentil stew

primer plato starters

pucherete al estilo montañés [poochair**e**tay al est**ee**lo montan-**yess**] black pudding and spicy sausage stew

puchero canario [pooch**ai**ro kanar-yo] casserole of meat, chickpeas and corn

puerro [pw**ai**rro] leek

pulpitos con cebolla [theb**o**-ya] baby octopuses with onions

pulpo octopus

puré de patata [poor**ay** day] potato purée, mashed

potatoes

purrusalda cod soup with leeks and potatoes

PVP price

queso [**kay**so] cheese

queso con membrillo [mem-**bree**-yo] cheese with quince jelly

queso de bola Edam

queso de Burgos soft white cheese

queso de cabrales [kabr**a**less] Spanish Roquefort-type cheese

queso de cerdo [th**ai**rdo] similar to the pork in a pork pie, usually in slices

queso de Idiazábal [eed-yath**a**bal] strong sheeps' cheese from the Basque country

queso del país [pa-**ee**ss] local cheese

queso de oveja [ob**ay**-H̱a] sheep's cheese

queso de Roncal strong sheep's cheese from Navarra

queso gallego [ga-y**ay**go] creamy cheese from Galicia

queso manchego hard, strong cheese from La Mancha

quisquillas [keesk**ee**-yass] shrimps

rábanos radishes

rabas squid rings fried in batter

rabo de buey [boo-**ay**] oxtail

ración [rath-y**on**] portion

ración pequeña para niños

245

[pekayn-ya – neen-yoss] children's portion

ragout de ternera [ragoot day tairnaira] veal ragoût

rape a la americana [rapay] monkfish with brandy and herbs

rape a la cazuela [kathwayla] monkfish casserole

rape a la plancha grilled monkfish

ravioles [rab-yoless] ravioli

raya [ra-ya] skate

raya con manteca negra skate in butter and vinegar sauce

redondo al horno [orno] roast fillet of beef

redondo de ternera [tairnaira] fillet of veal

redondo en su jugo [Hoogo] fillet of beef cooked in its own sauce

relleno [ray-yayno] stuffed; stuffing

remolacha beetroot

repollo [repo-yo] cabbage

repostería de la casa cakes and desserts made on the premises

requesón [rekay-son] cream cheese, curd cheese

revuelto de ajos [rebwelto day aHoss] scrambled eggs with garlic

revuelto de ajos tiernos [t-yairnoss] scrambled eggs with spring garlic

revuelto de espárragos trigueros [treegaiross]

scrambled eggs with asparagus

revuelto de sesos scrambled eggs with brains

revuelto de setas scrambled eggs with mushrooms

revuelto mixto [meesto] scrambled eggs with mixed vegetables

riñones a la plancha [reen-yoness] grilled kidneys

riñones al jerez [Haireth] kidneys in a sherry sauce

rodaballo [rodaba-yo] turbot

rodaballo al cava [kaba] turbot with champagne

romero [romairo] rosemary

romesco de pescado mixed fish

roscas sweet pastries

rosquillas [roskee-yass] small sweet pastries

rovellons [robay-yons] mushrooms (Catalan)

sal salt

salchicha sausage

salchichas blancas fried sausages with onions

salchichas de Frankfurt frankfurters

salchichón cured white sausage with pepper

salmón [sal-mon] salmon

salmón ahumado [a-oomado] smoked salmon

salmonetes [sal-monaytess] red mullet

salmonetes en papillote [papee-yotay] red mullet

cooked in foil

salmón frío [sal-mon free-o] cold salmon

salmorejo [salmor**ay**-Ho] thick sauce made from bread, tomatoes, olive oil, vinegar, green pepper and garlic, served cold with hard-boiled eggs and ham

salpicón de mariscos shellfish with vinaigrette dressing

salsa sauce

salsa ali oli/all-i-oli [alee-**o**lee] garlic mayonnaise

salsa bechamel béchamel sauce, white sauce

salsa de tomate [tom**a**tay] tomato sauce

salsa holandesa [oland**ay**sa] hollandaise sauce – hot sauce made with eggs and butter

salsa mayonesa [ma-yon**ay**sa] mayonnaise

salsa romesco sauce made from peppers, tomatoes and garlic

salsa tártara tartare sauce

salsa vinagreta [beenagr**ay**ta] vinaigrette dressing

salteado [saltay-**a**do] sautéed

sandía [sand**ee**-a] water melon

sandwich mixto [m**ee**sto] cheese and ham sandwich

sangre de cerdo [s**a**ngray day th**ai**rdo] pigs' blood

sardina sardine

sardinas a la asturiana [astoor-**ya**na] sardines in cider sauce

sardinas a la brasa barbecued sardines

sardinas a la parrilla [parree-ya] grilled sardines

sardinas fritas fried sardines

segundo plato main course

sesos brains

sesos a la romana brains in batter

sesos rebozados [rebotha**doss**] brains in batter

setas a la bordalesa [bordal**ay**sa] mushrooms cooked in red wine and onions

setas a la plancha grilled mushrooms

setas rellenas [ray-y**ay**nass] stuffed mushrooms

sobrasada soft red sausage with cayenne pepper

soldados de Pavia [pab**ee**-a] fillets of cod, marinaded and fried

solomillo al vino [solom**ee**-yo al b**ee**no] fillet steak with red wine

solomillo con guisantes [gees**a**ntess] fillet steak with peas

solomillo con patatas fritas fillet steak with chips/French fries

solomillo de cerdo [th**ai**rdo] fillet of pork

solomillo de ternera [tairn**ai**ra] fillet of veal

solomillo de vaca [b**a**ka] fillet

of beef

solomillo frío [free-o] cold roast beef

solomillo Roquefort [rokayfor] fillet steak with Roquefort cheese

sopa soup

sopa al cuarto de hora [kwarto day ora] soup made from ham, veal, chicken, almonds, vegetables and eggs

sopa castellana [kastay-yana] vegetable soup

sopa de ajo [day aHo] bread and garlic soup

sopa de almendras almond-based pudding

sopa de calducho clear soup

sopa de cola de buey [boo-ay] oxtail soup

sopa de fideos [feeday-oss] noodle soup

sopa de frutos de mar shellfish soup

sopa de gallina [ga-yeena] chicken soup

sopa del día soup of the day

sopa de legumbres [legoombress] vegetable soup

sopa de lentejas [lentay-Hass] lentil soup

sopa de marisco fish and shellfish soup

sopa de pescado fish soup

sopa de rabo oxtail soup

sopa de rabo de buey [boo-ay] oxtail soup

sopa de tortuga [tortooga] turtle soup

sopa mallorquina [ma-yorkeena] soup with tomatoes, meat and eggs

sopa sevillana [sebee-yana] fish and mayonnaise soup

sorbete [sorbaytay] sorbet

soufflé de fresones [fresoness] strawberry soufflé

suplemento de verduras extra vegetables

supremas de rodaballo [soopraymass day rodaba-yo] fish slices

tallarines [ta-yareeness] noodles

tallarines a la italiana [eetal-yana] tagliatelle

tapa de ternera rellena [tairnaira ray-yayna] stuffed veal hock

tapas appetizers

tarta cake

tarta Alaska baked alaska

tarta de almendra almond tart or gâteau

tarta de arroz [arroth] cake or tart containing rice

tarta de la casa tart or gâteau baked on the premises

tarta helada [elada] ice cream gâteau

tarta moca mocha tart

tartar crudo raw minced steak, steak tartare

tejos de queso [tay-Hoss day kayso] cheese pastries

tencas tench

tencas con jamón [Hamon] tench with ham

ternera [tairn**ai**ra] veal

ternera asada roast veal

tigres [**tee**gress] mussels in cayenne sauce

tocinillo de cielo [toth**ee**n**ee**-yo day th-**yay**lo] rich, thick crème caramel

todo incluido all inclusive

tomate [tom**a**tay] tomato

tomates rellenos [tom**a**tess ray-**yay**noss] stuffed tomatoes

tomatics a es forn baked tomatoes

tomillo [tom**ee**-yo] thyme

tordo thrush

tordos braseados [brassay-**a**doss] grilled thrushes

tordos estofados braised thrushes

torrijas [torr**ee**-Hass] sweet pastries

torta de chicharrones [cheecharr**o**ness] pie filled with assorted cooked and cured meats

torta de sardinas sardine pie

tortilla [tort**ee**-ya] omelette

tortilla a la paisana [pa-ees**a**na] omelette containing a variety of vegetables

tortilla aliada [al-y**a**da] omelette with mixed vegetables

tortilla al ron omlette with rum

tortilla a su gusto omlette made as the customer wishes

tortilla de bonito tuna fish omlette

tortilla de champiñones [champeen-y**o**ness] mushroom omelette

tortilla de chorizo [chor**ee**tho] spicy sausage omelette

tortilla de escabeche [eskab**e**chay] fish omelette

tortilla de espárragos asparagus omelette

tortilla de gambas prawn omelette

tortilla de jamón [Ham**o**n] ham omelette

tortilla de morcilla [morth**ee**-ya] black pudding omelette

tortilla de patata potato omelette

tortilla de sesos brains omelette

tortilla de setas mushroom omelette

tortilla española [espan-y**o**la] (cold slice of) Spanish omelette with potato, onion and garlic

tortilla francesa [franth**ay**sa] plain omelette

tortilla granadina omelette with artichokes, asparagus, brains and peppers

tortilla sacromonte [sakrom**o**ntay] vegetable, brains and sausage omelette

tortillas variadas [bar-y**a**dass] assorted omelettes

tostada toast

tostón sucking pig

tostón asado roast sucking

pig
tournedó fillet steak
tournedó a la salsa foie [fwa]
fillet steak in pâté sauce
trucha [troocha] trout
trucha ahumada [a-oomada]
smoked trout
trucha con jamón [Hamon]
trout with ham
trucha escabechada
marinated trout
truchas a la marinera
[mareenaira] trout in white
wine sauce
truchas molinera [moleenaira]
trout meunière – trout
coated in flour, fried and
served with butter, lemon
juice and parsley
trufas truffles (edible fungus)
trufas al jerez [Haireth] truffles
in sherry
turbante de arroz [toorbantay
day arroth] rice served with
steak, sausage, peppers and
bacon
turrón [toorron] nougat
turrón de coco coconut
nougat
turrón de Alicante [aleekantay]
hard nougat
turrón de yema [yayma]
nougat with egg yolk
turrón de Jijona [HeeHona] soft
nougat
txangurro [changoorro] spider
crab cooked in its shell
uvas [oobass] grapes
vaca estofada [baka] stewed

beef
verduras [bairdoorass]
vegetables
vieiras [bee-ay-eerass] scallops
vinagre [beenagray] vinegar
xoric amb patates [soreek am
patatess] tern with potatoes
(type of swallow)
yogur [yo-goor] yoghurt
zanahoria [thana-or-ya] carrot
zanahorias a la crema [krayma]
carrots à la crème
zarzuela de mariscos
[tharthwayla day mareeskoss]
shellfish stew
**zarzuela de pescados y
mariscos** fish and shellfish
stew

Menu
Reader
Drink

agua [**ag**-wa] water

agua mineral [meenairal] mineral water

agua mineral con gas fizzy mineral water

agua mineral sin gas [seen] still mineral water

agua potable [potablay] drinking water

Alella [alay-ya] region near Barcelona producing red, white and rosé wines

Alicante [aleekantay] region in the south producing red and rosé wines matured in oak casks

Ampurdán region at the foot of the Pyrenees which produces rosé wine

anís [aneess] aniseed-flavoured alcoholic drink

año vintage

aperitivo aperitif

batido milkshake

batido de chocolate [day chokolatay] chocolate milkshake

batido de fresa [fraysa] strawberry milkshake

batido de frutas fruit milkshake

batido de plátano banana milkshake

batido de vainilla [ba-eenee-ya] vanilla milkshake

bebida drink

bebidas alcohólicas alcoholic drinks

bebidas refrescantes soft drinks

cacao [kakow] cocoa

café con leche [lechay] coffee with milk (large cup)

café cortado coffee with milk (small cup)

café descafeinado [deskafay-eenado] decaffeinated coffee

café escocés [eskothayss] black coffee, whisky and vanilla ice cream

café instantáneo [eenstantanay-o] instant coffee

café irlandés [eerlandayss] black coffee, whisky, vanilla ice cream and whipped cream

café solo black coffee

café vienés [b-yenayss] black coffee and whipped cream

caña (cerveza) [kan-ya thairbay-tha] 250cc of draught beer

carajillo [karaHee-yo] black coffee with brandy

carajillo de ron black coffee with rum

carajillo de vodka black coffee with vodka

Cariñena [kareen-yayna] region in the north producing red and rosé wines

carta de vinos [day beenoss] wine list

Cava [kaba] Spanish champagne

cerveza [thairbay-tha] beer, lager

cerveza de barril draught beer

Chacolí fruity white wine produced in the Basque Country

champán [champan] champagne

champaña [champan-ya] champagne

chato glass of red wine

Cheste [chestay] region to the west of Valencia producing dry and sweet white wines

chiquito [cheekeeto] glass of red wine

chocolate caliente [chokolatay kal-yentay] hot chocolate

Cigales [theegaless] region in Valladolid producing light rosé wines

clara shandy

cóctel cocktail

Conca de Barbera [barbaira] region in Catalonia producing red and white wines

Condado de Huelva [welba] region in the south producing dry, mellow and sweet white wines

con gas fizzy, sparkling

coñac [kon-yak] brandy

corto (de cerveza) [thairbay-tha] 125cc of draught beer (1/2 caña)

cosecha vintage

cosechero [kosechairo] red wine of the last vintage

cubalibre [koobaleebray] rum and cola

cubata a spirit with a soft drink of lemon or cola

cubito de hielo [yaylo] ice cube

cucaracha [kookaracha] tequila and coffee-flavoured strong alcoholic drink

destornillador [destornee-yador] vodka and orange juice

espumoso sparkling

gaseosa [gasay-osa] lemonade

ginebra [Heenay-bra] gin

granizada/granizado [graneethada] crushed ice drink

hielo [yaylo] ice

horchata (de chufas) [orchata day] milk drink flavoured with tiger nuts

infusión [eenfooss-yon] herb tea

jarra de vino [Harra day beeno] jug of wine

jerez [Haireth] sherry

jerez amontillado [amontee-yado] pale dry sherry

jerez fino pale light sherry

jerez oloroso sweet sherry

jugo [Hoogo] juice

jugo de albaricoque [day albareekokay] apricot juice

jugo de lima [leema] lime juice

jugo de limón lemon juice

jugo de melocotón peach juice

jugo de naranja [naran-Ha] orange juice

jugo de piña [peen-ya] pineapple juice

jugo de tomate [tomatay]

tomato juice

Jumilla [Hoomee-ya] region in the south producing dry, light red wines and sweet white wines

kirsch strong alcoholic drink made from cherries

leche [lechay] milk

licor liqueur

licor de avellana [day abay-yana] hazelnut-flavoured liqueur

licor de manzana [manthana] apple-flavoured liqueur

licor de melocotón peach-flavoured liqueur

licor de melón melon-flavoured liqueur

licor de naranja [naran-Ha] orange-flavoured liqueur

limonada lemonade

lista de precios [prayth-yoss] price list

Málaga region on the south coast producing sweet and dry white wines

Mancha region of the interior producing mainly white, but also red wines

manzanilla [manthanee-ya] dry sherry-type wine; camomile tea

media de agua [mayd-ya day ag-wa] half-bottle of mineral water

menta poleo [polay-o] mint tea

Mentrida central region producing dark-coloured red wines

Montilla-Moriles [montee-ya-moreeless] region in Andalusia producing sherry-like white wines

mosto grape juice

Oporto port

orujo [orooHo] colourless, strong alcoholic drink made from wine

orujo de miel [m-yayl] orujo with honey

pacharán strong alcoholic drink made from sloes

Penedés [penedayss] region in Catalonia producing in particular sparkling white wines

Priorato [pree-orato] wine-growing region near Tarragona

refresco soft drink

reserva especial quality wine matured in casks

Ribeiro [reebay-eero] region in Galicia producing slightly sparkling red and white wines; type of white wine

Rioja [r-yoHa] region in the north producing some of the finest red and white wines

romeral wine

ron rum

sangría [sangree-a] mixture of red wine, lemonade, spirits and fruit

seco dry

semidulce [say-mee-doolthay] medium-sweet

sidra cider

sin gas [seen] still

sol y sombra [ee] brandy and anís

Tarragona region on the Mediterranean coast producing red and white wines

té [tay] tea

Tierra Alta [t-yairra] region in the province of Tarragona producing red and white wines

tila [teela] lime tea

tinto de Toro [teento] dry, red wine from Zamora

tónica tonic

tónica con ginebra [Heenebra] gin and tonic

Utiel-Requena [oot-yeel-rekayna] region in Valencia producing mild red and rosé wines

Valdeorras [balday-orrass] region in Galicia producing red and white wines

Valdepeñas [balday-payn-yass] central region producing pale and dark, fruity red wines; type of fruity red wine

Valencia [balenth-ya] region on the Mediterranean producing red and white wines

Valle de Monterrey [ba-yay day montairray] region in Galicia producing full-bodied red and white wines

vino [beeno] wine

vino blanco white wine

vino de aguja [day agooHa] slightly sparkling rosé and white wines

vino de jerez [Haireth] sherry

vino del país [pa-eess] local wine

vino de mesa [maysa] table wine

vino rosado rosé wine

vino tinto red wine

viñedo vineyard

Yecla region in the south producing smooth red and light rosé wines

zumo [thoomo] fruit juice

zumo de albaricoque [day albareekokay] apricot juice

zumo de lima [leema] lime juice

zumo de limón lemon juice

zumo de melocotón peach juice

zumo de naranja [naranHa] orange juice

zumo de piña [peen-ya] pineapple juice

zumo de tomate [tomatay] tomato juice

zurito [thooreeto] 125 cc of draught beer (1/2 caña)

zurracapote [thoorrakapotay] wine with sugar and cinammon